MOGHUL COOKI

JOYCE WESTRIP was born in southern India in 1929, moved to England in 1947 and has lived in Perth, Western Australia, since 1955. Fascinated by Indian history and culture since her childhood, she has visited the subcontinent on numerous occasions and is a collector of rare Indian cookbooks. She has presented radio programmes on Moghul cuisine as well as giving talks and classes on the subject.

MOGHUL COOKING
India's Courtly Cuisine

Joyce Westrip

DECORATIONS BY WALTER TOLLOY

Serif

London

First published 1997 by
Serif
47 Strahan Road
London E3 5DA

and

1436 Randolph Street
Chicago IL 60607

British Library Cataloguing-in-Publication Data. A catalogue record for
this book is available from the British Library.

Library of Congress Cataloging in Publication Data. A catalog record
for this book is available from the Library of Congress.

ISBN 1 897959 27 3

Designed by Sue Lamble

Printed and bound in Great Britain by
Biddles of Guildford and King's Lynn

Contents

FOREWORD

Joyce Westrip is a talented writer and avid researcher. I like to believe what she tells me – that it was my urging and gentle pushing and encouragement that has brought her Moghul cookbook to the point of being published.

Not only has she delved deep into historical documents, she has also made numerous trips to the land which has always held such fascination for her. She was born in India and lived there until, at the age of seventeen, she was sent 'home' to England. In those years she absorbed much of the country's culture from personal experience, and she has returned many times, drawn irresistibly to the land she loves. She shares her time in India with an almost palpable affection for the land and its people.

Even as a child she was interested in the preparation of food. She loved watching spices being ground and meals being cooked. Reading her descriptions not only brings the scene before me, but also adds sound and, almost, the aromas.

I for one will always be grateful that she chose Moghul cooking and that almost unbelievably lavish period to write about. She brings historical data to life, and her descriptions of life at court take us back to another era. Within these pages are emperors whose names are synonymous with power and uncountable wealth; their courtiers, queens and ladies and the jewels they wore; extravagant banquets and glimpses of grandeur beyond imagination.

After being introduced to the cast of characters who shaped the history of India, we are invited to partake of the kind of food they enjoyed. Spices and herbs are introduced, menus suggested, recipes explained in detail. Translated to modern times and methods, there is no need for an army of cooks and helpers nor, thankfully, for tasters to ensure that the food has not been poisoned!

Reading the introductory pages, I was delighted to find accounts of a Kashmiri *waazwaan* and a meeting with the former Maharani of Jaipur in Rajasthan. Both evoked memories of having had the same experience when myself visiting India and brought back vivid memories of being entertained by the gracious Maharani in a garden where peacocks strutted and uttered their shrill cries while the sun set in a torrent of red and gold.

A warm and charming hostess, Joyce Westrip loves to present the exquisite flavours of Moghul India when she entertains. Being a guest is akin to being invited to a *daawat-e-khass* – sitting at one of the tables under a colourful *shamiana* in the garden and enjoying lively conversation and delicious food.

I have no doubt that readers will be inspired to try the dishes and to stage their own Moghul feasts under Joyce Westrip's expert guidance.

Charmaine Solomon

ACKNOWLEDGEMENTS

This book would not have been possible without the encouragement, patience and understanding of my husband Charles. It was, however, the constant and enthusiastic urging from that guru of Asian cooking, Charmaine Solomon, which gave me the confidence to get started. The writing commenced, but there were times when it seemed to flag, and by some strange coincidence it was at these times, and often late at night, the telephone would ring and I would hear a gentle voice from 2,000 miles away asking 'Joyce, this is Charmaine, how is your cookbook progressing?' We would talk and, rejuvenated, I would forge ahead once again.

My son, Paul Hanlon, came to the rescue when the computer decided to be difficult.

Testing recipes was great fun with Paula and Walter Tolloy, Charmaine Surin, Mercedes Webb, and my sister Maureen Thomas.

I owe thanks to many friends who urged me on: Susan Watkins, Ruby Ottley, Sonia Phelan, Hazel Galbraith, Niranjula Galhenage, Melanie Anderson, Peggy Holroyde, Shaku Devagnanam, Margaret Fernandes Anil and Manek Kadam.

Glenys Edwards patiently typed and retyped while Mercedes Webb and Stephanie Kukura checked and re-checked the manuscript in its early stages. Ceridwen Morris finally put the work into shape on the computer.

In India historians and friends, chefs, managers, cookery writers and experts in the culinary arts of India, generously shared their recipes and their knowledge. Her Royal Highness Gayatri Devi of Jaipur, J. Inder Singh Kalra, Dorothy Sait, Joan and Krishna Reddy, Thrity Kuka, Anil and Manek Kadam, Harish Mathur, Satish Arora, Mohammed Imtiaz Quershi, Arvind Saraswat, Arvind Bhargava, Manjit Gill, J. Chadiok, Mohammad Islam, Eldred Sequeira, Ajit Kumar, O.P. Khantwal, Pradip Rozario, Avijit Chaturvedi and Rajiv Narain all gave of their knowledge of Moghul cooking.

Sri and Roger Owen were most generous with advice and with help in putting the proposal together to submit to a publisher.

The painting on the cover, of the Emperor Shah Jahan's son Dara Shikoh with courtiers in a garden, is taken from a transparency supplied from the Chester Beatty Library, Dublin. It appears in the fine two-volume publication by Linda York Leach, *Mughal and Other Indian Paintings from the Chester Beatty Library*, London 1995.

Caroline Davidson, my literary agent, was always encouraging and helpful, and persevered to find the right publisher.

My publisher and editor, Stephen Hayward, guided me with great sensitivity to making improvements along the way. I thank him for the faith he showed in an unknown author.

PREFACE

India has held me spellbound for as long as I can remember. I was born and brought up near Bangalore in the south of the country and lived there until I was seventeen when I left for England; later, I settled in Western Australia.

One of my favourite occupations when I was young was to watch the activity in the large kitchen, and my sister and I even had our own little grinding stones and stone rolling-pins. We would sit under the shade of a large tamarind tree in the garden and spend hours grinding leaves and petals for our make-believe curries.

I had my own 'pied piper' in India whose sound never failed to bring me scurrying to the kitchen, no matter what I was doing. This sound was, in fact, a rhythm – that of the grinding stone.

Tuk-a-ka-kut... tuk-a-ka-kut... tuk-a-ka-kut was the start of the rhythm made by the heavy, smooth, untapered stone rolling-pin being knocked on the lightly pitted flat grinding stone to break up knobs of fresh, juicy ginger or cloves of garlic. *Tuk-a-ka-ku*t had an accompaniment too, a sound all of its own which belongs very particularly to India – the tinkle of Jaya's rainbow-coloured glass bangles which went from her wrist to halfway up her forearm. Jaya was one of the helpers in the kitchen and her job was to grind the spices. She held the stone rolling-pin firmly between the palms of her hands and as the knobs of ginger were squashed the rhythm changed; stone rolled over stone, now with a pushing action. Back and forth went the stone and Jaya's bangles tinkled and danced up and down her arm.

Every now and again she would pause to flick a few drops of water or vinegar onto the flat stone, then her forefinger became a spatula as she curved it and scraped all round the stone towards the centre until all the bits of ginger were collected there. Then stone on stone again and back to the pushing rhythm, caressingly coaxing the ginger into a soft creamy texture. 'See now Missy, *masala* is right,' she would say. The spatula finger went into action once again and the *masala* was gathered together in a smooth mound and put onto a round *thali* or tray.

Jaya would be seated on the kitchen floor, her legs neatly tucked under and covered with her sari, during this grinding process which went on and on until a multitude of pastes of all hues and textures patterned the tray. The dark green of fresh coriander leaves, the palest of green if coriander leaves and coconut were ground together to make a chutney, the light brown of coriander seeds, a flaming red from long, shiny fresh chillies, mounds of creamy ginger and garlic, milky white coconut, brown tamarind and speckled heaps of mustard seeds, all waiting to be popped into *degchis* or pots to form the bases of mouth-watering dishes of lamb *korma*, fish *molee* or vegetable *aviyal*.

At a large kitchen table at the other end of the kitchen, onions were cut and sliced on a solid wooden block and chickens were chopped into pieces by Moonswamy. Even though I had wept earlier when I saw the chickens being chased round the garden by Moonswamy, who seemed to delight in wringing their necks, my crying was all too short-lived, as I used to enjoy helping him to pluck the birds. *Ghee* was sizzling away in pans. As the cook's assistants handed him onions and *masalas* or dry spices on demand, wonderful aromas started to fill the air. Sam, the cook, stood over the pots and stirred and stirred, waiting for the exact moment to throw in some cloves or cinnamon, to plop in a wet *masala* or to introduce the flavour of coconut or the tang of tamarind. He never referred to a recipe.

It was a happy kitchen, where there was always chatter, laughter and gentle teasing, and much haggling too when vendors came to the kitchen door with baskets of eggs, fruit or vegetables.

I was indeed lucky to have had this early interest and initiation into some of India's culinary mysteries. Lucky primarily because it was an unusual interest for someone of my background. Unlike so many well known writers on Indian cooking, I cannot claim to come from a dynasty of grandmothers and aunts steeped in that tradition. My maternal grandmother was as Irish as they come, of the 'Irish stew and no fancy food' brigade, but my grandfather, who had been born in Rangoon when his father was stationed there with the British army, enjoyed mildly spiced dishes. I had my first taste of *khichri* in grandfather's hill station home in Ootacamund. When as children we were recuperating from one or another type of fever we always knew we were on the road to recovery when grandmother's beef tea and 'pish pash' (a dish peculiar to the India of the Raj) appeared on the table. Potato chops and *brinjal* cutlets with just a hint of spice were grandfather's favourites, and the mere mention of them evokes in me strong memories of Ootacamund. Grandmother would tell us stories of the north-west frontier, where she began her young married life and where some of her seventeen children were born in tented army camps, and we would listen wide-eyed as we devoured our *khichri*.

Several maharajas had holiday palaces in Ootacamund, and trays of Indian sweets were often sent to my grandfather's house from the palaces. I can still recall the excitement I felt when a palace retainer walked up to the house with a tray laden with pink and white coconut sweets, golden *jalebis* and snow-white *barfi*.

Apart from making Christmas cakes and puddings, I don't believe my mother ever did any cooking in India, but she turned out to be a natural cook later in life. Retired from India, she turned her hand to all styles of cooking, from fancy European confections, cakes and pastries to Indian dishes, pickles and delicacies fit to grace the table of any *nawab*.

My parents did a lot of entertaining in India, and the spread of food on such occasions was always impressive. Days beforehand mother would discuss the menus with the head cook and, if he suggested certain dishes, she always wanted to know exactly what ingredients were to be used and how those dishes would be prepared and garnished, whether certain ingredients were still in season and all the other pieces of information which allow one to plan a fine meal. I was often listening by her side and would plead to be allowed to go to the markets with the servants. I loved the markets, especially those which sold flowers, fruit and vegetables. Perfume wafted down from colourful baskets of marigolds, roses and jasmine which were being threaded into garlands. Mounds of vegetables surrounded some of the stallholders, who sat on raised platforms, while others sat at floor level on mats with piles of chillies and ginger and garlic and onions in front of them and baskets of fresh green coriander piled up alongside. Tropical scents, above all from mangoes, melons, papayas, custard apples, wood-apples and jackfruit, permeated the air and increased my fascination with the foods of India.

No wonder I was spellbound. And how I missed it all when I had to leave at the age of seventeen to go to that other 'home', England. It all seemed so dull and grey and dreary by comparison. But as my grandmother was fond of saying, 'One door shuts and another one opens,' and for me the closing door in fact beckoned me to delve back into those early memories and experiment with the cooking of India. I did just that and have been involved in a love affair with the cooking of India ever since.

The more I experimented and cooked, the more I learned; and the more I learned, the more I wanted to know. And so started my interest in collecting books on the cooking of India. Indian cookbooks were scarce in the 1950s – the cooking of the subcontinent was still very much an oral tradition then. Now, however, I have built up a collection of more than 800 books on the subject.

Part of that library is made up of works written by, or dedicated to, royal personages. One in the Marathi language is by a Maharaja of Baroda, written in 1890, with a title that translates as *The Science of Soups*, although it contains a variety of recipes. Another is a collection of recipes from friends and relations of Her Highness Gayatri Devi, the former Maharani of Jaipur in Rajasthan. On one of my research visits there I was invited to meet several of the contributors to the book, and I learned a great deal about the cooking of Rajasthan from that visit. I was thrilled, too, to meet the Gayatri Devi, who was amused when I told her that as a teenager in India I used to collect pictures of her from the pages of newspapers and magazines – at that time she was considered one of the ten most beautiful women in the world. In this part of my collection I also have a wonderful book translated from the Persian and written in 1839 by a nobleman, with recipes from the kitchen of Nawab Uli Khan.

My collection also includes nineteenth-century works, many written as household manuals, for the British *memsahibs* who went out to India to join their husbands, with household hints and remedies, advice on how to employ servants, and recipes including some fine *biryani* and *pilau* dishes. Not all of these are published works. Some are handwritten into notebooks, at the end of diaries or even on loose sheets of paper. I love browsing through them, and in doing so am reminded of the many problems the *mem-*

sahibs were expected to deal with. Snake bites seem to have been a common occurrence, and I certainly remember one of our *malis* (gardeners) being bitten by a snake and watching as my father cut the puncture areas, sucked the venom and then poured permanganate of potash into the wound.

The regional part of my collection covers the entire subcontinent, including Pakistan and Bangladesh, from Goa with its Portuguese influence in the south to the cooking of the meat-eating Brahmin Pandits in Kashmir.

After I started to learn how to make the dishes, I became curious about the whole subject and discovered that, just as India is a country of legends, so there were many stories or legends associated with certain dishes. One of my early discoveries was that the Moghul dish *nauratna* or *navrattan* was dedicated to the nine courtiers of Akbar's court in the sixteenth century. They were known as his 'nine jewels' and the ingredients or garnishes, nine in number, are supposed to represent the colours of jewels. A *navrattan* is a colourful sight, containing diced vegetables like carrots, beans, peas, cauliflower florets and more, and garnished with grapes, cherry tomatoes, almonds and cashew nuts.

I became intrigued and wanted to know more about the Great Moghuls and their cuisine and so began a hunt to collect Moghul-style recipes. I travelled wherever the scent of the hunt led me to gather material. I talked to members of royal families in Rajasthan, Hyderabad and Lucknow; recipes were tracked down from old palace retainers who specialised in this dish or that. Others were coaxed from friends. I had lengthy talks with executive chefs and food and beverage managers of some of the Taj and Sheraton group of hotels (particularly from the palace-converted hotels). I met cookery writers and reviewers and acknowledged experts on classic Indian cooking like J. Inder Singh Kalra, President (Asia) of the International Wine, Food and Travel Writers' Association, and master chefs of this classic form like Satish Arora, Harish Mathur, Mohammed Imtiaz Quershi and Arvind Saraswat, who was Director of Kitchen Planning and Food Production for the Taj group. I led gourmet tours to India and feasted on grand banquets. Friends in high places in Hyderabad, like Krishna and Joan Reddy, people whose ancestors, and they themselves, having held high positions at the Nizam's court, fed me with legends and unforgettable *chowki* parties. My friend Ruby Ottley regaled me with stories of palace life when she was governess at the palace of the prime minister in Hyderabad; noble families in Lucknow, steeped in culture and tradition, took me back in time to the kitchens of the food-loving *nawabs* who vied with each other for culinary recognition and who poached on each other's preserves to bribe chefs away. Kashmiri Pandits, Brahmins who eat meat, and some of whom will now eat onions and garlic as well, were astounded by my enthusiasm and parted with jealously guarded secrets. I had a wonderful time and this book is the result.

INTRODUCING THE MOGHULS

There is plenty of historical evidence that the Moghuls looked to Persia as the fount of their culture, and it was the interweaving of Persian and Indian culture that became one of the most notable features of the Moghul empire.

For the Moghuls, Persia epitomised high culture. *Mughal* is Persian for Mongol and *Moghul* is the Indianised version of the word. Persian became the language of the court, and Persian customs, literature, music, painting and architectural styles merged with the best India had to offer. It is a similar fusion of Persian and Indian culinary styles that sets Moghul cooking apart from other Indian cuisines.

In 1526 Babur the Moghul nurtured the seeds of a culture that was to become inseparable from that of India more generally. Moghul rule had begun, bringing with it a continuity of administrative systems and dynastic stability. The last Moghul ruler was deposed by the British in 1858, although a decline set in after the death of Aurangzeb in 1707. Weak rulers followed one after the other, straining the political structure. The treasury was wickedly depleted in 1739 by Nadir Shah who, coming only to plunder, rode off with a grand booty including Shah Jahan's famous Peacock Throne and the Koh-i-Nor diamond. So when we speak of the Great Moghuls, it is generally with reference to Babur and his direct descendants, from Humayun to Aurangzeb, who gave India a stability that facilitated the flowering of a cultured and lavish lifestyle.

The Moghuls not only unified all but the southern tip of the subcontinent, they overwhelmed it, leaving behind a legacy of grandeur and opulence, a wealth of painting, architecture, literature and cuisine. Moghul India has been well documented by historians, but, like the chroniclers of many other cultures, they have neglected to record the historical significance of the Moghul contribution to India's culinary arts. Today when enthusiasts speak of the classical style of Indian cooking, they are referring to the legacy left by the Moghul dynasty – the Moghul or Moghlai style.

Eyes light up, the tongue caresses the lips and a knowing nod accompanies accolades when conversation turns to cooking in the Moghlai style. The adjectives used to describe it – princely, sublime, majestic, illustrious – leave no doubt about its royal status. It is food for kings and queens, courtiers and nobility, and also for modern-day enthusiasts. But before we enter the Moghul kitchen with its courtly recipes, it is worth taking a brief look at the history of the Moghul dynasty.

Babur was the founder of this great dynasty. His line was followed by direct descendants, starting with his son Humayun whose reign started in 1530; Akbar reigned from 1556 to 1605, Jahangir 1605 to 1627, Shah Jahan 1627 to 1658 and Aurangzeb 1658 to 1707. Although the power of the Moghul rule declined fairly rapidly after Aurangzeb, the grand lifestyle continued and magnificent tables with yet more innovative dishes found their way into the vast and wealthy palaces of the *nizams* of Hyderabad, the *nawabs* of Lucknow, the nobles of Lahore, the Rajput rulers and into the stately homes of the Pandits of Kashmir. The survival of a unique blend of Persian and Indian ingredients and methods was ensured, bringing to our tables dishes redolent of the days of the great Moghuls.

They were dishes that were aromatically marinated in *masalas* of ginger and onion, tinged with nutmeg, mace, cloves and cinnamon; dishes of rich sauces combining a perfect balance of a range of spices, yoghurt and cream, almonds and pistachios, the base to receive morsels of chicken or meat cooked in *ghee*; vegetable dishes with the nutty flavour of poppy seeds and sweetened with honey; extravagant rice dishes, *biryanis* and *pilaus*, each grain separate and full of flavour, garnished with cardamom and strands of saffron; silky-smooth, ice-cold desserts flavoured with essence of roses, decked with tissue-thin sheets of real gold or silver and decorated with a scattering of rose petals; drinks squeezed from fresh fruits. All were prepared to please the eye as well as the palate.

Babur was a Chaghati Turk with the blood of both Ghengis Khan and Timur in his veins. He was scholarly, a poet, sensitive to the fine things in life and, as were all the Moghul rulers, a lover of gardens in the Persian style – as today's visitor to Lahore and Kashmir can testify. He surrounded himself with Turkish and Persian intellectuals who, like himself, were as adept with pen and brush as they were at wielding the sword. He had seen the cultural achievements at his ancestors' capitals at Samarkand and Herat and he would clearly love to have taken those capitals – but it was not to be, so he turned his attention first to Kabul and then expanded down into northern India to enjoy its legendary spoils.

Babur was meticulous in keeping a journal which leaves us with a record of his Indian campaigns, and of life in the tented encampments – set up to a regulated plan with quarters for the women, the guards, the chiefs and nobles, the kitchens and out-houses. The tents themselves were luxurious, lined with carpets and fine fabrics.

Babur's first impressions of his new land express disappointment, perhaps because he was unfamiliar with the countryside and homesick for the cooler climate of Kabul. He thought Hindustan a country of few charms:

Of social intercourse, paying and receiving visits there are none; in handicraft and work there is no symmetry, method or quality; there are no good horses, no ice or cold water, no good bread or cooked food in the bazaars, no hot baths, no colleges, no candles, torches or candlesticks ... Except their large rivers and their standing waters which flow in ravines and hollows ... there are no running waters in their gardens or residences ... These residences have no charm, air, regularity or symmetry.

He does concede, however, that, 'Pleasant things in Hindustan are that it is a large country and has masses of gold and silver … and endless workmen of every kind.'

Babur soon set about planning and planting gardens and brought in seeds, plants and gardeners from Kabul and Persia to grow his favourites – melons (prized for their restorative power), peaches, apricots, pistachios, walnuts and almonds. He does not tell us a lot about the types of food he enjoyed, but there is much mention of bouts of wine drinking and of a refreshing drink called *julabmost* (sherbet). He talks of a sheep being made into kebabs; *chikhi*, a meat dish incorporating a paste of wheat flour and ginger which also appears later at Akbar's table and is still in the repertoire today. This gives us a clue that spices had found their way into the Moghul kitchen. Babur appeared to enjoy the luscious mangoes of his new land and gives instructions on two ways of eating them – 'Punch a hole in it,' he writes, 'and squeeze or suck the juice out, the other is to eat it like a peach.' He likened the Indian jackfruit (a member of the durian family) to a sheep's stomach stuffed and made into *gipa*, a thick soup, but makes no reference to the smell of the fruit, often repugnant on first encounter.

We do know that Babur employed Hindustani cooks – and that they were bribed to poison him. They made a good attempt, but as they were being watched they could not drop the poison powder directly into the cooking pot, so they hastily sprinkled it on the bread, probably *naan* or *roti*, and covered it with 'buttered fritters'. Besides, they had to have first taste from the cooking pot! Babur fell ill and reprisal was swift, certain and cruel – the negligent taster was cut into pieces and the cook was skinned alive.

Babur reaped rich rewards from his conquest of the Delhi sultanate and his reign saw the beginnings of the opulence and luxury associated with the Moghuls. The treasures of five kings fell into Babur's hands after the Battle of Panipet in 1526, but 'He gave it all away,' said his daughter Gul-Badan. Humayun, Babur's son, came back gloating with pride and clutching an enormous diamond believed to be the Koh-i-Nor (the Mountain of Light), so named later by the Persian plunderer, Nadir Shah. Babur nonchalantly returned it to Humayun to keep, but not before mentally noting its worth which, he calculated, would 'provide two and a half days' food for the whole world'. Babur divided much of the treasure among his loyal followers, including gifts to the ladies of the harem and to the female heads of household departments.

> To each *begum* is to be delivered as follows: one special dancing girl of the dancing girls of Sultan Ibrahim, with one gold plate full of jewels – ruby and pearl, cornelian and diamond, emerald and turquoise, topaz and cat's-eye – and two small mother-o'-pearl trays full of *ashrafis*, and on two other trays *shahrukhis*, and all sorts of stuffs by nines – that is four trays and one plate.

Babur died just four years later and Humayun became emperor at the age of twenty-two. He did not have his father's tenacity, nor his acumen in battle, and it was not long before he lost the kingdom, temporarily, to the Afghan chieftain Sher Shah (Sher Khan).

Humayun was forced to flee with his Persian wife Hamida and sought refuge at the court of Tahmasp, the Shah of Persia, in 1544. Here Humayun lived in the style of his ancestors at Samarkand and Herat. The Persian court of that time was considered a great artistic and cultural centre. The arrival of Hamida and Humayun was greeted with a welcome feast given by Tahmasp, and on each of the following days a banquet of five hundred dishes appeared:

Upon his auspicious arrival let him drink fine sherbets of lemon and rosewater, cooled with snow; then serve him preserves of watermelon, grapes and other fruits, with white bread just as I have ordered. For this royal guest prepare each drink with sweet attars and ambergris; and each day prepare a banquet of five hundred rare and delicious and colourful dishes ... O my son, on the day of his arrival give feast, tremendous and enticing, of meats and sweetmeats, milks and fruits to the number of three thousand trays.

Shah Tahmasp agreed to back Humayun in his attempt to recapture his kingdom in India, and announced his intention to provide Humayun with 12,000 of his best horsemen. When Humayun returned to reclaim his throne in 1555, the diamond, the Koh-i-Nor, stayed behind. It had started out on its travels – the Shah sent it to the Nizam Shah in the Deccan in India; in the seventeenth century it was in Shah Jahan's treasury; it was seized by Nadir Shah in 1739; was appropriated by the Sikh ruler of the Punjab, Ranjit Singh, and finally came into British hands when the Punjab was annexed in 1849. Today it is *the* jewel in the crown in the Tower of London.

Had Humaun not been forced into long exile, we might have been made more aware of his lifestyle and food habits. Of feasts there were many, often given by his aunts to celebrate birthdays or weddings. There was 'profusion and splendour', and we know that as early as 1533 Humayun was following a tradition of Hindu kings in being weighed against gold. Gul-Badan, Humayun's aunt, leaves us a description of the 'House of Feasting' commemorating his accession to the throne.

She describes the large room, with an octagonal tank in the centre and in the middle of the tank a platform spread with Persian carpets on which entertainers and musicians sat. In the hall was a jewelled throne sheltered by gold-embroidered hangings and long strings of pearls. In another room sat a gilded bedstead and *paan* dishes, from which we learn that the Hindu ceremonial custom of *paan* exchange had been introduced to the Moghul court. There are jewelled drinking vessels and utensils of pure gold and silver and tablecloths of choice gold brocade. It was indeed a grand occasion, but yet more sumptuous banquets and feasts and festivities were to take place as Moghul rule progressed.

Humayun's reign after his return from exile was not destined to be a long one, and he died just six months later in 1556. He turned to answer a call to prayer, tripped and fell down some stairs. Although Humayun's reign was brief, his stay in Persia made a deep impression on both himself and Hamida, and they made the initial contribution to the cultural synthesis which was to be the hallmark of Moghul style in India.

Humayun's tomb in Delhi is a monument raised by his older widow, Haji Begum, who is said to have camped on the site while the building was in progress. It marks the beginning of the development of Indo-Islamic architecture. Persian in style, and incorporating for the first time in India the Persian double dome, with the Indian *chatris* on the roof, it was the predecessor to many other buildings fusing the two styles – from Akbar's tomb at Sikandra to the perfection of the fusion in Shah Jahan's Taj Mahal at Agra.

The real flowering of the Great Moghuls began with Akbar's accession to the throne in 1556. Akbar followed sound policies with the appointment of Hindu Rajput nobles to high positions at court and marriage alliances with Rajput princesses, and his personal curiosity, interest and involvement ensured the stability of the Moghul dynasty. Under Akbar the arts and culinary matters were both raised to a level of state concern.

Birthdays, festivals, naming ceremonies and other special occasions were celebrated with a display of abundant wealth. Akbar's wonderful palace at Fatehpur Sikri (built to honour a prediction, by Sufi mystic Salim Chisti, that a son would be born) was the scene of great jubilation on these occasions. To celebrate Akbar's birthday, the buildings were adorned with pavilions and awnings of translucent gold tissue-like fabric to shelter the golden throne with its inlay of rubies and emeralds. Persian and Indian court musicians played. A pair of golden scales glittered in the sunlight as nobles, chiefs, courtiers and attendants watched. The Emperor was to be weighed – but no ordinary weigh-in this, no simple test to gauge the results of gargantuan meals prepared by hundreds of palace cooks. This was a show of benevolence. The Emperor sat on one of the scales and the other was balanced with gold and silver, rubies, diamonds and pearls, with clothes heavily embroidered in gold thread, and precious foodstuffs like almonds (also used as currency) – all later to be distributed for charity. Needless to say, the Emperor found much favour with his subjects.

The Moghul emperors accepted their vast wealth with a certain nonchalance. Ambassadors and foreign travellers to the courts of Jahangir, Shah Jahan and Aurangzeb have left their impressions of these displays of wealth and the extravagance of dress and jewels worn by those at court. Thomas Roe, England's first ambassador to India, spent long years at the court of Jahangir trying to establish an agreement for trade. He was getting ready to move camp and on one occasion watched as Jahangir was being robed by his attendants:

Then a nother came and buckled on his swoord and buckler, sett all over with great diamonds and rubyes, the belts of gould suteable. A nother hung his quiver with 30 arrowes and his bow in a case, the same that was presented by the Persian ambassador. On his head he wore a rich turbant with a plume of herne tops, not many but long; on one syde hung a ruby unsett, as bigg as a walnutt; on the other syde a diamond as great; in the middle an emralld like a hart, much bigger. His shash was wreather about with a chayne of great pearle, rubyes, and diamonds drild. About his neck hee carried a chaine of most excellent pearle, three double (so great I never saw); at his elbowes, armletts sett with diamonds; and on his wrists three rowes of several sorts. His hands bare, but almost on every finger a ring; his gloves, which were English, stuck under his girdle; his coate of cloth of gould without sleeves upon a fine semian as thin as lawne; on his feete a payre of embrodered buskings with pearle, the toes sharp and turning up.

French traveller Jean-Baptiste Tavenier was both dazzled and astounded by Shah Jahan's Peacock Throne. According to him it was six feet long and four feet wide. Four solid gold rods supported the base and twelve bars of gold rose up on three sides to support a canopy. The bars and rods were encrusted with large rubies and emeralds and the intervals between them were covered in diamonds and pearls. There were more than one hundred rubies, and the same number of emeralds. The underside of the throne was covered with pearls and diamonds, and the canopy was framed with a fringe of pearls. A peacock rose above the canopy, its gold body inlaid with a variety of precious stones, its tail composed predominantly of blue sapphires. An enormous ruby sat in its breast and from the ruby dangled a large pearl of about 50 carats. Fronds of golden flowers, again studded with precious stones, flanked the peacock. I can well understand Tavernier's stunned reaction. I saw the remains of the Peacock Throne when on a visit to Teheran to research the Indo-Persian links in Moghul cooking and was equally struck by its magnificence.

Even though the last of the Great Moghuls, Aurangzeb, was himself much more austere, lavish entertainments at court were still held for his large entourage and the expenses of running the palace were extraordinary.

Foreign travellers to both Persia and the Moghul courts have left their impressions of the lavish banquets and the types of dishes served. Manrique, Bernier, Manucci, Roe, Hawkins and Monserrate all wrote of their experiences in the land of the Moghuls.

Having glimpsed something of the extravagant courtly presentations and the fabulous wealth that supported the Moghul empire, we can begin to understand why the culinary style could not fail to be elevated into the surrounding extravaganza of state.

The fruits and vegetables for which Babur had pined were now grown in profusion – melons, peaches, apricots, walnuts, pistachios, almonds, plums, apples, pears, cherries, chestnuts and special grape varieties came together to combine with local produce like mangoes, oranges, limes, jackfruit, coconuts, pineapples, star fruit, plantains, tamarind, sugar cane and, of course, the full gamut of spices.

With more than 400 cooks in Akbar's kitchen, there was great potential for experimenting to produce perfect blends of marinades and sauces combining meats and fruits, and using spices for their aromatic and pungent attributes as well as for their medicinal qualities. Royal banquets became a focus of entertainment at the Moghul courts. We must pay our salaams to Abul Fazl, the philosopher poet and Akbar's favourite courtier and confidant, who introduces us to those dishes which became, and remain, the classical dishes of India – Moghul or Moghlai style.

Abul Fazl was an Indian-born Muslim, a scholar and a diplomat. He soon rose to the rank of prime minister and had command of 4,000 horsemen. He wielded an enormous amount of influence at court. We are indebted to Fazl for his meticulous recording and for his own great interest in food. His food consumption was gargantuan. His son sat by his side to serve him when he ate, while the kitchen superintendent stood by, watching closely to observe which dishes met Fazl's favour. This they would gauge if Fazl enjoyed a second helping of any particular dish. If he did not approve of a dish, he would, without uttering a word, indicate that his son taste it, and with great disdain the dish was passed to the superintendent to be removed and improved upon or never to be presented again.

When Abul Fazl was sent to the Deccan to relieve Akbar's drunken son from his command, he set off with 3,000 men. He lived in grand style during this time and his table was further embellished with dishes from that region. His daily fare apparently included 1,000 dishes, which were also relished by his officers. In another large tent nearby all-comers came to dine; *khichri,* one of the favourite dishes, was prepared in great quantities and distributed throughout the day. Today the very special cuisine of Hyderabad is a mixture of Moghul and Hindu influences, with a further injection of flavours from the south.

Back at the Moghul court we learn a lot from Abul Fazl about Akbar's policy on food. He philosophises on Akbar's pedantic concern for dishes presented at his table – every dish had to be perfect. Abul Fazl explains that,

The equilibrium of man's nature, the strength of the body, the capability of receiving external and internal blessings and the acquisition of worldly and religious advantages depend ultimately on the proper care being shown for appropriate food. This knowledge distinguishes man from beasts.

For Akbar, the right balance was more important than mere eating.

We learn too that Akbar ate only once in the course of 24 hours, but there was no fixed time for eating, so the kitchen staff were constantly at the ready, waiting for the royal command, and within an hour no fewer than 100 dishes were presented. With the ladies of his harem it was a different story – their kitchen staff were on the go from morning to night running back and forth with trays of delicacies to cater to special whims.

Only trustworthy and experienced staff were appointed to the royal kitchens. The kitchen supervisors and the kitchens were overseen by no less a figure than Prime Minister Abul Fazl himself. He tells us that, although he was entrusted with other important affairs of state, the kitchen departments fell particularly under his control, with, of course, the emperor being kept fully informed. The possibility of being poisoned was never far from an emperor's mind.

When the Moghuls were on the move, even a short journey was a mammoth organisational task. When the royal party set out for Kashmir, Abul Fazl ensured the efficiency of the travelling kitchens. One camp contained 100 elephants, 500 camels, 400 carts, 100 bearers, 500 troopers, 1,000 labourers, 500 site levellers, 100 water carriers, 50 carpenters, 30 leather makers and 150 sweepers. Then there were tent-makers, candle-makers and torch-bearers; the hundreds of tents included sixteen large kitchen tents.

Akbar had 300 wives, most of whom were Turkish or Persian, but it was his Rajput Hindu princesses and their relatives in administrative positions who helped to turn the Moghul foothold into a united Hindustan in the north of the subcontinent.

The imperial kitchen was run like a state department with a treasurer, storekeeper, tasters, clerks, and cooks from Persia and various regions of India. 'Every day,' Abul Fazl reports, 'such dishes are prepared as the nobles can scarcely command at their feasts, from which you may infer how exquisite the dishes are which are prepared for his Majesty.' The treasurer issued the budget on an annual estimate, purchases were made accordingly and the storehouse sealed with two individual seals, those of the superintendent of the stores and of the head of the kitchen. These two were responsible for daily expenditure, for receipts and for the servants' wages. Rice, according to the season in different areas, was purchased quarterly. Fowls were never kept for more than a month after fattening, and even animals such as sheep and goats were fattened by the cooks. An abundance of vegetables was supplied from the kitchen garden, which was supervised by horticulturalists from Persia.

Richness and variety were the dictates of food required from the emperor's kitchen. Dishes were prepared with the utmost care and presented on elaborate platters, some made in the palace workshops, others imported. Vessels were made of gold, silver, stone or terracotta; gold ladles were studded with jewels; special foods were served in the finest of Ming porcelain imported from China; goblets of gold, jade and silver were filled and refilled with sherbets and wines. Elaborate security measures were taken to ensure that there could be no tampering with the containers as they were escorted from the royal kitchens to the royal dining chamber:

During the time of cooking, and when the victuals are taken out, an awning is spread, and lookers-on kept away. The cooks tuck up their sleeves, and the hems of their garments, and hold out their hands before their mouths and noses when the food is taken out; the cook and the Bakawal taste it, after which it is tasted by the

Mir Bakawal, and then put into the dishes. The gold and silver dishes are tied up in red cloths, and those of copper and china in white ones. The Mir Bakawal attaches his seal, and writes on it the names of the contents, whilst the clerk of the pantry writes out on a sheet of paper a list of all vessels and dishes, which he sends inside, with the seal of the Mir Bakawal, that none of the dishes may be changed. The dishes are carried by the Bakawals, the cooks, and the other servants, and mace-bearers precede and follow, to prevent people from approaching them. The servants of the pantry send at the same time, in bags containing the seal of the Bakawal, various kinds of bread, saucers of curds piled up, and small stands containing plates of pickles, fresh ginger, limes and various greens. The servants of the palace again taste the food, spread the table cloth on the ground, and arrange the dishes; and when after some time his Majesty commences to dine, the table servants sit opposite him in attendance; first the share of the derwishes is put apart, when his Majesty commences with milk or curds. After he has dined, he prostrates himself in prayer. The Mir Bakawal is always in attendance. The dishes are taken away according to the above list. Some victuals are also kept half ready, should they be called for.

Ice was transported daily from the mountains to the capital; water was cooled by a drip system through saltpetre. Meals were accompanied by a great variety of breads from the Persian-style oven, from pear-shaped *naans* using milk and yeast and *ghee*, to the simple *chapati* using only flour and water to make a pliable dough rolled out into a circle and cooked dry on an iron plate. There were always numerous side-dishes of curds, pickles, achars, fresh ginger and limes. And to finish, many varieties of *paan*, betel leaves smeared with camphor and musk rolled up and accompanied by betel nuts. Abul Fazl enjoyed the taking of *paan* because, 'It renders the breath agreeable, and repasts odorous. It strengthens the gums, and makes the hungry satisfied, and the satisfied hungry.'

The taking of *paan* was an Indian custom adopted by the Moghuls early in their reign. Today betel leaf plays an important role in ceremonies such as birth and marriage, and on auspicious occasions. It has been endowed with digestive, medicinal, even magical qualities in some parts of India. The offering of *paan* after a meal is a ritual expected of the host.

The list of dishes commented upon by Fazl reveal that the royal cooks were by then making much use of the spices indigenous to India, even in the Persian-style dishes. No doubt Akbar's Hindu wives and his Rajput chiefs had a role in ensuring that dishes made with spices with which they were familiar were presented to the emperor.

Tempting dishes were sent to the emperor after his periods of fasting. *Murgh mussamman*, a forerunner of today's *murgh mussalam*, was one of the favourite dishes of the Rajput warriors that became fused into the Moghul style. To prepare it is a supreme test, even for expert cooks. The chicken has to be skilfully boned so that it remains whole, stuffed with well seasoned mince and rice and marinated in a spicy *masala* paste, placed on a rack in a heavy pan and cooked slowly in the oven in the *dum-phukt* manner in which the lid is sealed with dough. The method has changed little since the days of Akbar.

Akbar demanded nothing less than perfection from all his state departments, including the royal kitchen. One chicken dish had to be prepared 247 times before it was pronounced fit to bear the name *murgh akbari*. Persian culture introduced a richness to the rice dishes in the forms of the *pulao* or *pilau*, a Persian word meaning rice boiled with meats and spices. Akbar commanded that a special dish be created and dedicated to his nine favourite courtiers, one of whom, of course, was Abul Fazl. The nine were well known as 'Akbar's nine jewels' and the spectacular *pilau* with nine different jewel-coloured vegetables garnished with tiny grapes that resulted was called *navrattan*. Another of the 'nine jewels' was philosopher-wit Mullah Dopiaza. *Do-piaza gosht* is a full-flavoured meat dish using large quantities of both fried and ground onion introduced into the spices in two stages. It is still a favourite on Hyderabadi tables today.

Khichri, a simple dish from Gujerat in the west of India, caught Akbar's fancy and took on a more sophisticated form as cooks in the royal kitchens prepared it. Aurangzeb also enjoyed *khichri* and one version, *kichdi alamgiri* (Seizer of the Universe) was named for him. Being allowed to name a dish after an emperor was a great mark of prestige for the kitchen department and particularly for the cook who had created it. *Khichri* is still a popular dish and is often referred to as *kichdi*, a Hindi word meaning a mixture of pulses and rice.

Shahjahani biryani is an elaborate rice dish which combines the products of an extended empire. Rice is par-boiled, layered with lamb, chicken or vegetables cooked in a special *masala* of onions, ginger, crushed almonds and spices, spiced yoghurt and finally milk and *ghee*, and then sprinkled with saffron threads to complete the layers. Baked slowly in the oven, it is superb and well worth the effort involved. Mumtaz, the lady of the Taj, also has dishes that commemorate her name. *Murgh keema mumtaz mahal* is a very tasty chicken dish flavoured with poppy seeds and cashews on a bed of savoury minced lamb.

Abul Fazl mentions more than thirty dishes and their ingredients which were presented at Akbar's table and many of these dishes are still cooked in India today. He tells us that the emperor was subject to the influence of the numerous Hindu princesses who gained so great an ascendancy over him as to make him forswear beef, garlic, onion and the wearing of a beard. Akbar, a Muslim, went out of his way to introduce modified Hindu customs and heresies into the court assemblies to please and win over his Hindu subjects.

Jewellery was made incorporating Hindu motifs of the lotus, the ashoka tree, the elephant along with the tulip, the chrysanthemum and the gazelle of Islam. A deliberate policy of identifying with India was adopted. When Shah Jahan decided to try to conquer Samarkand, it was for the glory of his *Indian* empire. Both Akbar's son Jahangir and his son Shah Jahan had Hindu mothers. Akbar's courts were filled with Hindu entertainers, musicians, painters and philosophers.

Jahangir was also very fond of his food and wine. The now renowned dishes cooked in the *tandoor* oven were a favourite of his and his cooks were instructed to take their ovens whenever the emperor travelled. The clay *tandoor* oven came to India from Central Asia and today dishes like *tandoori murgh* are favourites wherever there are Indian restaurants.

Persian influences were certainly at work during Jahangir's reign. He married the daughter of a Persian nobleman employed at the Moghul court and she became one of the most influential women in the history of the Moghul empire. Nur Jahan counselled on state matters and also laid out gardens in Kashmir in the formal Persian style. She was an accomplished poet and a designer of clothes and jewellery. Her brother became a high-ranking official while her mother is credited as discovering attar of roses and her niece was wedded to the emperor Shah Jahan, builder of the Taj Mahal. This Persian quintet wielded much power, and under their direction banquets and festivals were celebrated in an even more lavish manner.

In 1590 Akbar chose Lucknow as one of the seats of government and, as the empire expanded, the city became an important seat of Muslim culture and learning. It was here that culinary skills reached new heights in the eighteenth and nineteenth centuries. In 1753 Shuja ud Daula established the independent court of Avadh (Oudh) and the court kitchens far surpassed those of his ancestors. He had six separate kitchens, supervised in a style similar to Akbar's. He spent great sums on food, the main kitchen receiving over 2,000 rupees per day for food alone, a very sizeable sum for those times.

As Lucknow became the centre of high society, expert cooks were brought in and the preparation of food became more and more elaborate as the cooks competed for supremacy. New dishes were created, and any that came from the kitchens of Lucknow were of the greatest interest to the nobility elsewhere in the subcontinent. Cooks were paid high salaries, and one *nawab*, Salar Jang, paid his cook the unprecedented sum of 1,200 rupees per month to prepare *pilaus*. His dishes became so renowned that other *nawabs* tried to bribe the cook into their service. At this time Lucknow specialised in several types of *pilau* with exotic-sounding names: *gulzar*, meaning garden, *nur* (light), *koko* (cuckoo), *moti* (pearl) and *chambeli* (jasmine). One Lucknow cook is said to have prepared a *khichri* of pistachios and almonds cut and shaped to resemble and replace the usual rice and pulses.

These highly specialised cooks guarded their secrets and there was much enticing of cooks from one household to another. Cooking had become an art form centred above all around rice dishes. This is well demonstrated in a *pilau* in which the rice was made to resemble pomegranate seeds, each grain being painted half red and half white so that it looked as if a dish of rubies had been set before the king.

For *moti pilau*, the rice was made to look like pearls. Tissue-thin sheets of pure gold and silver leaf were beaten into the yolk of an egg. This was mixed into the rice, which was then stuffed into the gullet of a chicken. The chicken was tied up with string and heated slightly, and the skin then cut to release the rice, which looked like pearls. The rice was then cooked with the meat of the *pilau*. One renowned Lucknow chef used to make a bird *pilau* in which the rice formed a type of pie from which small birds flew out when it was opened.

Today India specialises in two types of confectionery, that prepared by Muslims and that made by Hindus. *Halwa* is a typical Muslim sweetmeat and came to India via Central Asia. The Hindu variety, called *tar halwa* or *mohan bhog*, uses large quantities of *ghee*. Today's *jalebi* is often thought of as a typical Hindu sweetmeat, but Muslims claim that the name is a corruption of the Arabic *zalibya* introduced to India by Arab traders in the eighth century. Muslim-type sweetmeats include *barfi*, from the Persian word *baraf* meaning snow, a mouth-watering milk sweet, and *gulab jamun*, soft round balls steeped in syrup flavoured with rosewater.

When Shah Tahmasp of Persia offered hospitality to the Moghul Emperor Humayun early in the sixteenth century, he started another tradition that was to continue for hundreds of years. 'Let him drink fine sherbets of lemon and rosewater, cooled with snow,' he declared, and today in India cooling drinks are extremely popular, as are *nimbu pani* (lime juice), *lassi* (yoghurt diluted with water) and the sherbets or *sharbats* which can be bought from roadside stalls. In many households they are offered as a welcoming drink on a hot day. There is one sherbet that is very obviously Persian in origin, *badam sharbat*. Made from almonds, sugar and rosewater, *badam* means almonds in Persian. *Badam sharbat* is served both in Iran and in India. And so the Indo-Islamic fusion lingers on in these dishes handed down from the time of the Moghuls.

MENUS AND BANQUETS

As a general guide, main dishes are all served and set out at the same time and a small portion of each dish is taken along with the staple of rice or bread, sometimes both. Unless otherwise stated, the recipes which follow will serve four to six people generously. However, because traditionally several dishes are presented at a Moghul meal, an unexpected guest will not prove an embarrassment.

Choose an array of dishes that complement each other in flavour, texture and colour, and consider too a mixture of dry and sauce-based dishes. Usually, a main meal should consist of a combination of one or two meat, chicken or fish dishes, a couple of vegetable dishes, a lentil or pulse dish, a chutney, a pickle and always a *raita* or a bowl of yoghurt. There should be a rice dish or bread, or both. I often prepare a *pilau* or *biryani* as well as plain rice. No meal would be presented without a mound of crackly *pappadums*. Then, to complete the menu, glasses of a colourful *sharbat* or a milky white *lassi* and fresh fruit or one of the desserts.

I have given some suggestions for garnish and decoration, such as peas, fresh coriander leaves, rose petals, radish roses, julienne strips or flowers of chilli, raw onion rings (sometimes coloured), but there is so much more that can be done. If you have a garden free of chemical sprays, you can use the petals of any flower which is in bloom and seems appropriate.

In Moghul times dishes were presented to please the eye as well as the palate, so you may enjoy using your own ideas to present a meal to create a dramatic impression.

The Emperor Akbar's kitchens, with over 400 cooks to prepare food for his 300 wives and the royal entourage, turned out over 500 dishes daily to please and feed the emperor and his inner circle of courtiers and retainers. At short notice, 100 dishes would be presented. Even when the Emperor dined alone, as many as 40 dishes would be laid out before him.

As the empire spread, the elaborate banquets of the Moghul court were emulated at the palaces of the *nizams* of Hyderabad and the *nawabi* courts and mansions at Agra and in Bengal. The cooking style evolved further as each court tried to outdo the other in culinary innovation and presentation. A style resulted and is known today as Moghlai style.

Lavish court banquets became known by particular names which are still in use when food and entertainment is held on a grand scale. I have enjoyed the Moghul-style *chowki* banquets of Hyderabad; a *navrattan* feast in Agra; a *dawat* in Lucknow and similar lavish feasts in Delhi. All were memorable occasions. However, it was the Kashmiri *waazwaan* that I enjoyed most of all.

Kashmiri banquets are expected to be gargantuan feasts and we were, on one memorable occasion, offered seventy dishes at a Kashmiri *waazwaan*. In the event, we opted for twelve, which was more than sufficient. The lavish dining habits of Moghul days have not entirely disappeared from modern India and, although it is clearly impossible for the domestic cook in the West to emulate the extraordinary meals produced in Moghul India, it should be remembered that the recipes which follow come from a courtly cuisine. These dishes were intended to reflect the wealth and power of the imperial court as well as to give pleasure. These are recipes which deserve to be presented in as grand a style as is feasible in the modern dining room or kitchen.

HINTS AND BASIC RECIPES

CHILLIES

Much of the heat in chillies comes from the seeds and the membrane to which they are attached, so it helps to reduce the heat if the seeds are discarded. Use scissors to cut down the length of the chilli and shake or scrape free the seeds. Scissors are useful when cutting chillies as they minimise contact with the skin. Hands should be washed thoroughly after handling chillies.

COCONUT MILK

Coconut milk is extracted from the flesh of the coconut. This is done by steeping grated flesh in boiling water and pressing it through a sieve. Flesh from one fresh coconut should yield about three cups of coconut milk. Milk can be extracted from desiccated coconut and also made from creamed coconut. Tins of coconut milk are available from Indian shops and some supermarkets.

GARLIC, ONIONS AND GINGER

In the recipes which follow, quantities of garlic and ginger are given in teaspoons (tsps) and tablsespoons (tbsps). In the case of ginger, 4 cm/0.5 inches of the root will yield a tablespoon of grated ginger. As a rough guide, 3-5 cloves of garlic (depending on size) will yield 1 tablespoon when finely chopped. One large clove will give 1 teaspoon.

When a recipe calls for onions, garlic, ginger, chilli or coriander to be blended in a food-processor, add and blend the onions in short bursts after the other ingredients have been blended, to avoid a purée texture, because onions contain a lot of moisture.

The importance of the frying stages of the onions, garlic and ginger cannot be emphasised too strongly. The time it will take for the onions to lose their moisture and start changing colour will vary according to the type of oil, the size and thickness of the saucepan and the degree of heat used. Stirring is necessary to keep the ingredients from sticking. If this happens, add water, a little at a time, and continue stirring and cooking.

GARAM MASALA

Garam masala means 'hot spices'. It is a combination of spices which are dry-roasted and ground to a powder. *Garam masala* is usually added to a dish towards the end of the cooking process or just before serving. There are many versions of *garam masala*.

Moghul and Kashmiri *garam masalas* are highly aromatic and fragrant and give a certain character and lift to various dishes. Make them in small quantities and store in an airtight container.

Moghul Garam Masala

Use this *garam masala* for all the recipes in this book unless Kashmiri *garam masala* is specified.

1 tbsp light-coloured cumin seeds
2 tsp black cumin seeds
3 tsp cardamom seeds, extracted from pods
1½ tbsp black peppercorns
20 cloves
1 tsp fennel seeds
3 cinnamon sticks, each about 2.5 cm/1 inch, broken into tiny bits
1 tsp mace powder

Heat a small frying pan and separately dry-roast the light and black cumin seeds, cardamom seeds, peppercorns, cloves and fennel seeds until they begin to change colour and release their aromas. Do not allow them to burn. When cool, add the broken pieces of cinnamon to the roasted spices and grind to a fine powder in a coffee-grinder or spice-mill. Finally, mix in the mace powder and store in an airtight container.

Kashmiri Garam Masala

1 tsp black cumin seeds
2 tsp large brown cardamom seeds, extracted from pods
1 tsp light-coloured cardamom seeds, extracted from pods
1 tbsp black peppercorns
10 cloves
3 cinnamon sticks each about 2.5 cm/1 inch, broken into small bits
½ tsp saffron threads
½ tsp mace powder
1 tsp nutmeg powder

Heat a small frying pan and separately dry-roast the cumin seeds, cardamom seeds, peppercorns and cloves until they begin to change colour and release their aromas. Do not allow them to burn. When cool, add the broken pieces of cinnamon and saffron threads to the roasted spices and grind to a fine powder in a coffee-grinder or spice-mill. Mix in the mace and nutmeg powder. Store in an airtight container.

GHEE/CLARIFIED BUTTER

Indian sages used to refer to *ghee* as 'food that feeds the brain'. It was considered a source of energy and is used extensively in Moghul recipes. Fresh, unsalted butter is melted and simmered for lengthy periods to evaporate the moisture in the milk solids. The solids will turn into a brown residue which will remain at the bottom of the saucepan. Only the clear liquid *ghee* should be poured off and allowed to set. *Ghee* attains a high degree of heat before reaching smoking point.

SPICES

Many of the herbs and spices used in Indian cooking have been known in the subcontinent for thousands of years. They are important not only for their culinary and medicinal properties but also for their religious and social significance, and each herb and spice used in a recipe has a particular function besides that of enhancing the aroma and taste. Some are used for their preservative and anti-oxidant properties while others are added as an aid to digestion.

For further information on the subject of herbs and spices in Indian cooking, two fine works are highly recommended: Charmaine and Nina Solomon's *Encyclopedia of Asian Food*, Heinemann Australia 1996, and K.T. Achaya's *Indian Food, A Historical Companion*, OUP India 1994.

This list introduces the many spices and other flavouring ingredients that are used in Moghul cooking. In India and other Asian countries where the cuisines demand a high standard of freshness, spices and other ingredients are bought from the markets, as needed, on a daily basis. This is not always possible in Western countries, but if bought in small quantities most spices store well in airtight containers kept out of direct sunlight. To ensure that the spices you use are as fresh as possible, buy dried whole spices and grind them as required rather than buying them already ground.

English	Hindi	English	Hindi
ajowan	*ajwain*	coriander leaves	*hara dhania*
aniseed	*saunf*	cumin (light-coloured)	*jeera safaid*
asafoetida	*hing*	cumin (black)	*jeera kala*
basil	*goolal tulsi*	curry leaves	*cariya patta*
cardamom (large brown)	*bara elaichi*		*meetha neem*
cardamom (small light)	*chota elaichi*	fennel	*saunf, hasha*
cassia leaves	*tejpattar*	fenugreek	*methi*
chilli	*mirich*	mace	*javitri*
cinnamon	*dalchini*	mango powder	*amchoor*
cloves	*laung*	mixed spices (ground)	*garam masala*
coriander seeds	*sukha dhania*	mixed spices (whole)	*panch poran*

English	Hindi	English	Hindi
mustard seeds	*rai*	rose essence	*gulab ruh*
nigella	*kalonji*	rose water	*gulab jal*
nutmeg	*jaiphal*	saffron	*kesar*
pepper (black) or	*kala mirich*	sesame seeds	*til, gingelly*
peppercorns		screwpine essence	*kewra*
pomegranate seeds	*anardana*	tamarind	*imli*
poppy seeds	*khas khas*	turmeric	*haldi*

Crushed or bruised: use a pestle and mortar or put the spices between sheets of kitchen paper or a cloth, so that they do not scatter, and crush with a rolling pin.

Dry-roasted: dry-roasting of some seeds before grinding them to a powder or adding whole to a dish enhances both the aroma and the flavour. Care must be taken that the seeds do not burn or a bitter taste will result. Heat a small frying-pan over medium heat, sprinkle in the seeds and shake the pan lightly over the heat to toss and turn the seeds. As soon as they begin to smoke or change colour and release their aromas, remove them from the heat.

Ground or powdered: generally speaking, the quantities to be ground are small and the most efficient way to do this is in a coffee-grinder or spice-mill kept especially for that purpose. Sometimes the spices are ground to a coarse texture and sometimes they are ground to a fine powder. Ground or powdered spices are usually added after the frying of the onions, garlic and ginger. It is important to keep stirring. If the mixture is inclined to stick, add a tablespoon of water at a time and stir to prevent burning. When the spices are cooked the oil will start to separate out at the edges.

Whole or bruised: whole or bruised spices are often added when the *ghee* or oil begins to sizzle and before the onions, garlic and ginger are added. The spices are fried for a few seconds to release the seductive aromas into the oil.

Vegetable Stock (Akhni)

Akhni is a clear aromatic stock made without meat to be used instead of water when cooking vegetables to add to the flavour of the sauce. It can be made ahead and frozen.

1 tbsp ghee
1 tbsp crushed coriander
seeds
5 cm/2 inch cinnamon stick
10 peppercorns
1 tsp fennel seeds
2 large brown cardamoms,
bruised
1 finely chopped small onion
1 tsp finely chopped garlic
2 tsp grated fresh ginger
$1/2$ tsp salt
4 cups water

Heat the *ghee* in a heavy-bottomed saucepan, add the coriander seeds, cinnamon, peppercorns, fennel seeds and cardamom and fry for a few seconds; add the onion, garlic, ginger and fry for 3 minutes. Add the salt and water and bring to the boil, reduce the heat, cover and simmer for 5 minutes. Strain and discard the solids.

Meat Stock (Yakhni)

Yakhni is a rich stock made from the meat and bones of chicken or lamb and flavoured with garlic, ginger, onion and aromatic whole spices. It is used as the liquid for *pilaus* and *biryanis* and to enrich sauces for meat and chicken dishes. It can be prepared ahead and frozen.

750 g/1$1/2$ lb lamb shanks
1 roughly chopped large
onion
1 tsp finely chopped garlic
2 tsp grated fresh ginger
4 bruised cardamoms
20 peppercorns
5 cm/2 inch cinnamon stick
4 cloves
$1/2$ tsp salt
10 cups water

Place all the ingredients in a heavy-bottomed saucepan and bring to the boil. Reduce the heat, cover and simmer gently until the meat is falling off the bones. Allow to cool and then skim the fatty solids from the surface. Strain the liquid through a fine sieve and discard the solids.

Dahi (Yoghurt)

Yoghurt is favoured as a cooling agent and, in one form or another, often accompanies Moghul meals. It is used as a tenderiser and in marinations; it is added to sweet and savoury dishes and made into *raitas* and drinks like *lassi*. Yoghurt can easily be made at home. It is a source of Vitamins A and D, high in calcium, fat and protein. If you use commercial yoghurt, strain it through muslin or cheesecloth to drain of any extra moisture and leave a thicker, creamier texture.

When adding yoghurt to a dish, do so gradually to avoid curdling on making contact with heat.

If a thicker consistency and creamier texture is desired, add 2 tablespoons of full-cream powdered milk to the milk to be boiled.

Allow 8 hours or more for the yoghurt to set.

2 pints fresh milk
2 tbsp yoghurt

Bring the milk to the boil in a heavy-bottomed saucepan. Allow to cool, skimming off any skin that forms, until it is lukewarm. Add the yoghurt and mix well to dissolve the yoghurt into the milk. Pour into a glass or porcelain bowl and cover. Leave undisturbed in a draught-free place to set; this can take 8-12 hours.

WEIGHTS AND MEASUREMENTS

Weights and measurements for all the recipes in this book are given in metric, together with the British or imperial equivalent; for simplicity's sake, they have been rounded off to the nearest convenient equivalent and close approximations are given rather than the exact converted amount.

Cup measurements used in the recipes are metric. 1 cup equals 250 ml or 8 fluid ounces, and to keep things simple I have used the same size of measuring cup for solids like rice and lentils.

Spoon measurements are as follows. 1 teaspoon equals 5 ml or $\frac{1}{6}$ of a fluid ounce and 1 tablespoon equals 15 ml or $\frac{1}{2}$ a fluid ounce. Where spoon measures are indicated, I have used rounded or heaped spoonfuls; the text will indicate whether a level spoon measurement is required. The Australian and New Zealand tablespoon has a slightly larger capacity of 20 ml.

APPETISERS AND SNACKS

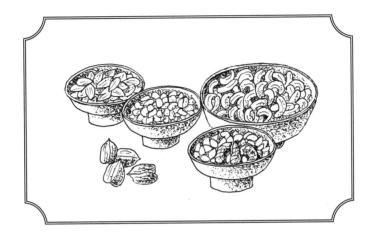

The Spanish Ambassador to Timur's court at Samarkand in the fifteenth century has left a vivid account of court banquets and the food served at them. After declaring himself Emperor of Hindustan, Babur pined for Samarkand and the foods of his home-land. Travellers through Uzbekistan today could be forgiven for momentarily thinking that they were in Pakistan or northern India. Culinary sights and aromas with Turko-Persian names like *naan, paratha, shashlik kebab, shorva, palav* and *samsas* (*samosas*) would all be familiar in flavour and appearance to the snacks in those countries. In Samarkand, Bukhara and Tashkent bazaars and market stalls sell snacks much as they did in the times of Timur and Babur, but now combining the same ingredients, such as spices, chillies and fresh coriander, as the stallholders in Peshawar, Lahore, Avadh or Delhi.

There is much to tempt the passer-by; snacking is an important part of the culture of all these countries and snacks are considered to be part of the daily diet. Roadside stalls and itinerant vendors selling snacks and nibbles are a familiar sight. Crisp and crunchy nibbles made from spiced chick-pea batter are piled high on trays and carts. Nuts are sprinkled with cumin and chilli and tossed in sizzling *ghee*. Spicy aromas pervade the air and crowds are drawn to stalls where freshly cooked savoury delicacies are prepared and devoured at all times of the day and night.

Immense importance is placed on hospitality. Muslims consider and treat the unex-pected guest as a gift from god, while Hindus believe that the unexpected guest could be a god in disguise. Both arrive at the same conclusion as far as plying the guest with snacks either freshly cooked or purchased from a nearby stall – *pakoras, parathas, samosas* or *kebabs* along with a cooling sherbet, lime juice, yoghurt drink or piping hot sweet tea or coffee.

As the Moghul Empire expanded and became stabilised, many of the foods of Samarkand, familiar to Babur, eventually came to Hindustan to be fused into an Indo-Persian style. Were Babur to return to Hindustan today and see the foods at roadside stalls, he could be forgiven if he thought he was back in his beloved Samarkand.

The snacks and appetisers that I have included are intended to be served in moderate quantities before the main meal, but you may like to consider preparing a variety of these savoury delicacies to serve with drinks.

Masala Bhona Badami Kaju

LIGHTLY SPICED NUTS

This nutty mixture, served warm, will prove very popular with a drink before dinner. When cool, the spiced nuts can be stored in an airtight container. To reheat, place in a low to moderate oven for 8-10 minutes.

Vegetable oil to cover the frying pan to a depth of 3 cm/1¹⁄4 inches
3 cups of assorted shelled nuts (cashews, almonds, peanuts, pistachios)
1 tsp cumin seeds
1¹⁄2 tsp garam masala
¹⁄2 tsp chilli powder
1 tsp salt

Heat the oil in a heavy-bottomed frying pan. When the oil begins to sizzle, add the cumin seeds. Lower the heat, add the nuts and keep stirring until they become a golden colour. Remove with a slotted spoon to absorbent paper. Transfer to a bowl while still warm and sprinkle with *garam masala*, chilli powder and salt; toss to coat the nuts.

Nimki

ॐ

CUMIN-FLAVOURED PASTRIES

Diamond-shaped wedges of golden fried dough are transformed into delectable nibbles with a nutty flavouring of black cumin seeds. They can be served warm or cold and will store well in an airtight container.

2 cups plain flour
1 tsp salt
1½ tsp black cumin seeds
½ tsp chilli powder
½ tsp garam masala
3 tbsp melted ghee
½ cup water
(approximately)

Sift the flour into a bowl and stir in the salt, cumin seeds, chilli powder and *garam masala*. Rub in the melted *ghee*. Gradually add the water and mix to a firm dough. Knead for 10-15 minutes to form a smooth pliable dough. Return to the bowl and cover with a moistened cloth. Set aside to rest for 30 minutes at room temperature.

Extra flour for dusting

Dust the rolling surface and rolling pin with flour. Roll the dough out thinly and cut into small diamond shapes.

Ghee or vegetable oil for deep-frying

Heat the ghee or oil in a heavy-bottomed saucepan until it begins to sizzle. When hot, fry a few of the shapes at a time, turning them to get an even golden colour. Remove with a slotted spoon and drain on absorbent paper.

Bhuna Jhinga

ॐ

MARINATED AND SHALLOW-FRIED PRAWNS

Large, raw prawns are shelled to their tails and deveined. Before being shallow-fried, they are lightly spiced and marinated in a paste of ginger, garlic and lemon juice to take on a subtle tangy flavour and a golden tinge. Serve with a bowl of cucumber *raita* (p.202). Large king-size prawns are preferable, if available. If you use a smaller variety of prawns or shrimps, the quantity will need to be increased. Frozen prawns must be properly thawed but, if pre-cooked, they will only require heating through at the frying stage.

12 large raw prawns; remove heads and shells, leaving the tail on; devein

To devein the prawns after shelling, use a sharp knife and make a shallow cut along the outer curve and lift or scrape out the gritty vein.

1 tsp turmeric powder
1/2 tsp chilli powder
1/2 tsp salt
1/2 tsp garam masala

Sprinkle the shelled and deveined prawns with turmeric, chilli powder, salt and *garam masala*. Set aside for 15 minutes.

2 tsp roughly chopped fresh ginger
1 tsp roughly chopped garlic
1 tbsp fresh coriander leaves
2 tbsp lime or lemon juice

Blend the ginger, garlic, coriander leaves and lime or lemon juice to a smooth paste in a food-processor. Rub the paste into the prawns and leave to marinate for 1 hour.

Vegetable oil for shallow-frying

Heat the oil and shallow-fry prawns, turning them until they are cooked.

Machhi Kebabs

ॐ

SPICY FISH BALLS

These delicious spicy fish balls are a party favourite. I make them into walnut-sized balls to be picked up with the fingers. To serve them as a first course, make them a little larger and flatten to a circle. Serve with a banana *raita* (p.205) or a tomato chutney (p.207). Peeling the potatoes after cooking them in their skins seems to give them a light floury texture. Select a firm, white-fleshed fish like cod for these tasty snacks.

1 tsp turmeric powder
2 tbsp lime or lemon juice
750 g/1½ lb firm white fish fillets

Mix the turmeric powder with the lime or lemon juice and sprinkle over and rub into the fish fillets. Set aside for 15 minutes.

1½ cups water	Put the water into a heavy-bottomed saucepan and add the marinated fish fillets. Cover the saucepan and poach the fish. Drain, allow to cool and set aside.
250 g/8 oz potatoes *½ tsp salt* *1 light-coloured cardamom pod, bruised*	Cover the potatoes with water, add the salt and cardamom pod and cook. Allow the potatoes to cool. Peel the cardamom-flavoured potatoes and put them in a bowl with the cooked fish fillets.
1 roughly chopped small onion *2 tsp roughly chopped fresh ginger* *1 tbsp fresh coriander leaves* *1 fresh green chilli, seeds discarded* *2 tbsp water*	Blend the onion, ginger, coriander leaves, chilli and water to a smooth paste in a food-processor.
½ tsp salt *2 tsp ghee* *1 tsp dry-roasted cumin seeds* *1 tsp garam masala*	Add the blended paste to the fish and potato mixture and mix in the salt, *ghee*, dry-roasted cumin seeds, *garam masala* and mash all together. Do this by hand to make sure all the ingredients are well integrated.
A small bowl of water to moisten fingers	Moisten your fingers and form walnut-sized balls of the fish and potato mixture.
Vegetable oil for deep-frying *2 eggs, yolks and whites beaten together in a small bowl* *125 g/4 oz breadcrumbs spread on a plate*	Heat the oil in a heavy-bottomed saucepan. Dip the spicy fish balls into the beaten egg, roll in the bread-crumbs and deep-fry a few at a time until a deep golden brown. Drain on absorbent paper.

Aloo Tikki

🐚

SPICED PEAS IN MASHED POTATO

Garden peas are cooked with ginger, coriander, mint and spices and mashed to a coarse texture before being buried in a casing of savoury mashed potato and then shallow-fried to a golden brown. These can be rounds of about 5 cm/2 inches, but you can make them smaller or larger as you prefer. Serve with a coriander (p.208) or tomato chutney (p.207). The main ingredient for the filling can, of course, be varied with other vegetables or even minced or ground meat or fish. Without the chilli, these potato 'cakes' are very popular with young children.

For the filling:
1 tbsp ghee
1 tsp cumin seeds
2 tsp finely chopped fresh ginger
1 finely chopped fresh green chilli, seeds discarded
1/2 tbsp finely chopped fresh coriander leaves
1/2 tbsp finely chopped fresh mint leaves
2 tsp coriander powder
1/2 tsp salt
1/2 tsp ground black pepper
1 tsp garam masala
3/4 cup shelled green peas
1 tbsp lime or lemon juice
3 tbsp water

Heat the *ghee* in a small heavy-bottomed frying pan, add the cumin seeds and fry for a few seconds to release their aroma. Add the fresh ginger, chilli, coriander leaves, mint leaves, coriander powder, salt, pepper and *garam masala* and fry for 2 minutes. Lower the heat. Add the peas and stir for 1 minute. Add the lemon juice and water; cover and cook on a low heat for 4 minutes or until the peas are cooked.

Add a little water if the liquid is absorbed before the peas are cooked. Test by squashing a couple of peas. Drain, cool and mash the peas to a coarse texture.

For the casing:
750 g/1 1/2 lb potatoes
2 tbsp cornflour
1 tsp salt
1 finely chopped fresh green chilli, seeds discarded

Boil the potatoes in their skins, allow them to cool, then peel and mash them. Put the mashed potatoes into a bowl and add the cornflour, salt, chopped chilli and coriander or mint leaves and mix well.

Moisten your fingers and divide and roll the mashed mixture into portions of the size you require. Take each

1/2 tbsp finely chopped fresh coriander or mint leaves
2 eggs, yolks and whites beaten together

ball between your palms and flatten it slightly with a depression towards the centre. Put a little of the savoury pea filling in the centre, bring the edges together and roll lightly into a ball with moistened fingers. Flatten between your palms to make kebabs and dip in the beaten egg.

Ghee or vegetable oil for shallow frying

Heat a little *ghee* or oil to coat a heavy-bottomed frying pan and shallow-fry the kebabs on a medium heat. Use as little ghee as possible, adding more as necessary until the kebabs are golden brown on both sides.

Shahi Murghi Pakoras

CHICKEN IN BATTER

Bite-sized pieces of chicken are penetrated with the flavours of garlic, chilli, cumin and saffron, dipped in batter and deep-fried to emerge as succulent morsels. Serve with coriander chutney (p.208) or a *raita* of your choice. Meat or vegetables can be used instead of chicken; if you substitute vegetables, allow only 15 minutes for each of the marinations.

Allow 1$\frac{1}{2}$ hours for marination.

For the pakoras:
500 g/1 lb skinned chicken breasts cut into fairly large bite-sized pieces
1/4 tsp saffron threads, steeped for 15 minutes in 1 tbsp hot milk
1 tsp chilli powder
2 tsp cumin powder
1 tsp salt
2 tbsp lime or lemon juice, mixed with 1/2 tsp crushed garlic

Put the chicken pieces in a bowl and sprinkle them with the steeped saffron threads, chilli powder, cumin powder and salt. Turn the mixture from time to time to allow the flavours to penetrate into the chicken pieces for 30 minutes. Trickle the garlic-flavoured lime or lemon juice over chicken pieces and mix well. Allow to marinate for a further hour.

For the batter:
6 tbsp chick-pea flour
1 tbsp rice flour
1 tsp cumin seeds
3/4 tsp salt
1/2 tsp garam masala
1/2 tsp turmeric powder
1/4 tsp bicarbonate of soda
1/2 cup water

Vegetable oil for deep-frying

Sift the chick-pea and rice flour into a bowl. Then mix in the cumin seeds, salt, *garam masala*, turmeric powder and bicarbonate of soda. Gradually add the water to make a fairly thick batter. Allow the batter to stand for about 20 minutes. Whisk just before dipping the ingredients for deep-frying.

After the marination period, heat the oil in a heavy-bottomed saucepan until it is sizzling hot. Dip the chicken pieces in the batter, lower the heat and deep-fry as many as the pan will take in a single layer without over-crowding. Cook for 4 minutes or a little longer if the pieces are thick, turn them over and cook for another 4 minutes. Remove with a slotted spoon to drain on absorbent paper.

Samosa Keema Peshawari

SPICY SAMOSAS

I will never forget driving across the border from Afghanistan to Peshawar in Pakistan on a bitterly cold and blustery day and being greeted at the border with wonderful aromas tempting weary travellers to linger at the roadside stalls. I succumbed, and after devouring several *samosas* filled with delicately spiced meat I begged the recipe from the stall-keeper who told me the recipe had been in his family since the times of Shah Jahan. A drop or two of screwpine essence with a touch of nutmeg and mace lifts these *samosas* to great heights. It was these last three ingredients, I was told, that makes the Peshawari *samosa* different to any other. These quantities will make about 18 *samosas*.

For the pastry:
1 cup sifted self-raising flour
1/2 tsp salt

Put the sifted flour and salt into a bowl. Rub in the melted *ghee* and *kewra* essence. Gradually add the water and mix and knead until the dough becomes soft

2¹/2 tbsp melted ghee

2 drops kewra (screwpine) essence

¹/3 cup lukewarm water

1 tsp melted ghee to moisten fingers

and leaves the side of the bowl. If more water is needed to achieve this, add a few drops at a time and continue kneading for about 10 minutes, your fingers moistened with melted *ghee.*

Cover with a damp cloth or plastic wrap and set aside at room temperature for 30 minutes. Meanwhile prepare the filling.

For the filling:

2 tbsp ghee

1 finely chopped medium onion

1 tsp finely chopped fresh ginger

¹/2 tsp finely chopped garlic

1 tsp coriander powder

1 tsp cumin powder

¹/2 tsp turmeric powder

¹/2 tsp chilli powder

¹/2 tsp Kashmiri garam masala

Heat the *ghee* in a heavy-bottomed saucepan, fry the onion, ginger and garlic until the onion starts to change colour. Lower the heat, add the coriander, cumin, turmeric, chilli and *garam masala* and fry for 2 minutes.

185 g/6 oz lean minced meat (lamb is traditionally used)

¹/2 tsp salt

1 tbsp lime or lemon juice

¹/2 cup warm water

¹/4 tsp grated nutmeg

3 drops kewra (screwpine) essence

1 tbsp finely chopped fresh mint leaves

1 finely chopped medium onion

1 finely chopped large fresh green chilli

Raise the heat a little, add the mince and stir and mash it against the side of the pan to prevent lumps from forming. Add the salt, lime or lemon juice, warm water and stir. Cover, lower the heat and cook for 10-15 minutes or until the mince is cooked and the moisture is absorbed. The mixture should be fairly dry. Add the nutmeg, *kewra* essence, fresh mint leaves, onion and chilli; stir well to combine. Remove from the heat and allow to cool.

Extra flour for dusting

Lightly knead the rested dough. Divide into 9 balled portions. Press each ball with your palm to flatten it out and cover with a moistened cloth or plastic wrap. Dust the work surface and rolling pin with the extra flour.

Work with one flattened portion at a time. Roll out into
10 cm/4 inch circles and cut into two semi-circles.

Put a generous teaspoon of the filling on one half of
a semi-circle, leaving the edges free. Brush round the
edges with water. Fold the free half of a semi-circle over
the filling to form a triangle and press the edges firmly
to seal. Repeat until all the *samosas* are ready for deep-
frying.

Oil for deep-frying

Heat the oil in a deep, heavy-bottomed saucepan until it
begins to sizzle. Reduce the heat and gently fry the
samosas a few at a time, turning and spooning oil over
until the samosas are a rich golden colour. Remove with
a slotted spoon and drain on absorbent paper.

SOUPS

The Hindi word for soup is *shorva* or *shorba*, which means broth. Except on restaurant menus, soups appear only rarely in India. When soups are served in the home, they are usually presented with the main dishes and not separately at the beginning of the meal as they are in Western countries. The recipes which follow are for creamy-textured soups which are not intended as hearty meals in themselves. They will be enjoyed if served in the Western way as starters for Moghul meals.

There is evidence from early writings that soups were enjoyed by Timur at Samarkand, his capital, in the fourteenth century, and substantial soups or *shorvas* are still served in Uzbekistan. Babur's memoirs mention *gipa*, a dish which is reputed to be one of the oldest soups in the history of Persian cuisine. In Iran thick soups or *ash* (pronounced to rhyme with squash) are considered a major part of the daily diet and are as popular today as they were in the sixteenth century in the days of Shah Tahmasp of Persia, with whom the Moghul Emperor Humayun took refuge. There is little doubt that soups were served as a part of Moghul banquets, and those that I have included reflect the influence of Persia in their use of almonds, pomegranates and yoghurt.

Yakhni Shorba

AROMATIC LAMB BROTH

In many parts of the Muslim world soups are served at the end of the day to break fast during the month-long period of Ramadan. This light lamb broth is delicately flavoured with cardamom, cinnamon, fresh herbs and saffron. The heat comes from the black pepper. Served hot garnished with fresh coriander leaves, the broth is a pleasing introduction to a Moghul meal.

1 kg/2 lb lamb shanks
7 cups water
1 tsp salt
2 small light-coloured cardamoms, bruised
5 cm/2 inch cinnamon stick
1 tsp ground black pepper
2 cloves
1 tbsp grated fresh ginger
1 tbsp coriander powder
1 tbsp finely chopped fresh coriander leaves

Put all the ingredients except the yoghurt and saffron threads in milk into a heavy-bottomed saucepan and simmer gently for about 1 hour or until the stock is reduced to about 4 cups. Allow to cool. Skim the fat off the surface and discard the cardamom pods, cinnamon stick and cloves.

1 cup lightly whisked yoghurt
1/4 tsp saffron threads, steeped for 15 minutes in 1 tbsp hot milk

Discard the meat and bones. Strain the stock through a fine sieve. Return it to the pan and bring it to the boil. Lower the heat, gradually add the yoghurt and saffron threads in milk and stir gently. Continue simmering for 5 minutes.

Badami Shorba

ALMOND-FLAVOURED SOUP

I know that my guests will enjoy some subtle surprises when I serve this almond-flavoured soup, which is made slightly aromatic with its hints of cardamom and saffron. It may be served hot, but it is also delicious ice-cold as a start to a Moghul meal on a hot summer's day.

250 g/8 oz blanched almonds
2 tbsp milk

Blend the almonds and milk to a smooth paste in a food-processor and set aside.

2 tbsp butter
1 tsp grated fresh ginger
2 lightly bruised cardamom pods
2 tsp plain flour
2 cups milk
1 tsp sugar
1/4 tsp ground white pepper
1/2 tsp salt

Heat the butter in a heavy-bottomed saucepan, add the grated ginger and bruised cardamom pods and sauté for a couple of seconds. Add the flour and continue stirring for about 1 minute. Remove from the heat and stir in the milk gradually to avoid lumps forming; add the sugar, pepper and salt, return to the heat and simmer for 3 minutes.

2 1/2 cups hot water
1/4 tsp saffron threads, steeped for 15 minutes in 1 tbsp hot milk
1/2 cup cream

Mix the almond paste into the hot water and add to the saucepan. Add the steeped saffron threads and simmer for about 10 minutes. Discard the cardamom pods. Fold the cream into the soup just before serving.

2 tsp butter
1 tbsp flaked or slivered almonds

Heat the butter in a small frying pan and toss the almonds until golden. Just before serving, sprinkle the almond flakes over the soup.

Dahi Shorba

⤎

LAMB AND YOGHURT SOUP

This palate-pleaser is a combination of yoghurt and split peas in a lamb stock flavoured with cumin, a light dash of ground pepper and chilli powder. Served with a crusty Western-style bread, it is an ideal soup for an autumn lunch.

Allow the split peas to soak in water for about one hour; this will soften them, thus speeding up the cooking time and also helping to make them more digestible.

1 tbsp butter
1 finely sliced large onion
¹/4 tsp finely chopped garlic
250 g/8 oz shank of lamb;
cut meat into pieces and
reserve the bone
¹/4 cup dried yellow split
peas; cover with water and
soak for 1 hour
¹/2 cup well rinsed rice
1¹/2 tsp salt
¹/4 tsp cumin powder
¹/2 tsp turmeric powder
¹/2 tsp ground black pepper
¹/4 tsp chilli powder
6 cups water

Heat the butter in a heavy-bottomed saucepan, sauté the onion and garlic until light brown, add the meat pieces and cook until they turn brown. Add the soaked split peas, rice, salt, cumin, turmeric, pepper and chilli powder and mix well. Add the water and the bone. Cover the saucepan and simmer gently for 1 hour, stirring occasionally.

2 cups lightly whisked
yoghurt

Remove the bone and discard. Leave the soup on a gentle simmer. Remove the meat and grind to a paste in a food-processor. Skim off any fat globules that may have surfaced on the soup. Return the meat paste to the saucepan and gradually stir in the yoghurt.

A few finely cut rings of the
green end of a spring onion

Serve hot, garnished with spring onion rings.

Nizam's Nimbu Shorba

?●

LEMON-FLAVOURED SOUP

Nourishing, rich, tangy and spicy, this creamy-textured soup is thickened with mashed potato and coconut milk. This recipe comes from the palace kitchen of a former prime minister of Hyderabad. I enjoyed it and many other superb Hyderabadi dishes at the home of my late friend Rubina Ottley, who was a governess at the palace for many years. If limes are available, use lime juice in preference to lemon juice.

I often start preparing this soup a day ahead; it then only needs to be finished about 10 minutes before serving.

First stage:
6 cups water
2 lamb shanks, washed
1 roughly chopped onion
$^1/_2$ tsp salt
$^1/_4$ tsp ground black pepper
5 cm/2 inch piece
cinnamon stick
6 cloves
1 tsp cumin seeds
2 light-coloured cardamom
pods, lightly bruised at tip
8 peppercorns

Place the water and all the ingredients for the first stage in a heavy-bottomed saucepan. Bring to the boil and simmer for about 1 hour or until the meat starts to fall away from the bone. Remove the bones and meat, shred the meat and discard the bones. Discard the cinnamon stick and the cardamom pods.

Strain the liquid through a sieve over a bowl. When cool, skim off the fat. Return the shredded meat to the stock and refrigerate until working on the next stage.

Second stage:
$1^1/_2$ tbsp butter
2 finely chopped onions
1 tsp grated fresh ginger
1 tsp turmeric powder
1 tsp garam masala
1 tsp coriander powder
$^1/_4$ tsp chilli powder
3 medium potatoes, peeled
and finely diced
1 tsp salt

Heat the butter in a heavy-bottomed saucepan, add the onions and ginger and fry until the onions start to change colour. Add the turmeric, *garam masala*, coriander powder and chilli powder, stir and fry for 2 minutes. If the mixture is inclined to stick, sprinkle in a little water and continue stirring. Add the diced potatoes to the mixture and coat well. Add the salt, the prepared stock, the lime or lemon juice and chopped coriander leaves. Bring to the boil and then simmer for 30 minutes. Strain through a sieve over a bowl and reserve the solids; return the stock to the pan. Purée the solids and

5¹/2 cups stock as previously prepared for the first stage
2 tbsp lime or lemon juice
¹/4 cup finely chopped fresh coriander leaves

add to the stock. If preparing ahead, cool and refrigerate.

¹/2 cup coconut milk
2 tbsp lightly whisked yoghurt

Heat the soup, gradually adding the coconut milk and yoghurt. Bring to the boil, then lower the heat and simmer for 4 minutes. Serve hot.

Anarkarli Shorba

POMEGRANATE SOUP

Pomegranates were relished at Moghul courts and it was believed by some that they were the fruit in the Garden of Eden. When Jahangir beheld the beauty of a flower-seller he called her his beautiful Anarkarli (Pomegranate Blossom), but the ill-fated young woman was entombed alive by Akbar for daring to acknowledge Jahangir's attentions. This delectable soup dedicated to the flower-seller is thickened with a purée of split peas, lentils, rice, spinach and leek and flavoured with the syrup of pomegranate. I sometimes add a sprinkling of chopped mint leaves as a garnish.

Allow 1 hour for soaking the split peas.

1¹/2 tbsp butter
1 finely chopped large onion
¹/2 cup yellow split peas; rinse, cover with water, soak for 1 hour and drain
¹/4 cup rinsed masoor dal (lentils)
¹/2 cup well rinsed rice
6¹/2 cups water
1 tsp salt
¹/2 tsp ground black pepper

Heat the butter in a heavy-bottomed saucepan and sauté the chopped onion until it turns a light golden brown. Drain and add the split peas, lentils and rice and stir to coat. Add the water, bring to the boil, lower the heat and simmer for 15 minutes. Add the salt, pepper, coriander, leek and spinach; simmer gently for 10 minutes.

*2 tbsp finely chopped fresh
coriander leaves and stalk
1 finely chopped small leek
120 g/ ¼ lb fresh spinach,
rinsed and finely chopped*

2 tbsp syrup of pomegranate
or
*1 cup juice extracted from
fresh pomegranate*

Strain the mixture through a sieve and return the stock to the pan. Purée the solids and return to the stock. Add the pomegranate juice and continue to simmer gently for 10 minutes.

MEAT

Moghul cuisine boasts an incredible number of spiced lamb and kid dishes cooked in a variety of ways, and master chefs in India and Pakistan boast that they could cook a different lamb dish for every day of the year. Cooking methods vary from skewered barbecue-style spit-roasted or grilled kebabs, or shallow-fried kebabs of minced meat; *samosas* or pastry cases filled with meat and deep-fried; whole legs of lamb or kid and cubes of meat marinated and cooked in the *tandoor* clay oven; countless sauce-based, curry-style dishes cooked on the stove top or in the oven; finally, there is an endless repertoire of *pilaus* and *biryanis* combining layers of meat with rice.

The Emperor Humayun records that beef in Hindustan was tasteless and tough. Hindu administrators and officials were numerous at the Moghul court, and no doubt in deference to them and to the Rajput Hindu wives, beef was not eaten, although there is no evidence that it was strictly forbidden. Pork, of course, is forbidden to Muslims, but the Moghuls hunted wild boar, which was enjoyed by the Hindu Rajputs. Sir Thomas Roe, the English Ambassador to the Moghul court, was presented with a wild boar shot by the Emperor Jahangir, who 'kindly requests that the tusks be returned'.

There is no reason why beef or pork should not be substituted for many of the lamb dishes, and if goat or kid meat is available, do substitute it for any of the meat dishes; the loose-textured flesh of goat or kid allows for easy penetration of spices and marinades.

Goshtaba

ॐ

MEATBALLS IN YOGHURT AND CREAM

Cubes of lamb are finely ground or minced to a smooth texture, kneaded together with aromatic spices and formed into balls which are then very gently simmered in milk, yoghurt and cream. This dish is only one of the highlights of a Kashmiri banquet. To enjoy the delicate aromatic flavours, serve it with a light *pilau* or plain white rice. I ask my butcher to pass lean lamb cubes through his finest mincer blades twice. Test the smoothness by rubbing some across your fingers. The kneading process will further smooth the mince.

Kashmiris will spend at least a couple of hours pounding cubes of meat until they are happy with the smoothness of texture. No wonder cooks were so highly prized that after one particular banquet Babur's daughter Princess Gulbadan was heard to say words to the effect that, 'Such food had not been sighted since the Cook of Divine Contrivance placed a dish of the Sun on the table of the Heavens.'

For the meatballs:
750 g/1½ lb lean lamb,
off the bone
2 tsp grated fresh ginger
1 tbsp ghee

Pass the meat, ginger and *ghee* through finest mincer twice or divide into 3 portions and chop each portion to a near paste-like texture in the food-processor.

½ tsp nutmeg powder
1 tsp cardamom powder
1 tsp chilli powder
1 tsp Kashmiri garam
masala
1½ tsp salt
4 tbsp arrowroot,
mixed to a smooth paste
with 3 tbsp water

Add the nutmeg, cardamom, chilli, Kashmiri *garam masala* and salt to the meat paste mixture and knead in. Add the arrowroot paste and knead together until well combined and velvety smooth. Moisten your fingers and form balls a little smaller than a golf ball. Cover with plastic wrap or a damp cloth and set aside in a refrigerator to become firm.

For the sauce:
4 tbsp ghee
3 large brown cardamom
pods, bruised

Heat the *ghee* in a heavy-bottomed saucepan, add the cardamom pods and cinnamon stick and fry for a few seconds to release their aromas. Add the chopped onions and ginger and fry until the onions become

2 cm/³/4 inch cinnamon stick
2 finely chopped onions
2 tsp grated fresh ginger
2 tsp cumin powder
2 tsp coriander powder
1 tsp Kashmiri garam masala
¹/2 tsp chilli powder
¹/2 tsp salt
1 tsp sugar
¹/2 cup cream
2 cups milk
1 cup yoghurt
¹/2 cup water

translucent. Lower the heat.

Add and stir in the cumin, coriander, *garam masala*, chilli powder, salt and sugar and fry for 2 minutes.

Lightly whisk together the cream, milk, yoghurt and water and gradually stir into the mixture; simmer for about 7 minutes.

¹/2 tsp saffron threads, steeped for 15 minutes in 1 tbsp hot milk

Add the steeped saffron threads and milk and simmer for 2 minutes. Gently add the meatballs and roll them in the sauce to coat them. Cover the pan and simmer gently on a low heat for about 30 minutes. Turn the meatballs carefully every 10 minutes or so to ensure even cooking. Discard the cardamom pods and the cinnamon stick.

1 tbsp chopped fresh mint leaves

Gently remove the meatballs to a serving dish and pour the sauce over them. Scatter with chopped fresh mint leaves.

Tabak Maas

CARDAMOM-FLAVOURED LAMB CHOPS

Chops make their appearance in various guises during a Kashmiri feast and this is one of several versions of this Kashmiri dish. These chops are delicious as a starter and are also a popular picnic snack. The main flavouring is cardamom, both from the large brown pods and from cardamom powder. The chops are first cooked in cardamom-flavoured milk and then fried and finally simmered in yoghurt and spices and flavoured with saffron and Kashmiri *garam masala*.

8 lamb chops scored twice with a sharp knife across the outside fat to prevent curling when cooking
2 cups milk
3 large brown cardamom pods, bruised
1/2 tsp salt

Place the chops in a heavy-bottomed saucepan with the milk, cardamom pods and salt and bring to the boil. Lower the heat, cover and simmer for 10 minutes. Turn the chops over once during this time. Remove and drain on absorbent paper. Discard the liquid.

5 tbsp ghee
2 finely chopped medium onions
1 tbsp grated fresh ginger
1 tsp finely chopped garlic
1 tsp chilli powder
1/2 tsp turmeric powder
1/4 tsp cardamom powder
1/4 tsp ground black pepper
1 tsp salt

Heat the *ghee* in a heavy-bottomed frying pan, fry the drained chops so that they brown well on both sides. Remove to a plate. Add the chopped onions, ginger and garlic to the remaining oil and stir-fry for 3 minutes. Add the chilli powder, turmeric, cardamom, black pepper and salt; stir-fry for a further 2 minutes.

1 tsp fennel seeds
8 cloves
2 cm/3/4 inch cinnamon stick

Grind the fennel seeds, cloves and cinnamon in a coffee-grinder or spice-mill and add to the mixture.

1 1/2 lightly whisked cups yoghurt
1/2 cup water
1/4 tsp saffron threads, steeped for 15 minutes in 1 tbsp hot milk
1/2 tsp Kashmiri garam masala

Gradually stir in the yoghurt, return the chops to the frying pan and simmer uncovered for 5 minutes. Stir in the water and the saffron threads and milk and continue cooking until all the liquid is absorbed and the chops are tender. Some oil will have separated out. Lift the chops and shake free of any remaining oil. Arrange the chops on a serving platter. Sprinkle with the *garam masala.*

Kashmiri Kamargah

❧

SPICY LAMB RIBS IN BATTER

Members of the highest of the caste system in India, Brahmins are strictly vegetarian except in Kashmir where they are known as Pandits. Kashmiri Pandits are renowned for their distinctive cuisine and are proud of having adopted the finer elements of the Moghul art of cooking. The Moghuls in turn had taken on the finer elements of Persian and Rajput styles. I was invited to a wedding and treated to a *mishani*, a marriage feast of seven different lamb dishes. One of the dishes was spiced and seasoned ribs of lamb coated in a chick-pea and rice-flour batter and deep-fried. The only way to eat them is with your fingers. Lamb chops may be used instead of ribs.

For the ribs:
8-10 *tender ribs from breast*
of lamb, separated into pairs
1 tsp salt
1/2 tsp chilli powder
1 tbsp roughly chopped
fresh ginger
3-4 cups milk
3 tsp fennel seeds
4 light-coloured cardamoms,
bruised
4 large dark brown
cardamoms, bruised
5 cm/2 inch cinnamon stick
4 cloves
8 peppercorns

Put the ribs into a wide heavy-bottomed saucepan. Sprinkle the salt and chilli powder over them, add the ginger and pour milk over all. Add the whole spices. Bring gently to the boil and then simmer on a low heat for 30 minutes, stirring across the bottom of the pan from time to time. After half an hour there should be very little liquid left. Take out the ribs and discard the remainder of the liquid.

For the batter:
1 cup chick-pea flour
2/3 cup self-raising rice flour
or plain rice flour
1/2 tsp baking powder
1/4 tsp nutmeg powder
1/4 tsp mace powder

Sieve together all the dry ingredients. Make a batter in the food-processor or by gradually adding the water to the dry ingredients and whisking. Set aside.

¹/₂ tsp chilli powder
¹/₂ tsp salt
1 cup water

Ghee or vegetable oil for deep-frying
6 tbsp lightly whisked yoghurt

Heat the *ghee* in a frying pan. Dip the ribs in the whisked yoghurt, then in the batter. Fry them until crisp and golden, drain on absorbent paper and serve.

Kashmiri Rojan Josh

LAMB IN A RICH SAUCE

Meat-eating Kashmiri Brahmin Pandits of the high priestly class claim this *rojan josh* as their speciality. Using fewer spices than the *shahi rojan josh* (pp.60-2) and omitting the lengthy marination, this dish is one of the most popular served to guests in Kashmiri homes. Powdered ginger replaces root ginger and onions and garlic, said to overheat the blood and to cause wanton passions, are absent. Traditionally, mustard oil would be used, but it is neither to everyone's taste nor always readily available. *Ghee* and vegetable oil have been substituted.

Yoghurt drained of whey creates a thick tangy sauce for the meat. Drain the 3 cups of yoghurt through a muslin bag or cheesecloth for 1 hour.

2 tbsp ghee
2 tbsp vegetable oil
4 cloves
5 cm/2 inch cinnamon stick
2 large dark brown cardamoms, bruised
4 small light-coloured cardamoms, bruised

Heat the *ghee* and the oil in a heavy-bottomed saucepan. Add the cloves, cinnamon and bruised cardamom pods. Fry for a few seconds to release their aromas into the oil.

750 g/1¹/₂ lb lean lamb, cut into 5 cm/2 inch cubes

Add the cubed meat and a pinch of asafoetida and turn and stir until the cubes turn a light brown. Add the

A pinch of asafoetida
3 cups lightly whisked
yoghurt, drained of whey for
1 hour

drained yoghurt to the meat, stir to mix well, reduce the heat and simmer for 15 minutes.

2 tsp coriander powder
1 tsp cumin powder
2 tsp chilli powder
1/4 tsp mace powder
1/4 tsp nutmeg powder
1 tsp paprika
2 tsp fennel powder
2 tsp ginger powder
1 tsp salt
1/2 tsp ground black pepper

Add the spice powders of coriander, cumin, chilli, mace, nutmeg, paprika, fennel, ginger and the salt and pepper. Stir well and continue to simmer for another 15 minutes or until the oil starts to separate out.

1/2 tsp saffron threads,
steeped for 15 minutes in
1 tbsp hot milk
2 tsp Kashmiri garam masala

Add the saffron threads and milk and *garam masala* and cover and simmer until the meat is tender, stirring occasionally. The sauce should be thick and aromatic.

1 fresh red chilli, seeds
discarded and cut into
julienne strips

Garnish with strips of fresh red chilli.

Jahangiri Gosht

LAMB MARINATED IN GINGER AND SPICES

Lamb cubes are first steeped in a marinade of yoghurt flavoured with grated fresh ginger and saffron threads and then simmered in a sauce with ginger, chilli powder, nutmeg and mace. This aromatic delicacy was served to me on a frosty morning high up in the mountains of Kashmir at Gul Marg. Served with plain rice, mint *raita* (p.203) and a relish, it was just the dish to counter the cool mountain air.

Allow 1 hour for marination.

750 g/1½ lb lean lamb
½ tsp saffron threads,
steeped for 15 minutes in
1 tbsp hot milk
1 tbsp grated fresh ginger
2½ cups lightly whisked
yoghurt

Cut the lamb into 5 cm/2 inch cubes. Stir the saffron threads and milk with the ginger and the yoghurt in a bowl. Add the cubes of lamb, mix well and leave to marinate for 1 hour.

3 tbsp ghee or vegetable oil
3 cloves
5 cm/2 inch cinnamon stick
1 large brown cardamom
pod, bruised
4 light-coloured cardamom
pods, bruised

Heat the *ghee* in a heavy-bottomed saucepan, add the cloves, cinnamon and cardamom pods and fry for a few seconds to release their aromas. Add the meat and marinade, bring to the boil and cook, stirring until most of the liquid has evaporated.

1 tsp salt
1 tsp ginger powder
1 tsp chilli powder
1 tsp black pepper
¼ tsp nutmeg powder
¼ tsp mace powder
2 cups hot water
1 tsp garam masala

Add the salt, ginger powder, chilli, black pepper, nutmeg and mace. Stir well and cook for 5 minutes. Add the pint of hot water, cover and simmer for 30 minutes or until most of the liquid is absorbed. Add the *garam masala*, stir and cook for 5 minutes. Discard the cinnamon stick and cardamom pods.

Fresh coriander leaves

Serve garnished with a sprinkling of coriander leaves.

Shahi Rojan Josh

&

LAMB IN A SAUCE OF MANY SPICES

The name of this dish means royal red meat. Succulent pieces of marinated lamb are cooked in a sauce made with fourteen spices. The finished appearance should have a reddish tinge which will come from ground red chillies. Paprika mixed with chilli powder adds its own flavour and the dish can still live up to its name 'red meat' without being too hot with chillies. Check your spice shelf for ingredients before starting, as this is a dish which runs the gamut of spices.

Allow a marination time of 4-6 hours, or overnight if convenient.

For the marinade:
2 lightly whisked cups yoghurt
1 tsp saffron threads, steeped for 15 minutes in 1 tbsp hot milk

Add the steeped saffron threads and milk to the yoghurt and set aside.

1 tbsp roughly chopped fresh ginger
2 tsp roughly chopped garlic
1 tbsp fresh coriander leaves
3 dried red chillies
1/2 tsp ground black pepper
1 tsp salt
1/4 tsp asafoetida
2 tbsp water
750 g/1 1/2 lb lean lamb cut into cubes

Blend the ginger, garlic, coriander leaves, chillies, pepper, salt, asafoetida and water to a smooth paste in a food-processor. Stir in the yoghurt and saffron threads. Add the meat cubes and mix to coat the meat. Cover and set aside to marinate for 4-6 hours or refrigerate overnight.

For the masala:
1 roughly chopped small onion
2 tbsp roughly chopped fresh ginger
1 tbsp roughly chopped garlic
1 tbsp water

Blend the onion, ginger, garlic and water to a smooth paste and set aside.

5 cm/2 inch cinnamon stick, broken into small pieces
8 cloves
12 peppercorns
2 tsp poppy seeds
1 tsp cardamom seeds
1 tsp black cumin seeds
3 tsp coriander powder
2 tsp cumin powder
1/2 tsp turmeric powder

Grind the cinnamon, cloves, peppercorns, poppy seeds, cardamom and cumin seeds in a coffee-grinder or spice-mill. Put into a bowl and mix to a paste with the coriander powder, cumin, turmeric, chilli, paprika, nutmeg, mace, salt, vinegar and water.

1 tsp chilli powder
1 tsp paprika
1/2 tsp nutmeg powder
1/4 tsp mace powder
1/2 tsp salt
3 tbsp white wine vinegar
3 tbsp water

3 tbsp ghee or vegetable oil
1 finely sliced large onion

Heat the *ghee* or vegetable oil in a heavy-bottomed saucepan and fry the onion to a light golden colour. Add the blended mixture of onion, ginger and garlic and continue frying for 3 minutes.

Add the paste of spices. Lower the heat and stir for about 5 minutes or until the *ghee* starts to separate out from the spices.

3 large, ripe tomatoes,
puréed
2 tbsp finely chopped fresh
coriander leaves
1 cup hot water

Add the puréed tomatoes, coriander leaves and water. Stir and simmer for 3 minutes. Increase the heat and add the meat cubes and the marinade. Stir and mix well to coat all the meat. Turn the heat to low, cover and cook for about 1 hour, or until the meat is cooked and tender. Stir occasionally to prevent sticking.

2 tsp garam masala
A sprig of coriander leaves

Ten minutes before completion, sprinkle in the *garam masala*. Remove to a serving dish and garnish with a sprig of fresh green coriander.

Khubani Gosht

APRICOT-FLAVOURED LAMB

There are numerous apricot orchards in Kashmir and the combination of apricots and raisins brings a delicate piquancy to this lamb dish, which adapts well if chicken is used as an alternative.

If convenient, strain the cup of yoghurt overnight through cheesecloth to drain it of whey. It should be firm and of a soft cheesy texture. The yoghurt is flavoured with spices and the meat is marinated before being cooked in a sauce sweet with raisins and dried apricots. Serve with a lentil or vegetable dish with plain rice.

Allow 1 hour for marination.

1 cup yoghurt, drained of whey
1 tsp cumin powder
1 tsp coriander powder
1/2 tsp turmeric powder
1/2 tsp ground black pepper
1 tsp salt
1/2 tsp chilli powder
2 tsp Kashmiri garam masala
500 g/1 lb cubed lean lamb

Place the strained yoghurt in a bowl and fork through lightly to loosen it. Add the cumin powder, coriander, turmeric, ground black pepper, salt, chilli powder and the Kashmiri *garam masala* and combine. Add and mix in the cubed meat and marinate for 1 hour, stirring occasionally to make sure the meat is well coated.

1/4 cup seedless raisins
6 dried apricots, slivered
1 cup warm water
2 tbsp crushed almonds

Soak the raisins and apricots to soften in the warm water for 15 minutes. Drain and set aside with the crushed almonds.

1 tbsp ghee
2 tbsp vegetable oil
2 finely sliced onions
1 tsp finely chopped garlic
1 tbsp grated fresh ginger

Heat the *ghee* and oil in a heavy-bottomed saucepan, add the sliced onions and continue frying on a low heat until the onions soften. Add the chopped garlic and ginger and continue stirring and cooking until the onions start to turn a golden brown. Add the drained apricots and raisins and the crushed almonds. Fry for a few seconds, then add the meat and the marinade. Simmer for 1 hour or until the meat is tender, stirring occasionally.

1/4 cup finely chopped fresh coriander leaves
1/2 tsp saffron threads, steeped for 15 minutes in 1 tbsp hot milk

About 5 minutes before the end of the cooking, add the chopped coriander leaves and the saffron threads and milk.

1 tbsp yoghurt

Fold in the yoghurt before serving.

Shahi Korma

&

NUTTY-FLAVOURED BRAISED LAMB

This is a royal dish of lamb braised in a spicy sauce of yoghurt thickened with almonds and poppy seeds and enhanced with the delicate fragrance of saffron. The bite of heat comes from dried red chillies and peppercorns. Strain the yoghurt through cheesecloth or muslin over a bowl. Make this a priority as it needs to strain for at least 1 hour to drain the whey, leaving a thick, soft cheesy consistency which should then be lightly loosened with a fork.

Jahangir was obsessed with Kashmir and utterly charmed by the delicate mauve-blue petals of the saffron flower. In his memoirs he calls them 'a page that the painter of destiny had drawn with the pencil of creation. The buds of heart break into flowers from beholding it.'

1 roughly chopped onion
2 tsp roughly chopped fresh ginger
4 cloves garlic
3 dried red chillies, seeds discarded
3 tbsp water

Blend the onion, ginger, garlic, chillies and water to a smooth paste in a food-processor and set aside.

10 black peppercorns
2.5 cm/1 inch cinnamon stick
1½ tbsp white poppy seeds
2 tbsp blanched almonds or unsalted cashew nuts
½ tsp cardamom seeds
4 cloves
1 tsp black cumin seeds

Grind the peppercorns, cinnamon, poppy seeds, almonds or cashew nuts, cardamom seeds, cloves and black cumin seeds in a coffee-grinder or spice-mill.

1 tbsp ghee
1 tbsp oil
1 finely sliced large onion

Heat the *ghee* and oil in a heavy-bottomed saucepan and fry the onion until it begins to turn golden. Add the smooth-blended *masala* paste from the first stage and the ground nuts and spices and stir-fry for 2 minutes.

1 tsp mace powder
1¹/2 tsp coriander powder
1 tsp cumin powder
2 tsp garam masala
1¹/2 tsp salt

Add the mace, coriander powder, cumin powder, *garam masala* and salt. Continue frying until the oil starts to separate out. Add a little water and stir across the bottom of the saucepan to prevent sticking.

750 g/1¹/2 lb lean lamb cut into medium-sized cubes
¹/2 tsp saffron threads, steeped for 15 minutes in 2 tbsp hot milk
1¹/2 cups yoghurt, strained through cheesecloth for 1 hour, then lightly forked through

Add the cubed meat and stir to coat well with the spicy *masala*. Mix in the threads of saffron and milk and the strained yoghurt. Simmer gently for about 1 hour or until the meat is tender, stirring occasionally to prevent sticking.

Fresh coriander leaves

Serve with a garnish of coriander leaves.

Kashmiri Moghlai Gosht

LAMB IN A GINGER-FLAVOURED SAUCE

This lamb dish is redolent of Moghul influence in the vale of Kashmir. Although the amount of ginger seems 'heady', you will be surprised that in the end it does not dominate the flavour. The spices are bruised and not ground, and each retains its individual flavour within the sauce. It is a family favourite and I sometimes substitute beef or chicken for a change.

When the dish is cooked some *ghee* or oil will rise to the top, you may wish to spoon this off, although Kashmiris would not do so!

5 tbsp ghee or oil
3 finely chopped large onions
4 tsp finely chopped garlic
6 tbsp grated fresh ginger

Heat the oil in a heavy-bottomed saucepan. Fry the onions until they start to soften, add the garlic and ginger, continue frying and stirring until the onions start to change colour. If the mixture tends to stick, add a little water and stir across the bottom of the pan.

2 tsp turmeric
2 tsp chilli powder
8 large tomatoes
1 tsp salt
750 g/1½ lb diced lean lamb

Add the turmeric and chilli powder, then chop and add the tomatoes and salt, stir and cook for a couple of seconds to combine the mixture. Add the cubed meat, stir well and simmer for 5 minutes to partly seal the meat.

3 tsp bruised cumin seeds
2 tsp bruised black cumin seeds
2 tsp bruised cardamom seeds
10 bruised cloves
½ cup water
6 tbsp lightly whisked yoghurt
2 tsp Kashmiri garam masala

Mix in the bruised spices, cook for 10 minutes, then add the water and the yoghurt, stirring continuously. Simmer on a low heat until the meat is cooked and tender, for about 45 minutes. Add the *garam masala* and simmer for another 3-4 minutes.

Fresh coriander leaves or spring onions

Serve with a garnish of fresh coriander leaves or spring onions rings.

Dalcha Hyderabadi

SWEET AND SOUR LAMB WITH LENTILS

This tasty dish is said to have originated in Turkey and then been further embellished with the flavours of India. It is a combination of lentils and meat with the sour-sweet tang of tamarind and hot with fresh and powdered chilli. Only a small quantity of meat is used in this dish, a lunchtime favourite in Hyderabad. Serve with plain rice or *paratha* (pp.193-4) and a light vegetable dish accompanied by a beetroot *raita* (p.204).

Tamarind is sold either in pulp form or in concentrate. If you use the concentrate, follow instructions to obtain 3 tablespoons of diluted juice.

250 g/8 oz masoor dal
(split red lentils)

Pick over the lentils for grit or stones and wash well in a colander with running water. Put in a heavy-bottomed saucepan, cover with water and soak for 15 minutes. Drain but leave the *dal* in the pan.

3 cups water
1/2 tsp salt
1 tsp turmeric
2 tsp coriander powder
1/2 tsp chilli powder

Cover the lentils with 3 cups of water, add the salt, turmeric, coriander and chilli powder. Bring to the boil, then lower the heat and simmer gently for about 30 minutes or until cooked. Test whether the lentils can be mashed with the back of a wooden spoon against the side of the pan, then mash the lentils in the remaining liquid and set aside.

3 tbsp ghee
1 tbsp vegetable oil
4 light-coloured cardamoms,
bruised
1 large brown cardamom,
bruised
5 cm/2 inch cinnamon stick
4 cloves
1 tsp cumin seeds
1/2 tsp fenugreek seeds
1 finely chopped onion
12 curry leaves, fresh or
dried

Heat the *ghee* and vegetable oil in a separate heavy-bottomed saucepan. Pop in the whole spices, bruised cardamoms, cinnamon stick, cloves, cumin seeds and fenugreek seeds and fry for about 30 seconds to release their aromas. Add the finely chopped onion and curry leaves and fry until the onion starts to change colour.

1 roughly chopped
medium onion
2 tsp roughly chopped
fresh ginger
2 tsp roughly chopped garlic
3 fresh green chillies, seeds
discarded
2 tbsp water

Blend the onion, ginger, garlic, fresh green chillies and the water to a smooth paste in a food-processor, stir into the frying mixture and continue frying for about 4 minutes.

250 g/8 oz lean lamb
cut into cubes
1 tsp salt
1 1/2 cups water

Add the cubes of meat and stir and turn until they are browned. Add the salt and water; cover and simmer for 50 minutes, after which the meat should be tender.

3 tbsp tamarind pulp, steeped for 15 minutes in 4 tbsp hot water
2 tbsp finely chopped fresh coriander leaves
1 tsp garam masala

Push the steeped tamarind pulp through a sieve to extract 3 tablespoons of juice and add to the meat. Then add the mashed *dal*, coriander leaves and *garam masala* and stir to mix well; simmer, uncovered, very gently for 10 minutes. Put into a serving dish and prepare the garnish immediately.

1 tbsp ghee
2 fresh red chillies, seeds discarded, cut into strips
2 cloves garlic, cut into strips

Heat the *ghee* in a small frying pan until sizzling, toss in the chilli and garlic strips, pour over the *dalcha* and serve.

Do-Piaza Gosht

LAMB BRAISED IN A RICH ONION SAUCE

Do (pronounced doe) means twice, *piaz* means onion: lamb, with onions, twice. This dish was a favourite at the Moghul court and its name is a play on one of the emperor Akbar's 'jewels', his courtier Mullah Dopiaza. At this distance of time, no one is quite sure how 'onions, twice' should be understood. Some say the onions should weigh twice as much as the meat, others that the onions should be introduced at two separate stages – the first time fried, the second time raw. The version that follows comes from Hyderabad. Serve with plain rice.

The crisp-fried onion for the garnish can be brought in jars from most Indian grocers, and it is a good idea to have a jar to hand.

For the paste:
3 roughly chopped medium onions
2 tsp roughly chopped garlic
2 tsp roughly chopped fresh ginger
2 roughly chopped large fresh red chillies

Put all the ingredients for the paste into a food-processor, blend until smooth and set aside.

2 tsp cumin powder
1 tbsp coriander powder
2 tbsp fresh coriander leaves
1 tsp turmeric powder
4 tbsp yoghurt

For the meat:
3 tbsp vegetable oil
3 tbsp ghee
3 finely sliced medium
onions
4 cloves
5 cm/2 inch cinnamon stick
6 light-coloured cardamom
pods, bruised
1 tsp black cumin seeds
10 crushed black
peppercorns
8-10 curry leaves
750 g/1½ lb lean lamb, cut
into 5 cm/2 inch cubes

Heat the *ghee* and oil in a heavy-bottomed saucepan and fry the sliced onions until they are brown and crisp. Take them out with a slotted spoon and drain on absorbent paper. Set aside.

Fry the cloves, cinnamon, cardamom, cumin seeds, peppercorns and curry leaves in the remaining oil for a few seconds to release their aromas. Add the chunks of meat; stir and fry until they are browned, then remove them into a bowl with a slotted spoon.

1 tbsp ghee

Add another tablespoon of *ghee* to the saucepan, heat it and add the blended paste. Lower the heat and stir-fry the mixture until the oil begins to separate out. This should take about 7 minutes.

1¼ tsp salt
2 cups hot water

Add the meat and any juices that have drained off. Stir to coat the meat well with the paste. Add the salt and simmer for 10 minutes. Add the hot water, cover the saucepan and simmer for about 30 minutes.

1 tbsp blanched almonds,
slivered or flaked
1 tsp garam masala

Add the reserved fried brown onions, slivered almonds and *garam masala* and simmer for a further 10 minutes. Discard the cinnamon stick and remove the meat and sauce to a serving platter.

For the garnish:
2 tbsp fried slivered almonds
2 tbsp crisp-fried onion

Garnish with an outer circle of the fried slivered almonds and scatter the crisp onions over the meat in the centre of the dish.

Kalia Nizam ul Mulk

AROMATIC LAMB

Morsels of lamb are coated with generous quantities of ginger, garlic and chilli, teased and sweetened with honey and raisins and made aromatic with threads of saffron and drops of rose essence. Finally, soft cheesy yoghurt is folded into the meat mixture. Serve with *kulchas* (p.199), another bread or plain rice. If convenient, strain the yoghurt overnight through a sieve lined with a muslin bag or cheesecloth, cover and refrigerate. The yoghurt should be fully drained of whey and be of a soft cheesy texture. In addition, a couple of hours should be allowed to marinate the meat in a blended *masala* paste.

This aromatic lamb dish is said to have been a favourite of the Regulator of the Realm, who became known as Asaf Jah of the Deccan. When Nizam ul Mulk, vizier to the Moghul emperor, set out in 1724 from the Moghul court at Delhi with a large cavalcade to resume his appointment as viceroy of the Deccan, Aurangzeb conferred on him the title of Asahf Jah, or 'Equal in Rank to Asaf', the great seer who was one of Solomon's ministers. This title came to identify the Jah dynasty of Hyderabad, which ruled the largest state in India for seven dynasties.

For the paste:
1 roughly chopped
medium onion
3 tbsp roughly chopped
fresh ginger
1 tbsp roughly chopped garlic
2 tsp chilli powder
1 tsp turmeric powder
2 tsp coriander powder
1 tsp paprika
1$\frac{1}{2}$ tsp salt
2 tbsp water

Put all the ingredients for the paste into a food-processor and blend until smooth. Rub the paste into the meat cubes and marinate for two hours. Set aside.

For the sauce:
4 tbsp ghee
4 light-coloured cardamom
pods, bruised
750 g/1$\frac{1}{2}$ lb lean lamb, cut
into 5 cm/2 inch cubes

Heat the *ghee* in a heavy-bottomed saucepan, add the bruised cardamom and fry for a few seconds; then add the cubes of meat and the marinade. Cook on a high heat for 5 minutes, stirring and turning the meat.

1/4 cup water *1 cup milk*	Add the water and the milk. Lower the heat and cook until most of the liquid has been absorbed but the mixture remains moist.
2 tbsp ghee *2 finely sliced medium onions* *3 tbsp slivered almonds* *2 tbsp seedless raisins* *2 tbsp fresh coriander leaves* *2 tsp honey* *1/2 tsp saffron threads, steeped for 15 minutes in 1 tbsp hot milk*	Heat the *ghee* in a small frying pan and fry the onion until it is crispy brown. Drain by removing with a slotted spoon and add to the meat mixture. Add the slivered almonds to the remaining *ghee* and fry until golden; remove to the meat mixture with a slotted spoon. Now fry the raisins, keeping them moving in the pan until they puff up. Remove and add to the meat mixture. Add the coriander leaves, honey and saffron threads in milk. Stir to mix. Cover and simmer for 15 minutes, stirring occasionally.
4 cups yoghurt, strained of whey *4 drops rose essence* *1 tsp garam masala*	While stirring, gradually add the strained yoghurt. Cover and simmer for 15 minutes. Add the rose essence and *garam masala* and simmer for 5 minutes. Remove to a serving dish.
For the garnish: *1 tbsp blanched almonds, flaked or slivered* *Rose petals*	Garnish with blanched almonds and a scattering of rose petals.

Raja Haleem

🖤

LAMB SIMMERED WITH CRACKED WHEAT

Abdul Fazl Akbar's biographer tells us that *haleem* was a favoured dish at the court of Akbar. Later at the palace kitchens of Hyderabad it was cooked by *booas*, specialist women cooks who jealously guarded their culinary secrets. Each *booa* was assigned four helpers who, for a price, were happy to divulge the secrets to other cooks.

   There are many fine family recipes for Hyderabad's dish of mashed wheat grain and spiced meat. From the family of Raja Bahadur Venkatrama Reddy (*kotwal* to the last reigning Nizam of Hyderabad) comes this simplified version of that unusual dish. On a sunny afternoon at the family home, while Krishna regaled us with tales of the golden era in the history of Hyderabad, our nostrils flared continuously as dishes were being prepared by Joan and her assistants. It was a meal to be remembered. We scooped up the delicious food with Hyderabad's legendary leavened bread (p.199).

The crisp-fried onion for the garnish can be bought in jars from most Indian grocers. Allow 1 hour to soak the cracked wheat in water.

125 g/4 oz cracked wheat; rinse, cover with water, steep for 1 hour and drain

Cover the drained wheat with fresh water and bring to the boil in a heavy-bottomed saucepan. Lower the heat and stir from time to time. If the mixture is inclined to stick, add a little more hot water. Simmer until the grains are tender and mushy and can be mashed against the side of the saucepan with the back of a wooden spoon. Drain off the excess liquid and blend or mash to a thick purée. Set aside.

3 tbsp ghee
2 tbsp vegetable oil
3 finely sliced large onions
1¹/2 tbsp grated fresh ginger
2 tsp finely chopped garlic
1 tsp turmeric powder
2 tsp chilli powder
1¹/2 tsp salt
500 g/1 lb lean lamb cut into bite-sized cubes

While the wheat is cooking, heat the *ghee* and oil in another heavy-bottomed saucepan. When sizzling, add the sliced onion and fry for 2 minutes. Add the ginger and garlic and continue frying until the onion starts to change colour. Add the turmeric, chilli and salt; cook for 2 minutes. Add the cubed meat and stir-fry, turning the cubes until sealed and well browned.

2 cups water
¹/2 tsp saffron threads, steeped for 15 minutes in 1 tbsp hot milk

Add the water and saffron threads in milk. Mix well and simmer until the meat is tender.

2 tbsp blanched almonds
2 tbsp cashew nuts
1 tbsp poppy seeds
2 tbsp fresh mint leaves
2 tbsp fresh coriander leaves
1¹/2 cups yoghurt

Blend the almonds, cashew nuts, poppy seeds, mint leaves, coriander leaves and yoghurt, gradually adding the yoghurt until the mixture becomes a liquid paste.

5 cm/2 inch cinnamon stick
6 cloves

Stir the blended paste into the meat mixture. Add the cinnamon, cloves, cumin seeds and bruised cardamoms

2 tsp black cumin seeds
4 light-coloured cardamoms,
    bruised
1 tbsp garam masala

and the *garam masala* and bring to the boil. Simmer, stirring from time to time until most moisture is absorbed. Fold in the mashed wheat grains and simmer gently for 10 minutes.

2 tbsp crisp-fried onion
4 spring onions chopped
    into rings
2 radishes, grated
1 tbsp chopped mint leaves
1 tbsp chopped coriander
    leaves
2 limes or lemons cut into
    wedges

To garnish, fold in the spring onion rings and grated radish. Sprinkle the crisp-fried onion, chopped spring onion, mint and coriander leaves over the surface and fork through. Serve with lime or lemon wedges which can be squeezed at table.

Tamatar Gosht

LAMB CHOPS IN A SPICY TOMATO SAUCE

This is a light and appetising dish in which lamb chops are braised in a creamy tomato-based sauce with flavourings of both light and black cumin seeds. Aromas of cardamom, cumin and mustard seeds are released in hot oil in which the chops are then sealed. The sauce is enriched with fried onions blended into a garlic and ginger paste. The sealed chops are returned to the sauce towards the end of the cooking time. Serve with spinach and potato (pp.157-8) or cauliflower and nuts (p.142) and plain rice or any of the breads.

2 roughly chopped onions
2 tsp roughly chopped garlic
2 tsp roughly chopped
    fresh ginger
2 tbsp water

Blend the onion, garlic and ginger with the water to a smooth paste in a food-processor and set aside.

4 tbsp oil
2 finely sliced large onions
4 cloves
4 light-coloured cardamoms,
    bruised

Heat the oil in a heavy-bottomed frying pan. Add the finely sliced onions and sauté until the onions start to change colour. Add the cloves, cardamom, light and black cumin seeds, mustard seeds (which will pop and splutter), chilli strips and turmeric and stir-fry for

1 tsp light-coloured cumin seeds
1 tsp black cumin seeds
1/2 tsp dark mustard seeds
2 fresh red chillies, seeds discarded, cut into strips
1 tsp turmeric
8 lamb chops, 2 per person, according to size and preference

1 minute. Place the chops in the pan and fry to seal them on all sides. Remove from the pan and set aside. Add the blended paste to the pan and fry for a further 3 minutes or until the raw smell disappears.

1 tsp salt
1/2 tsp ground black pepper
1 kg/2 lb well ripened tomatoes, puréed
1/2 cup water
1/2 cup lightly whisked yoghurt

Stir in the salt, pepper, puréed tomatoes, water and yoghurt. Bring to the boil and simmer for 5 minutes. Place the sealed chops in the sauce and simmer gently for 10-15 minutes or until the chops are tender.

1 tsp Kashmiri garam masala
1 tbsp finely chopped fresh coriander leaves

A couple of minutes before completion, mix in the *garam masala* and the chopped coriander leaves.

Shahi Raan

MARINATED LEG OF LAMB

No book on Moghul cooking would dare to omit this royal speciality, a whole leg of lamb with all the fat removed, smothered in yoghurt and spices and impregnated with almonds, cashews, poppy seeds and raisins.

And then there are specialities of specialities. The *raans* of Lucknow, Lahore, Kashmir, Delhi, Hyderabad all claim Moghul heritage. Which should we choose? Time after time I was asked, 'Do you have a recipe for *raan*?' If my answer was yes, I was told, 'Oh! but ours is far superior to that one, you must take our recipe.' Try this version from the tables of the connoisseurs of Lucknow and present it at table fully garnished and ready to carve. Serve with spicy cauliflower florets with potato (p.159) and a mint *raita* (p.203).

Start preparing the leg of lamb to allow for overnight marination. The parchment-like outer skin and all the surface fat is removed so that the full flavours of the marinade penetrate the flesh; your butcher may do this for you. For the sake of appearances, the protruding bone can also be cut as close to the meat as possible.

Allow 6-8 hours for preparation and marination time.

2.5 kg/5 lb leg of lamb

Trim off the parchment-like covering skin and all surface fat. If convenient, cut the protruding bone as close to the meat as possible and set aside.

For the paste:
2 roughly chopped onions
3 tsp roughly chopped garlic
3 tbsp roughly chopped fresh ginger
3 fresh green chillies
1 tsp ground black pepper
1/2 tsp cardamom powder
3 tsp coriander power
2 tsp cumin powder
1 tsp turmeric powder
1/4 tsp mace powder
1/4 tsp nutmeg powder
1 tbsp almonds
1 tbsp cashew nuts
1 tbsp poppy seeds
1 1/2 tsp salt
3 tbsp lime or lemon juice
2 tbsp water

Blend all the ingredients for the paste in a food-processor until smooth. Divide into two portions and set aside.

For the marinade:
1 1/2 cups lightly whisked yoghurt
1/2 tsp saffron threads, steeped for 15 minutes in 1 tbsp hot milk

Combine the yoghurt with the saffron threads and milk. Stir in half of the blended paste. Set aside for 1 hour, so that all the flavours become well integrated.

For the meat:
2 tbsp seedless raisins
1 tbsp honey

Meanwhile, start preparing the meat for the two stages of marination. Make 3-4 deep diagonal slits across the rounded side of the flesh. Push and rub the remaining

2 tbsp melted ghee
1 tsp garam masala

portion of the blended paste into these slits. Pop a few raisins into each slit and set the leg of lamb aside for 1 hour in a dish that can be covered for baking.

Spoon the yoghurt and paste marinade into the slits and spread all over the meat. Leave in this marinade for 4-6 hours or cover and refrigerate overnight. If convenient, turn the lamb and spoon over the marinade and juices during this time.

Pre-heat the oven to 210°C/410°F/gas mark 6. With the (rounded) top side face up, dribble the honey and the melted *ghee* over the meat. Sprinkle with the *garam masala*. Cover the baking dish and bake the lamb for 30 minutes, basting occasionally. Then reduce the oven heat to moderate and bake until the lamb is cooked through to your liking. Baste from time to time. Lift out of the juices to a flat carving tray or platter.

For the garnish:
Large onion rings to surround outer edge of the serving platter. Divide into 3 portions; one portion remains natural; colour one portion red by steeping in beetroot juice or in small bowl of water coloured with cochineal or vegetable colouring and one portion yellow in a small bowl of water coloured with two teaspoons of turmeric powder
Rose petals
Roasted almonds; allow one for the centre of each onion ring

Garnish with an inner ring of rose petals cushioning the lamb and an outer ring of large onion rings, alternating red, white and yellow. Place a golden almond or cashew in the centre of each onion ring. Set aside.

2 tbsp yoghurt or cream
1 cup stock or water

Add the yoghurt or cream and the stock or water to the juices remaining in the baking dish and stir and simmer over a medium heat to a sauce consistency. Put into a separate sauceboat. Carve at the table into chunks or slices and spoon over the sauce.

Palak Gosht

🌿

LAMB WITH SPINACH AND TOMATO

A lightly spiced, easily prepared dish combining lamb with a creamy coating of spinach and tomato tempered with spices. Discard the cinnamon stick and cardamom pods before serving. Serve with chick-pea flour bread (p.198) and a side dish of sweet and sour lentils (pp.162-3). The recipe adapts well to beef.

2 roughly chopped onions
2 tsp roughly chopped fresh ginger
1 tsp roughly chopped garlic
2 fresh green chillies
2 tbsp water

Blend the onion, ginger, garlic, chillies and water in a food-processor until smooth and set aside.

1 tbsp ghee
2 tbsp oil
5 cm/2 inch cinnamon sticks
1 tsp black cumin seeds
2 large brown, cardamom pods, bruised

Heat the *ghee* and oil in a heavy-bottomed saucepan. Fry the cinnamon sticks, cumin seeds and large cardamom pods for a few seconds to release their aromas. Add the blended paste and continue stirring while frying for about 5 minutes.

1 tsp turmeric powder
1 tsp coriander powder
750 g/1½ lb lean lamb cut into fairly large cubes
1½ tsp salt
2 large tomatoes, puréed
500 g/1 lb spinach well washed and roughly chopped (including stalks)
½ tsp ground black pepper
2 tbsp yoghurt

Add the turmeric and coriander powder and fry until the oil separates out from the *masala* paste mixture. If required, add a little water to prevent sticking. Add the meat cubes and mix well to coat. Bring to the boil, lower the heat and simmer for 15 minutes. Add the salt and the puréed tomatoes and simmer for a further 5 minutes; stir in the chopped spinach, pepper and the yoghurt. Cover and simmer for 40 minutes or until the meat is tender.

1 tbsp ghee
1 finely sliced large onion

If you are not using prepared fried onion, heat the *ghee* in a small frying pan and, while the meat is cooking, fry the finely sliced onion until brown and drain it on absorbent paper. Put the meat and sauce in a serving dish and sprinkle the surface with the fried onion.

Shami Kebabs

🍃

FRAGRANT AND SPICY MINCE KEBABS

Kebabs made from finely minced lamb or chicken were enjoyed by the warriors of Rajasthan. The Moghuls adopted and refined the spiced kebabs in their kitchens and the smooth-textured delicately flavoured *shami kebab* resulted.

This mouth-watering snack, appetiser or savoury can be prepared ahead and gently re-heated. Make larger kebabs for a first course and serve them with salad.

To make well formed, smooth kebabs, have a bowl of water to hand to moisten your hands as you shape the kebabs.

Allow 1 hour for the split peas to soak and soften for the first stage and a further couple of hours to refrigerate and for the mixture to become firm.

100 g/4 oz channa dal or yellow split peas; rinse well, cover with water, leave for one hour and drain
450 g/1 lb finely minced lean lamb
1 cup water
1 finely chopped large onion
1 tbsp grated fresh ginger
1 tsp finely chopped garlic
10 roughly ground black peppercorns
6 roughly ground cloves
1 tsp roughly ground cumin seeds
1/2 tsp roughly ground cardamom seeds
1 finely chopped fresh green chilli
1 tsp salt

Add the soaked and drained split peas to the mince, onion, ginger, garlic, peppercorns, cloves, cumin, cardamom, chilli and salt, mix well and simmer for 30 minutes in a heavy-bottomed saucepan, stirring occasionally to prevent sticking. Moisture should evaporate to leave a fairly dry mixture when finished. Allow to cool and set aside.

1 finely chopped large onion
1 small fresh green chilli, finely chopped

Add the onion, chilli, mint, coriander leaves and chick-pea flour to the cooked mince mixture, then process very briefly in a food-processor, taking care not to let

1 tbsp finely chopped mint leaves
1 tbsp finely chopped fresh coriander leaves
3 tbsp chick-pea flour

the mixture acquire a paste texture. If you feel apprehensive about this, knead the mixture by hand until it is smooth. Cover and refrigerate for 2 hours or more so that the mixture becomes firm.

1 lightly beaten egg
1 tbsp lightly whisked yoghurt

Remove the mince from the refrigerator and add and knead in the beaten egg and the yoghurt.

1 finely chopped medium onion
Raisins
Slivered almonds
A bowl of water to moisten fingers and palms

Divide the kebab mixture into 8 portions for larger-sized kebabs or into 16-20 for snacks. Moisten your hands, form each portion into a ball, make a depression in the ball and put in a couple of pieces of onion, a raisin and a slivered almond. Pinch the mixture together to close the depression. Roll into a ball, then flatten out to form a round patty about 5.5 cm or 2½ inches in diameter.

Oil for shallow frying

Heat the oil in a shallow frying pan and fry the kebabs over a gentle heat, turning once or twice to get an even brownness on both sides. Too much oil can cause them to split. Drain on absorbent paper and serve hot.

Padishah Kofta Kari

MEATBALLS IN A CURRY SAUCE

The Moghul courts at Delhi and Agra favoured these almond-flavoured meatballs simmered in a smooth sauce. Without the sauce, the *koftas* are a tremendous hit with pre-dinner drinks. The meatballs can be formed easily if you use a small bowl of water to moisten your hands when rolling the balls. It may be more convenient to make the sauce ahead of the *koftas*. Serve with cumin-flavoured *pilau* (p.176) and beans coated with sesame seeds (p.153).

When Babur set his sights on Delhi little did he know that the Moghul Empire was to become the greatest since Rome. On 27 April 1526 the reign of the great Moghuls of India began. Babur, who had already declared himself Padishah (Emperor), preparing for battle said, 'I put my foot in the stirrup of resolution, set my hand on the rein of my trust in God, and went forward against Sultan Ibrahim whose throne at that time held the capital of Delhi and the dominion of Hindustan.'

For the koftas:

750 g/1½ lb finely minced lean lamb

1 very finely chopped onion

2 tsp grated fresh ginger

½ tsp finely chopped garlic

½ tsp chilli powder

1 tsp cumin powder

1 tbsp finely chopped fresh coriander leaves

½ tsp salt

½ tsp ground black pepper

1 tsp garam masala

1 tbsp blanched and ground almonds

1 tbsp chick-pea flour

1 tbsp lime or lemon juice

2 eggs, beaten together, reserve half

Put the finely minced meat, chopped onion, ginger, garlic, chilli and cumin powder, chopped coriander leaves, salt, pepper, garam masala, ground almonds, chick-pea flour, lime or lemon juice and half the beaten egg into a bowl. Reserve the remainder of the egg for dipping the meatballs before frying. Knead well by hand and rub the mince through your fingers to combine the ingredients and attain a smooth texture. Divide into 20 portions.

20 pieces slivered blanched almonds

20 seedless raisins

Have a bowl of water alongside to moisten your fingers. Roll each portion into a ball, flatten slightly, make a small depression in the centre and put a slivered almond and a raisin in the depression. Close the depression by pinching the meat together and roll into a ball. Repeat this process until all 20 meatballs are formed.

Vegetable oil for deep-frying

Heat the vegetable oil in a deep, heavy-bottomed frying pan, using enough oil to come half-way up the meatballs. Dip the meatballs in the reserved beaten egg. Lower the heat to medium. Fry as many meatballs as will fit in the pan comfortably in a single layer, turning them gently, or shake the pan to roll the meatballs over until they become an even light brown on all sides. Remove with a slotted spoon to absorbent paper and set aside. If the sauce has not already been made, strain the remaining oil and use for the sauce.

For the sauce:
4 tbsp ghee or vegetable oil;
if meatballs are already
fried, use some of the
remaining oil
3 finely chopped onions
2 tsp grated fresh ginger
1/2 tsp finely chopped garlic
1 tsp turmeric powder
2 tsp coriander powder
1 tsp cumin powder
1 tsp chilli powder
1 tsp garam masala
3 large ripe tomatoes,
blanched, peeled and puréed
1 tsp salt
1/2 tsp ground black pepper
1 cup yoghurt
1/2 cup water
2 tbsp roughly chopped fresh
coriander leaves

Heat the *ghee* or oil in a heavy-bottomed saucepan. Add the onions, ginger and garlic and fry until the onion starts to change colour. Add the turmeric, coriander, cumin, chilli and *garam masala* and stir-fry for 3 minutes. Stir in the tomato purée, salt and pepper. Lower the heat and simmer for a further 3 minutes. Lightly whisk the yoghurt and water together and gradually stir in the whisked yoghurt and water and the coriander leaves. Simmer for 2 minutes. Gently add the meatballs, allowing them to simmer undisturbed for 3 minutes and then shake the pan to move them around in the sauce or very carefully turn them over individually. Cover and simmer on a low heat for 20 minutes.

1 tbsp lime or lemon juice

Sprinkle the lime or lemon juice over and stir gently. The *koftas* should be quite firm at this stage and are not likely to break easily.

For the garnish:
1 tbsp slivered and roasted
almonds

Garnish with the slivered almonds.

POULTRY

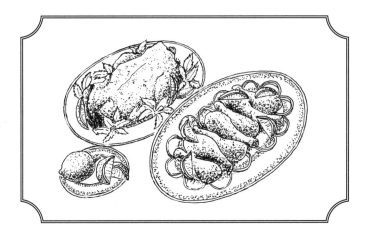

The domestic chicken was the year-round favoured fowl in Moghul dishes, while peacock, goose, pheasant, partridge, quail and parrot were all considered part of the seasonal hunts. Chicken was, and still is, considered a delicacy and a luxury item in India.

Imperial kitchens were responsible for rearing breeds of chicken specially for banquets and often for a particular dish. The palace chickens were hand-fed with pellets fragrant with saffron and rose essence, they were massaged daily with oils of musk and sandalwood. Only when they were considered sufficiently plump and exudingly fragrant were they deemed ready for the emperors' tables.

The Emperor Akbar set a particularly high standard for the preparation and presentation of chicken dishes, and one dish was prepared over 200 times before he was satisfied that it could bear his name.

Careful attention was paid first to the skinning of the chicken before it was prepared with saffron, spices and marinades. Either whole or cut into pieces, it was often combined with other ingredients such as minced or ground lamb, apricots, sultanas and nuts, particularly almonds, to appear as exotic dishes of whole chicken stuffed with minced lamb (pp.98-100), chicken pieces in an apricot purée (pp.96-7) or in an almond sauce (pp.91-2). I can almost inhale the wonderful fragrances of saffron, rose, musk and sandalwood rising from the steam of the chicken *pilaus* or *biryanis* that were presented for the emperor's approval.

The skin of the chicken is always removed to allow the spices and marinades to penetrate the flesh. Poulterers or butchers will do this if asked; in most supermarkets the job is done before the chicken pieces are packaged for display.

When using boneless chicken pieces I prefer to use either the breast or thigh fillets. If this is not convenient, chop the boned pieces into smaller portions.

Most restaurant-goers will be familiar with *tandoori* chicken dishes. *Tandoori* style is a method of cooking, initially confined to the north-west of India, that has gained great popularity in most parts with meat-eating members of the population. It is a style that is said to have come to Delhi, and then spread to other parts, with the influx of refugees from the north-west after Partition in 1947.

There has been a phenomenal rise in the popularity of *tandoori*-style dishes since the 1960s. The name comes from the earthenware oven, called the *tandoor*, which is heated red hot with coals. Marinated chicken, meat or fish is fed onto long skewers and grilled by heat both from the hot ash of the coals and the reflected heat of the oven walls. The meat is cooked quickly and emerges dry on the outside but succulent and moist on the inside, with a particular flavour from having been cooked in the clay oven. *Tandoor* ovens are also commonly used for baking flat breads.

Tandoor comes from the Arabic word *ta-noor*, meaning oven. It is said the *tandoor* oven came to India from Central Asia and Afghanistan and quite probably found its way into the North-West Frontier Province (now in Pakistan) with Babur and his camp followers. In time the robust camp-style of cooking chunks of meat over coals was refined and improved with the addition of spices and marination techniques of Hindustan to elevate the 'frontier' style of food into Moghlai style. The Moghul Emperor Jahangir is said to have been particularly fond of his breads and meats cooked in the *tandoor*.

Strictly speaking, the term *tandoori* should refer only to dishes that are cooked in an earthenware *tandoor* oven, but the word has gained common usage and has become acceptable in recipe books and restaurants even though no such oven is used. Barbecuing over hot coals gives a good result. Home-cooked *tandoori*-style food is often oven-baked, grilled or barbecued.

Chicken is the most popularly cooked ingredient in the *tandoori* style, but fish, meat and vegetables are also prepared for cooking in the *tandoor* oven. *Tandoori*-style chicken dishes appear in this chapter and I have included a fish dish in *tandoori* style in the appropriate chapter (pp.123-4). Most *tandoori* dishes are served with onion rings, slices of cucumber and wedges of lemon and accompanied by a mint chutney (p.207).

Murgh Tandoori

CHICKEN MARINATED IN YOGHURT AND SPICES

Chicken pieces with a lemony tang, traditionally coloured red, are marinated overnight and cooked in an earthenware oven. This version can be oven-baked, grilled or barbecued. *Tandoori* dishes are usually served with a mixed salad accompanied by *naan* (pp.191-2) and a mint chutney (p.207).

There are many recipes for *tandoori*-style dishes and it would be unusual to find two the same. This version with flavours of nutmeg and saffron is in the Moghul style. Jahangir was extremely fond of *tandoor* dishes and his cooks were instructed to take *tandoori* ovens whenever the emperor travelled. It is, however, only in more recent times that the popularity of *tandoori* dishes has spread south of the Punjab.

Allow a marination time of 4-6 hours or overnight. Before cooking the chicken, preheat the oven to 200°C/400°F/gas mark 6 for about 15 minutes.

First marination:
8 skinned chicken pieces
1 tsp saffron threads, steeped for 15 minutes in 1 tbsp hot water
2 tsp salt
4 tbsp lime or lemon juice

Wash the chicken pieces and pat them dry with kitchen paper. Make a couple of deep diagonal slits across the thickest part of each piece with a sharp knife. Combine the steeped saffron threads and water with the salt and lime or lemon juice and rub well into the chicken pieces, particularly into the cuts. Leave to marinate for 1 hour. Drain the liquid off from time to time and pour over the chicken pieces.

Second marination:
1 roughly chopped small onion
2 tsp roughly chopped fresh ginger
1 tsp roughly chopped garlic
1 tbsp water

Blend the onion, ginger, garlic and water in a food-processor until smooth. Set aside.

2 tsp coriander seeds
2 tsp cumin seeds
1 lightly whisked cup yoghurt
1 tsp white pepper

Dry-roast the coriander and cumin seeds in a small frying pan and then grind them in a spice-mill or coffee-grinder. Add to the yoghurt, along with the blended paste, the pepper, *garam masala*, chilli, nutmeg and the food colouring (if used). Mix well to combine, allow the

1 tsp garam masala
1/2 tsp chilli powder
1/2 tsp nutmeg powder
Edible red food colouring
(optional)

flavours to integrate for 20 minutes and then strain through a fine sieve. Set aside. Coat the chicken pieces with the marinade. Marinate for 4-6 hours or overnight, covered, in refrigerator.

Cooking the chicken:
2 tbsp melted ghee

Pre-heat the oven to 200°C/400°F/gas mark 6. Remove the chicken pieces from the marinade and arrange them in a single layer on a rack in a shallow baking tray. Bake for 15 minutes. Brush with the melted *ghee* and bake for a further 10 minutes. Pierce with a skewer or fork to check if cooked through. Breasts will cook through more quickly than legs and thighs.

Murgh Tikka

TANDOORI-STYLE CHICKEN KEBABS

Succulent morsels of chicken, first sprinkled with lemon juice and then marinated in spiced and seasoned yoghurt, are threaded onto skewers and cooked in the oven. They may also be cooked under a pre-heated grill or over a barbecue. They make a light first or starter course. To serve as snacks, cut each breast into smaller portions. Serve with slices of cucumber, tomato, radish, onion, a mint chutney (p.207) and any of the breads.

Allow a marination time of 4-6 hours or overnight if convenient. Pre-heat the oven for about 15 minutes before cooking the chicken.

First marination:
6 skinned chicken breasts
1 1/2 tsp salt
2 tbsp lime or lemon juice
1/2 tsp saffron threads,
steeped for 15 minutes in
1 tbsp hot milk

Cut each chicken breast into 4 equal portions. Combine the lime or lemon juice and the salt and rub over the chicken pieces. Sprinkle with the saffron threads and milk and set aside to marinate for 30 minutes.

Second marination:
*1 roughly chopped
small onion
2 tsp roughly chopped
fresh ginger
1 tsp roughly chopped garlic
1 tbsp water*

Blend the onion, ginger, garlic and water in a food-processor until smooth.

*1 cup lightly whisked
yoghurt
1 tsp coriander powder
1 tsp cumin powder
1/2 tsp chilli powder
1 tsp garam masala
1/2 tsp ground white pepper
1/4 tsp nutmeg powder
1/4 tsp cardamom powder
Edible red food colouring
(optional)*

Put the blended paste into a bowl and stir and mix in the yoghurt. To this add the coriander powder, cumin, chilli, *garam masala*, white pepper, nutmeg, cardamom and food colouring and stir well to combine. Allow the flavours to integrate for about 20 minutes, then strain through a fine sieve. Pour over the chicken pieces and coat well all over. Allow to marinate for 4-6 hours or cover and refrigerate overnight.

Pre-heat the oven to 200°C/400°F/gas mark 6 for about 15 minutes. Thread the chicken pieces onto skewers and balance them across a shallow baking tray to catch the juices or set in rows on a rack in a baking tray.

Cooking the chicken:
2 tbsp melted ghee

Brush with half the melted *ghee* and cook for 5 minutes in the pre-heated oven. Turn the skewers over, brush with the remainder of the melted *ghee* and put back into the oven for 10 minutes or until the chicken pieces are cooked through but remain moist. The cooking time will depend on the thickness of the meat.

Murgh Makhani

ॐ

CHICKEN IN A BUTTERY TOMATO SAUCE

Marinated chicken pieces are first grilled and then simmered in a buttery, cumin-flavoured sauce. Traditionally, the chicken is cooked in the *tandoor* clay oven over charcoal and then immersed and simmered in the tomato-based sauce, rich with butter and cream. This is a popular way of using left-over *tandoori* chicken pieces, but although I have a clay *tandoor* oven in my garden, I have yet to prepare this dish from any left-overs. In this recipe the chicken is grilled, but it can also be barbecued over charcoal to give it an authentic smoky flavour.

Maharani panch rattan, which uses five varieties of lentils (pp.161-2), will partner this dish well. Serve with one of the breads and garnish with a swirl of cream speckled with chopped coriander leaves.

Allow about 4 hours for marination.

For the chicken:
750 g/1³/4 lb skinned chicken breasts
2 tbsp lime or lemon juice

Cut the chicken into 5 cm/2 inch pieces; dribble the lime or lemon juice over the chicken pieces and set aside for about 30 minutes.

For the marinade:
3 tbsp yoghurt
1 tsp chilli powder
1 tsp garlic pounded to a paste
1 tsp garam masala
3 tsp cumin powder
1 tsp salt

Prepare the marinade by combining the yoghurt, chilli powder, garlic paste, *garam masala*, cumin powder and salt. Spoon over the chicken pieces and coat well. Leave to marinate for 2-3 hours, turning the pieces occasionally.

For the sauce:
6 roughly chopped large, ripe tomatoes
300 g/10 oz butter
3 tsp cumin powder
1 tsp ground white pepper
1 tsp garam masala
1¹/2 cups double cream
¹/4 cup roughly chopped fresh coriander leaves
¹/2 tsp saffron threads, steeped for 15 minutes in 1 tbsp hot milk

Meanwhile, prepare the sauce. Put the tomatoes into a heavy-bottomed saucepan and simmer for 5 minutes. Pass through a fine sieve and return to the saucepan. Add the butter and stir while simmering until the mixture is reduced to a fairly thick consistency.

Add the cumin powder, pepper and the *garam masala*. Continue cooking for about 2 minutes. Add the cream, the coriander leaves and the saffron threads in milk. Stir to mix and set aside.

Pre-heat the grill for about 5 minutes. Thread the chicken pieces on skewers and spoon over any marinade drippings. Arrange the skewers on a greased baking tray; par-grill and turn the skewers so as to seal the chicken pieces evenly on all sides, then slide the pieces off the skewers into the sauce. Stir to mix and simmer gently until tender.

Murgh Mumtaz Mahal

CHICKEN FLAVOURED WITH CARDAMOM AND CLOVES

'When Mumtaz-i-Mahal departed this world, the Virgins of Paradise opened the gates to admit her,' reads a Persian inscription on the tomb of Shah Jahan's beloved Mumtaz Mahal.

This chicken dish is aromatic with cloves and a generous quantity of cardamom, a spice considered a luxury in Moghul times. The chicken pieces are first fried in oil made aromatic with the spices and later added to a smooth tomato-based sauce. It is fittingly dedicated to the 'Exalted One of the Palace'.

1 kg/2 lb skinned chicken breasts
2 tbsp lime or lemon juice

Cut the chicken breasts into large bite-sized pieces. Arrange the pieces in a single layer in a dish and trickle the lime or lemon juice over them. Set aside for 30 minutes. Turn the pieces over a couple of times.

4 tbsp ghee
4 tbsp vegetable oil
8 cloves
12 bruised cardamom pods
2 tsp dry-roasted cumin seeds

Heat the *ghee* and the oil in a heavy-bottomed saucepan. Add the cloves, cardamom pods and the dry-roasted cumin seeds and fry for about 2 minutes to release their aromas. Add the chicken pieces in a single layer and fry gently for a few seconds to seal in their juices. Remove with tongs or a slotted spoon to a bowl and set aside.

3 finely chopped large onions
2 tbsp grated fresh ginger
2 tsp finely chopped garlic
1 tsp chilli powder
1 tsp turmeric powder
1½ tsp salt
1 tsp ground black pepper
2 tbsp blanched and pulverised almonds

Add the chopped onion, garlic and ginger to the remaining spiced oil and continue to stir-fry until soft. Add the chilli powder, turmeric, salt and pepper and the pulverised almonds and fry gently for a few seconds.

4 large tomatoes; blanch, remove skins and purée
1 tsp garam masala

Add the puréed tomatoes, *garam masala*, chopped coriander leaves and water and stir and simmer for 2 minutes. Put the chicken pieces in with any juices that

*¹/₂ cup roughly chopped
fresh coriander leaves
¹/₂ cup water
4 tbsp lightly whisked
yoghurt*

have collected. Stir to coat the chicken and then simmer gently for about 20 minutes. Gradually add the lightly whisked yoghurt and simmer for about 7 minutes. Spoon off any oil that rises to the surface and discard the cardamom pods.

*1 tbsp slivered roasted
almonds*

Remove to a serving bowl and scatter the slivered almonds over the surface.

Shahjahani Murgh

CHICKEN IN A NUTTY SAUCE

'Chicken for the Sovereign of the World' is the translation of the name for this dish in which chicken pieces are coated in a nutty yoghurt sauce made aromatic with gentle hints of mace, nutmeg and saffron. Removing the skin from the chicken ensures that all the flavours will penetrate the flesh. If any of the pieces are on the large side, cut them into halves; you may prefer to substitute boneless chicken breasts or thighs.

Shah Jahan invariably took his midday meal in the harem. Seated on rich carpets protected with white calico, the emperor was flanked by beautiful maidens. Two were chosen to wait on him. Eunuchs passed delicacies from the kitchen in dishes of gold and silver to the girls who presented them to the emperor. As many as fifty different dishes were arrayed before Shah Jahan while music played and jewel-bedecked dancing girls whirled for the emperor's pleasure.

*2 roughly chopped medium
onions
2 tsp roughly chopped garlic
2 tsp roughly chopped
fresh ginger*

Blend the onions, garlic and ginger in a food-processor until smooth. Set aside.

*3 tbsp blanched almonds
2 tbsp pistachio or
cashew nuts
1 tbsp walnuts
1 cup water*

Put the almonds, pistachios or cashews and walnuts in a food-processor, gradually add the water and blend to a smooth paste in a food-processor. Set aside.

3 tbsp ghee
3 tbsp vegetable oil
2.5 cm/1 inch cinnamon
stick
8 small, light-coloured
cardamom pods, lightly
bruised
2 tsp cumin seeds
4 cloves
8 skinned chicken pieces

Heat the *ghee* and oil in a heavy-bottomed saucepan, add the cinnamon stick, cardamom pods, cumin seeds and cloves and fry for a few seconds to release their aromas. Put as many pieces of chicken as will fit into the base of the pan and fry until golden brown. Remove the chicken pieces with a slotted spoon to a bowl and conserve as much oil as possible in the pan; set the chicken pieces aside.

Lower the heat and add the blended onion paste to the remaining oil; stir-fry until the onion starts to change colour.

2 tsp cumin powder
$1/2$ tsp nutmeg powder
$1/4$ tsp mace powder

Add the cumin powder, nutmeg and mace and fry for about 1 minute.

1 cup lightly whisked
yoghurt
$1^1/2$ tsp salt
$1/2$ tsp saffron threads,
steeped for 15 minutes in
1 tbsp hot milk
2 tbsp seedless raisins

Add the blended paste of nuts, stir and continue cooking until the oil starts to separate out. Gradually mix in the yoghurt while continuing to stir. Put the chicken pieces in with any juices that have collected and add the salt, saffron threads and milk and the raisins. Stir to mix well. Cover and simmer for 15 minutes, turning the chicken pieces occasionally.

$1/2$ cup cream
1 tsp garam masala

Stir in the cream, add the *garam masala*, cover and simmer gently until chicken is tender. Discard the cinnamon stick and cardamom pods.

2 tbsp crushed pistachios or
walnuts
2 hard-boiled eggs, shelled
and cut into thin rings

Serve garnished with a scattering of nuts and circles of hard-boiled egg.

Badami Murgh Akbari

&

CHICKEN IN ALMOND SAUCE

Travellers, Jesuits and ambassadors to the Moghul courts all recorded their impressions of lavish court ceremonies. The weighing of the emperor against valuables which were then distributed to the people was one such occasion. Sir Thomas Roe, the English ambassador to the Jahangir's court, was sceptical whether precious metals were in fact distributed, as they were kept in bags and not visible. The French physician François Bernier writes of Aurangzeb, 'On the third day of the feast the Emperor caused himself to be weighed,' and in his description solid golden scales glitter in the sunlight, the emperor sitting on one of the scales while the other was loaded with precious metals, diamonds, rubies, pearls, elaborate brocades and valuable foodstuffs. We can safely assume that almonds were among those foodstuffs.

Almonds were introduced to India by the Moghuls. Dishes were created in the emperors' kitchens and a sense of great anticipation filled the banquet halls when a newly created dish using highly prized almonds was put before the king to celebrate a special occasion.

Chicken pieces are coated with a sauce of puréed tomatoes combined with yoghurt and a paste of almonds. Coriander, which is the main spice, adds to the nutty flavour. If the chicken pieces are on the large side, cut them in half.

6 tbsp blanched almonds
2 tbsp hot milk

Blend the almonds and milk in a food-processor until smooth. Set aside.

3 tbsp ghee
3 tbsp vegetable oil
4 finely chopped medium onions
2 tsp finely chopped garlic
2 tsp grated fresh ginger
5 cm/2 inch cinnamon stick
1 tsp turmeric powder
2 tbsp coriander powder
1 tbsp cumin powder
1 tsp cardamom powder
1/2 tsp fennel powder
1 tsp chilli powder
1/2 tsp ground black pepper
2 tsp salt

Heat the *ghee* and oil in a heavy-bottomed saucepan; lower the heat and gently fry the onions for 1 minute. Add the garlic, ginger and the cinnamon stick and stir-fry until the onion starts to change colour.

Add the turmeric, coriander, cumin, cardamom, fennel, chilli, pepper and salt. Keep stirring and continue to stir-fry for 4 minutes. If the mixture is inclined to stick, gradually add a little water and stir.

3 large ripe tomatoes, skins removed and puréed
1/2 cup finely chopped fresh coriander leaves
8 skinned chicken pieces

Add the puréed tomatoes, fresh coriander and the blended almond paste. Simmer for 3 minutes and then add the chicken pieces and turn and coat them well in the sauce. Cover the pan and cook for about 20 minutes or until the chicken is almost cooked.

2 cups lightly whisked yoghurt
1 tsp garam masala

Add the yoghurt gradually and stir in to mix well. Then add the *garam masala* and simmer until the chicken is cooked. Discard the cinnamon stick.

2 tbsp slivered almonds, fried to a golden colour in 2 tsp hot ghee

Serve with a scattering of slivered almonds.

Murgh Kaleji

MARINATED CHICKEN LIVERS

This dish of chicken livers is lightly spiced and fairly dry. The livers are halved and marinated and then fried and simmered in half-sour cream. Serve it as a starter the Indian way by scooping morsels onto wedges of ballooned *chapati* (pp.195-6) or with hot buttered toast as a supper dish. If you plan to serve this as part of a larger meal, you will find that any of the potato combinations or the spicy mashed turnips (pp.158-9) will combine to make a substantial and tasty meal.

Allow 1 hour for marination.

500 g/1 lb washed and drained chicken livers

Cut the livers into halves, put in a bowl and set aside.

2 roughly chopped medium onions
1/2 tsp roughly chopped garlic
2 tsp roughly chopped fresh ginger

Blend the onions, garlic, ginger, chilli, cumin, turmeric, salt and the lime or lemon juice in a food-processor until smooth. Add the paste to the chicken livers and stir gently to coat all the pieces. Marinate for about 1 hour, occasionally turning the livers in the marinade.

*1 roughly chopped fresh
green chilli*
2 tsp cumin powder
1 tsp turmeric powder
1 tsp salt
2 tbsp lime or lemon juice

1 tbsp ghee
1/2 cup half-sour cream
1/2 tsp ground black pepper

Heat the *ghee* and toss in the livers and the marinade. Cook gently on a low heat for 10 minutes, then stir in the half-sour cream and black pepper and simmer gently for 5 minutes or until the livers are cooked. Overcooking tends to dry and toughen the livers.

*1 tbsp roughly chopped fresh
coriander leaves*

Garnish with a sprinkle of fresh coriander leaves and serve with *chapatis*, *rotis* or *puris*.

Murgh Nawabi Wajid Ali Shah

STUFFED CHICKEN BREASTS IN AN ALMOND SAUCE

The scent of saffron pervades this dish of chicken breasts. It reminds us of an era of grandeur which was drawing to a close with the reign of Wajid Ali Shah King of Avadh (Oudh). Food reflected the opulent lives of the wealthy epicures among his subjects and the *nawabs* presented banquet after banquet, vying for praise and recognition. Raw materials were especially bred for particular dishes and chickens were fed musk and saffron from the moment they hatched so that their flesh exuded these fragrances.

To moisten the breadcrumbs, the *nawabs'* cooks used a kind of condensed milk called *khoa*. This takes a great deal of preparation and I use double cream instead.

I serve this as a lunch dish with a bowl of mixed salad or with rice. The quantities given here will feed four hungry people, or eight as part of a larger meal.

Pre-heat the oven to 160°C/320°F/gas mark 3 for about 20 minutes before cooking the stuffed chicken breasts.

For the chicken:
8 skinned chicken breasts

Flatten the chicken breasts by firmly rolling over each one a couple of times with a rolling pin.

For the marinade:
1 small onion
*2 tsp roughly chopped
fresh ginger*
1 tsp roughly chopped garlic
1/2 tsp garam masala
1/2 tsp chilli powder
1/2 tsp salt
1 tbsp lime or lemon juice

Blend the onion, ginger, garlic, *garam masala*, chilli powder, salt and lime or lemon juice to a smooth paste in a food-processor. Rub this into the chicken breasts and leave them to marinate for 30 minutes or longer.

For the stuffing:
4 tbsp double cream
8 tbsp bread crumbs
1 finely chopped large onion
2 tbsp grated fresh ginger
*2 fresh green chillies, seeds
discarded, finely chopped*
*1/2 cup finely chopped fresh
coriander leaves*
1/2 tsp salt
1 tsp garam masala
2 tbsp lime or lemon juice

Mix the ingredients for the stuffing into a bowl and stir until well combined. Lay the chicken breasts on a board, divide the stuffing equally among them and roll up each breast with the stuffing inside. Secure with a couple of cocktail sticks.

1 tbsp melted butter

Grease a baking tray with a little of the melted butter. Arrange the chicken breasts on the tray, with the joint underneath. Brush them with the remaining melted butter and bake in the pre-heated oven until they are cooked and golden and the juices have stopped running. The time required will depend on the size of the chicken breasts.

For the sauce:
2 tbsp blanched almonds
1 tbsp desiccated coconut
1/2 cup hot water
2 tbsp ghee
1 finely chopped large onion
2 tsp finely chopped garlic
1 tbsp grated fresh ginger

Blend the blanched almonds, desiccated coconut and hot water to a paste and set aside. Heat the *ghee* in a heavy-bottomed saucepan wide enough to take the chicken breasts in a single layer. Fry the onions, garlic and ginger gently until they start to change colour. Add the almond and coconut paste and continue frying for 3 minutes.

*1/2 cup lightly whisked
yoghurt*

Reduce the heat, gradually add the yoghurt and simmer for 3 more minutes. Add the salt, saffron threads and

1/2 tsp salt
1/2 tsp saffron threads,
steeped for 15 minutes in
2 tbsp hot milk
1 tsp garam masala

For the garnish:
1 tbsp slivered roasted almonds
Varak (silver leaf)

milk, stir and continue simmering. Then carefully transfer the chicken breasts into the pan and sprinkle with the *garam masala* and spoon the sauce over them. Simmer for a further 3-4 minutes and transfer the chicken pieces and sauce onto a serving platter.

Flutter a piece of silver leaf (if used) onto each chicken breast. Garnish with the roasted almonds and serve immediately.

Murgh Salar Jung

२&

CHICKEN IN A CASHEW AND COCONUT SAUCE

Salar Jung is the name of a noble dynasty in nineteenth-century Hyderabad. I have not been able to establish the exact connection between this family of distinguished administrators and this dish of chicken pieces embedded in a creamy saffron-flavoured sauce, but no doubt they enjoyed it and it is even possible that one of them invented it. Pale-coloured dishes such as this were intended to simulate the silvery white of the moon and were presented on certain full moon nights, a custom no doubt introduced to the Moghul courts by the emperors' Rajput wives and administrators to celebrate their festival called Kauvre Chauth.

For a main dish, allow two pieces of chicken per person and a marination time of 4-6 hours, or overnight if convenient.

For the chicken:
8 skinned chicken pieces

For the marinade:
1 1/2 cups yoghurt
1/2 tsp garam masala
1/2 tsp salt
1/2 tsp saffron threads,
steeped for 15 minutes in
1 tbsp hot milk

Put the chicken pieces in a single layer on a dish and prick them with a fork.

Lightly whisk together the yoghurt, *garam masala*, salt, saffron threads and milk. Rub the chicken pieces with this mixture, coat them well and marinate for 4-6 hours; alternatively, cover them and refrigerate overnight. If possible, turn the pieces or spoon the marinade over them from time to time.

For the sauce:
1 cup desiccated coconut
2 cups hot water
2 tsp white poppy seeds
10 raw cashews
1 cup hot water

2 tbsp ghee
1 tbsp vegetable oil
2 finely sliced large onions
3 tsp grated fresh ginger
1 tsp finely chopped garlic

*3 dried red chillies, crushed
into tiny pieces*
1 tsp fennel seeds
*2 light-coloured cardamom
pods, bruised*
1/2 tsp coriander powder
1/2 tsp cumin powder
1/2 tsp salt
1/2 tsp ground black pepper

Steep the coconut in the hot water for 30 minutes, then blend at high speed. Strain the liquid through a sieve, extracting as much coconut milk as possible and set aside. Blend the poppy seeds and cashews while gradually adding the hot water and set aside.

To make the sauce, heat the *ghee* and oil in a heavy-bottomed saucepan and fry the sliced onion, ginger and garlic until the onions turn a pale golden colour.

Add the crushed chillies, fennel seeds, cardamom pods, coriander, cumin, salt and pepper. Lower the heat and cook gently for 3 minutes.

Add the mixture of poppy seeds and cashews. Continue cooking and stirring for about 3 minutes, until the oil begins to separate out. If the mixture starts to stick to the pan, add a couple of tablespoons of water.

Add the chicken pieces and the marinade. Mix them in and turn frequently to coat all the pieces. Simmer for 6 minutes. Gradually stir in the extracted coconut milk and simmer for about 35 minutes or until the chicken is cooked but not falling off the bone. Remove the chicken and sauce to a shallow serving platter. Discard the cardamom pods and serve.

Murgh Khubani

MARINATED CHICKEN IN APRICOT SAUCE

Lightly spiced and marinated chicken pieces are complemented here by an aromatic spicy sauce made sweet with flavourings of sultanas and apricots. The cream added just before serving is optional; it does, however, add a smooth richness to the apricot sauce. The whole spices of cinnamon stick and cardamom pods are usually discarded just before serving, but they can be left in if they are not easily accessible for removal. I do not mind the unexpected crunch of a cinnamon stick or cardamom pod. Serve with plain rice and lightly spiced corn kernels (p.000).

Allow 2 hours for marination.

750 g/1¹/₂ lb skinned chicken breasts	Cut the chicken into large bite-sized pieces and set aside.
¹/₂ cup finely chopped dried apricots *¹/₄ cup sultanas* *¹/₂ cup hot water*	Steep the apricots and sultanas in the hot water for 30 minutes and set aside.
1 cup lightly whisked yoghurt *2 tsp coriander powder* *1 tsp cumin powder* *¹/₂ tsp turmeric powder* *1 tsp salt* *¹/₂ tsp ground black pepper* *¹/₂ tsp chilli powder* *1 tsp Kashmiri garam masala*	Put the yoghurt into a bowl and add the coriander, cumin, turmeric, salt, pepper, chilli powder and *garam masala*. Mix well. Add the chicken pieces and leave to marinate for 2 hours.
2 tbsp ghee *2 cm/1 inch cinnamon stick* *2 lightly bruised cardamom pods* *2 finely sliced medium onions* *2 tsp grated fresh ginger* *1 tsp finely chopped garlic*	Heat the *ghee*, add the cinnamon stick and cardamom pods and fry for couple of seconds to release their aromas. Add the onions, ginger and garlic, lower the heat and stir-fry until the onion starts to change colour.
¹/₂ tsp saffron threads, steeped for 15 minutes in 1 tbsp hot milk *1 tbsp finely chopped fresh coriander* *2 tbsp cream (optional)*	Add the chicken and the marinade and simmer gently for 10 minutes. Then stir in the apricots and sultanas and the liquid in which they have been soaked. Add saffron threads in milk and chopped coriander leaves and simmer for 5 minutes. Discard the cinnamon sticks and cardamom pods, fold in the cream and serve.

Murgh Mussalam

🐦

WHOLE CHICKEN STUFFED WITH MINCED LAMB

'For its preparation all the bones of a fowl were taken out through the neck, the fowl remaining whole, and then ...' Abul Fazl describes the intricate procedure of preparing *murgh mussalam*. The preparation of this dish was often considered the test of a good cook, but today home cooks and even many restaurant chefs skip the process of boning the chicken.

This aromatic stuffed chicken, garnished in glittering silver leaf, is an instance of a popular Rajput dish which was adopted by Akbar's court and overlaid with Moghul influences. In Akbar's kitchens it would no doubt have been prepared under the super-vision of the prima donnas of the kitchen, the *rakabdars*, who served their dishes on silver plates.

Restaurants often request 24 hours notice for this order and it is advisable to start preparing the chicken the day before. Prepare the *murgh mussalam* in three stages, assembling and preparing a tray of ingredients for each stage so as not to confuse proportions of ingredients used sometimes in all three stages. The chicken will not be deboned for this version. Use poultry shears to cut the chicken at the table. Cut down the breast bone and open the two halves, inhale the rich and fragrant aromas and cut into quarters to serve.

Allow for marination overnight. Before starting the third stage of instructions, pre-heat the oven for about 20 minutes to 180°C/350°F/gas mark 4.

First stage:
1.5 kg/3 lb skinned chicken
2 tbsp lime or lemon juice
1 tsp salt

Put the skinned chicken into a dish and prick it all over with a fork. Combine the lime or lemon juice and salt and rub over the chicken. Set aside for 15 minutes.

1/2 cup yoghurt
1 roughly chopped small onion
1 tsp roughly chopped fresh ginger
1 tsp roughly chopped garlic
1/2 tsp cinnamon powder
1/2 tsp chilli powder
1/2 tsp turmeric

Blend together in a food-processor the yoghurt, onion, ginger, garlic, cinnamon, chilli and turmeric and smear over the chicken. Cover and refrigerate to marinate overnight.

Second stage:
*1/2 cup well rinsed
basmati rice
4 cups boiling water
1/4 tsp salt*

*2 tbsp ghee
10 roughly chopped
cashew nuts
10 blanched and roughly
chopped almonds
20 roughly chopped
pistachio nuts
2 tbsp sultanas*

*1 tbsp ghee
1 tbsp oil
1 tbsp grated fresh ginger
1/2 tsp finely chopped garlic
1/2 tsp chilli powder
1/2 tsp cardamom powder
1/2 tsp garam masala
1/2 tsp salt
150 g/5 oz finely minced
lean lamb or chicken
2 tbsp water
1 tbsp chopped fresh mint
leaves*

2 hard-boiled eggs

Third stage:
*1 tbsp blanched almonds
2 roughly chopped large
onions*

Put the rice into a pan of boiling water, add the salt and par-boil for 5 minutes. Drain, set aside and allow to cool.

Heat the *ghee* in a small frying pan and toss the nuts and sultanas until nuts become light golden and the sultanas puff up. Set aside.

Heat the *ghee* and the oil in a heavy-bottomed saucepan; fry the ginger and garlic for a couple of seconds. Add the chilli, cardamom, *garam masala* and salt and fry for about 1 minute. Then add the mince, water and chopped mint leaves and stir to mix well. Press the mince against sides and bottom of pan while cooking to prevent lumps forming. Reduce the heat, cover and simmer until the liquid is almost evaporated. Allow to cool.

Combine the par-boiled rice with the fried nuts and sultanas. Add to the cooked spiced mince and mix well with a fork to spread grains of rice and the nuts through the mince. Divide into two portions.

Stuff half the mixture into the tail end of the marinated chicken and push up towards neck end. Take one of the whole, shelled hard-boiled eggs and push it into the centre of this portion. Repeat with the other half of the filling and the other hard-boiled egg. Stitch or secure the cavity securely. Double up the legs to bring drumstick ends over the cavity and skewer or tie the ends together.

Pre-heat the oven to 180°C/350°F/gas mark 4 for about 20 minutes while preparing the coating.

Blend the almonds, onion, ginger, garlic and water in a food-processor until smooth and set aside.

1 tbsp roughly chopped
fresh ginger
1 tsp roughly chopped garlic
2 tbsp water

4 cloves
2 tsp white poppy seeds
8 black peppercorns
1/2 tsp cardamom seeds

Coarse-grind the cloves, poppy seeds, peppercorns and cardamom seeds in a coffee-grinder or spice-mill and set aside.

2 tbsp ghee
1 tbsp oil
1/2 tsp turmeric powder
1 tsp coriander powder
1/2 tsp cumin powder
1 tsp garam masala
1/2 tsp chilli powder
1/4 tsp mace powder
1 tsp salt
1 cup lightly whisked
yoghurt
1 tsp saffron threads,
steeped for 15 minutes in
1 tbsp hot milk
Oil or melted ghee

Heat the *ghee* and oil in a heavy-bottomed frying pan. Add the blended paste and fry for 4 minutes. Add the ground spice mixture and fry gently for a few seconds before adding the turmeric, coriander, cumin, *garam masala*, chilli, mace and salt. Stir and cook until the oil starts to separate out. This should take about 5 minutes. If the mixture is inclined to stick, add a little water and stir. Gradually add the yoghurt and the saffron threads in milk. Simmer gently for 2 minutes until all the flavours have integrated. Allow to cool.

Line a baking tray with foil brushed with oil or melted *ghee*. Place the chicken on the lined baking tray, folding in the neck skin.

Smear and coat the chicken all over with the cooled mixture. Bake in the pre-heated oven for about 1 hour. Baste frequently with the juice drippings that collect in the baking tray. Test that the chicken is cooked by pushing a skewer through the thickest part of the thigh; the juices should run clear.

When the chicken is cooked, cut the string from the drumsticks and cavity. Carefully transfer the chicken to a platter, breast side up, and pour over any remaining juices.

The garnish:
2 hard-boiled eggs
Fresh coriander leaves
Varak (silver leaf)

Surround the chicken with a scattering of coriander leaves and space rings of hard-boiled egg around it. If available, flutter silver leaf over the breast part.

Murgh Lajawab Shahi

❦

STRIPS OF CHICKEN WITH NUTS AND SULTANAS

A dish chosen by royalty. The word *shahi* means royal and it is said that if the emperor approved of a dish and said *'Lajawab'* the chef would be well rewarded. Here chicken breasts are cut into julienne strips and impregnated with flavours of nuts, spices and sultanas to contrast with the bite of chilli. Serve this dish, which comes from the rich cuisine of Lahore, with one of the breads and a cauliflower or *dal* dish, or both. This recipe is both easy to prepare and extremely tasty.

500 g/1 lb skinned chicken breasts
1/2 tsp salt
1/2 tsp saffron threads
1 1/2 cups hot milk

Sprinkle the salt over the chicken breasts and put them in a heavy-bottomed saucepan large enough to take them in a single layer. Sprinkle the saffron threads into the hot milk, pour it over the chicken breasts and poach them gently for 15 minutes. Allow to cool in the liquid, then drain and discard the liquid and cut the chicken into julienne strips. Set aside.

1 roughly chopped small onion
20 cashew nuts
20 blanched almonds
1 tbsp desiccated coconut
1/2 cup hot water

Blend the onion, cashew nuts, almonds, coconut and water together in a food-processor until smooth and set aside.

2 tbsp ghee
1 tbsp oil
1 tbsp cumin seeds
1 finely chopped large onion
3 tsp grated fresh ginger
1 tsp finely chopped garlic
1/2 tsp cardamom powder
2 tsp chilli powder
1 tsp turmeric powder

Heat the *ghee* and oil and fry the cumin seeds for a few seconds. Add the onion and stir-fry until the onion becomes transparent. Stir-fry the ginger, garlic, cardamom, chilli and turmeric powder for 3 minutes, then add the blended onion paste. Lower the heat and continue to cook and stir for a further 4 minutes.

1 cup lightly whisked yoghurt

Gradually add the yoghurt, coriander leaves, salt, pepper and *garam masala*. Simmer gently for 3 minutes.

2 tbsp chopped fresh coriander leaves
1 tsp salt
1/2 tsp ground black pepper
1 tsp garam masala
2 tbsp sultanas, steeped for 15 minutes in 4 tbsp hot water

Add the chicken strips and the steeped sultanas and simmer for a further 5 minutes.

3 fresh red chillies

Serve garnished with flowers made from fresh chillies. To make chilli flowers, hold the chilli at the stem end and with sharp scissors make as many cuts as possible from point to stem; be careful not to cut right through. Shake to discard seeds. Put in a bowl of iced water to curl.

Bahadurshahi Murgh

CHICKEN WITH WHOLE SPICES AND PEPPERCORNS

Chickens were specially prepared for Moghul tables and for particular dishes. Before chilli was introduced to India by the Portuguese, pepper was the ingredient used to give heat and flavour and it is probable that chickens reared for this dish would have been fed a diet heavy with pepper.

Bahadurshahi or 'Royal Champion' was a title of honour conferred by the Great Moghuls. This chicken dish can be prepared quickly and appears to belie the grand title bestowed upon it. Whole cloves and peppercorns give the sauce a bite without the sensation of chilli heat. If the chicken pieces are on the large side, cut them in half. These quantities will serve 4 people as a main course.

3 tbsp ghee
5 cm/2 inch cinnamon stick
2 large brown cardamom pods, bruised
8 cloves

Heat the *ghee* in a heavy-bottomed saucepan and fry the cinnamon, cardamom, cloves and peppercorns for a few seconds to release their aromas. Add the onions, ginger and garlic and stir-fry until the onions start to change colour.

12 peppercorns
2 finely sliced large onions
2 tsp grated fresh ginger
1 tsp finely chopped garlic

2 tsp garam masala
1 tbsp coriander powder
2 tsp cumin powder
1 tsp turmeric powder
1½ tsp salt
1 tbsp chopped fresh mint
leaves
2 tbsp chopped fresh
coriander leaves
2 peeled and chopped
tomatoes
1½ cups lightly whisked
yoghurt

Add the *garam masala*, coriander, cumin, turmeric and salt and keep stirring and frying for 3 minutes or until the oil starts to separate out. Add a little water if the mixture is inclined to stick. Stir in the chopped mint, coriander leaves and the chopped tomatoes and simmer gently for a couple of minutes. Gradually stir in the yoghurt and bring to the boil.

8 skinned chicken pieces
1 tbsp finely chopped mint
leaves

Add the chicken pieces and turn several times to coat well. Cover and simmer gently or until the chicken pieces are tender but not falling off the bone. Discard the cinnamon stick and the cardamom pods. Serve with a scattering of chopped mint leaves.

Murgh-Keema Mumtaz Mahal

CHICKEN WITH SPICY MINCED LAMB

Chicken and minced lamb are here served together but cooked separately. The chicken pieces are simmered in a spicy sauce while the mint-flavoured mince remains moist and crumbly. Poppy seeds and cashew nuts give the sauce a nutty flavour and the dried red chillies provide a piquant bite. Beef or pork may be used instead of minced lamb. If the chicken pieces are large, cut them in half.

This dish is named after Shah Jahan's beloved Mumtaz Mahal, who died giving birth to her fourteenth child. A legend tells that her dying wish was that Shah Jahan should never remarry and that he build a tomb over her grave that would become a point of pilgrimage for all the world to admire – and so we have that greatest of architectural monuments to love, the Taj Mahal.

The presentation of this dish is quite spectacular with the special effects of the garnish and decoration.

For the chicken:
4 tsp roughly chopped garlic
2 tbsp roughly chopped fresh ginger
4 dried red chillies
1 tbsp water

Blend the garlic, ginger, dried chillies and water together in a food-processor until smooth. Divide into 2 portions and set aside.

3 tbsp poppy seeds
20 cashew nuts
2 tbsp water

Blend the poppy seeds, cashew nuts and water to a paste in a food-processor and set aside.

2 tbsp oil
2 tbsp ghee
1/2 tsp cardamom seeds
8 cloves
3 finely sliced onions
1 tsp turmeric powder
3 chopped or blended medium tomatoes
4 cups water
1 tsp salt
6-8 skinned chicken pieces

Heat the oil and the *ghee* in a heavy-bottomed saucepan. Fry the cardamom seeds and cloves for a few seconds to release their aromas. Fry the onions for about 3 minutes and add one portion of the blended paste of garlic, ginger and chilli. Continue to stir-fry for a further 5 minutes. If the mixture is inclined to stick, add a little water. Add the turmeric and stir in the blended poppy seed and nut paste. Add the tomatoes and bring to the boil. Add the water and bring back to the boil, then put in the chicken pieces and salt, ensuring that the pieces are well coated with the sauce. Bring to the boil, lower the heat and leave to simmer gently until the chicken is cooked and the sauce is fairly thick, stirring from time to time.

For the mince:
500 g/1 lb minced lamb
1/2 tsp turmeric powder
1 finely chopped tomato
1 tbsp finely chopped fresh mint leaves
1 tsp salt

While the chicken is simmering, put the mince and the reserved portion of the garlic, ginger, chilli paste into a small saucepan. Add the turmeric, tomato, mint leaves and salt. Cook the mince mixture, stirring and mashing occasionally with a fork to prevent lumps from forming. If inclined to stick, add a little water. The finished consistency should be crumbly but moist.

For the garnish:
Fresh coriander leaves
Sufficient onion rings to
surround edge of the platter
The same number of roasted
cashew nuts or almonds

Serve on a large oval platter, leaving the edge clear for decoration. In the dish or bowl part of the platter, form an outer ring with the mince. Put the chicken pieces in the centre of this ring and spoon the sauce over the chicken pieces. Garnish with coriander leaves where the chicken meets the mince.

Colour the onion rings with cochineal or by steeping them in beetroot juice. Place the ruby-red onion rings around the edge of the platter and place a roasted cashew nut or almond in the centre of each onion ring.

Gul Murgh Kebabs

🌸

ROSE-SCENTED CHICKEN KEBABS

Gul means rose, and here we have delicately flavoured rissoles of finely minced chicken tinged with essence of roses. The kebabs are easy to prepare and equally delicious hot or cold. Portions can be made smaller to be served as snacks or larger as a first course. Traditionally cooked in barbecue style over charcoal to impart a smoky flavour, the kebabs can be grilled or shallow-fried. They should be served with rose-scented raisin chutney (p.211).

The mixture will need to be refrigerated for a couple of hours to become firm before shaping the kebabs. The kebabs can be formed round metal skewers for easy turning on the barbecue or under the grill. Alternatively, they can be formed into balls, lightly flattened and shallow-fried, as they are in this recipe.

750 g/1½ lb finely minced
skinned chicken
2 finely chopped large
onions
1 tbsp grated fresh ginger
2 tsp finely chopped garlic
1 fresh green chilli, seeds
discarded, finely chopped

Put the minced chicken into a bowl, add the onions, ginger, garlic, chilli, coriander leaves, cumin seeds, mace and nutmeg powder, *garam masala*, chick-pea flour, ground pepper, salt, rose essence and the lightly beaten egg. Knead well to combine thoroughly. Cover and refrigerate for about 2 hours so that the mixture becomes firm.

Divide into equal portions of 8 or 12 and with moist-

*¹/₂ cup finely chopped fresh
coriander leaves*
1 tsp light cumin seeds
¹/₂ tsp mace powder
¹/₂ tsp nutmeg powder
2 tsp garam masala
3 tbsp chick-pea flour
¹/₂ tsp ground black pepper
¹/₂ tsp salt
3 drops rose essence
1 lightly beaten egg

ened fingers and palms form into a ball and then flatten lightly into circles.

Oil for shallow-frying

Shallow-fry on a low heat until both sides are a golden brown.

*1 tbsp finely chopped
fresh mint*
Cucumber rings

If serving as a snack, place a small bowl of the rose-scented raisin chutney in the centre of a platter as a dip. Surround the bowl with the kebabs and wedge cucumber circles between them. Scatter with chopped fresh mint leaves.

Do Mirich Murghi

CHICKEN WITH CHILLI AND PEPPER

'Twice-chillied chicken' is the name given to these morsels of cubed chicken to which the chilli is added in both fresh and powdered form and another taste of heat is added with black pepper. Despite these spices, it is not searingly hot. A favourite lunch dish which can be prepared very quickly, it is delicious with ballooned *chapatis* (pp.195-6), tomato chutney (p.207) and a *raita*. The garnish of raw onion rings will introduce another dimension of flavours.

4 tbsp ghee or vegetable oil
4 cloves
1 tsp cumin seeds

Heat the *ghee* or oil in a heavy-bottomed saucepan, add the cloves, cumin and mustard seeds and fry for a couple of seconds to release their aromas. The mustard seeds

1 tsp black mustard seeds
1 finely chopped onion
1 tsp finely chopped garlic
2 tsp grated fresh ginger
1 large fresh red chilli, seeds discarded, cut into strips
1 large fresh green chilli, seeds discarded, cut into strips
1 tsp turmeric powder
1 tsp coarsely ground black pepper
1 tsp chilli powder
2 tsp garam masala
750 g/1½ lb skinned chicken breast cut into bite-sized pieces

will start to pop. Add the onion, garlic and ginger and fry until the onions become a light golden colour. Add the strips of red and green chilli, the turmeric, black pepper, chilli powder and *garam masala* and stir-fry for 2 minutes. Add the chicken and stir and cook for about 3 minutes to seal the chicken pieces.

2 tbsp roughly chopped fresh coriander leaves
2 medium tomatoes, cut into wedges
1 tsp salt
2 tbsp lightly whisked yoghurt

Stir in the coriander leaves, tomato wedges and salt. Reduce the heat and simmer for 5 minutes. Add the yoghurt and mix well, cover and simmer on a low heat until the chicken is cooked.

1 small onion cut into rings
Fresh coriander leaves

Serve hot, garnished with a scattering of onion rings and coriander leaves.

Kebabs Murghi Gosht

MINT-FLAVOURED CHICKEN AND LAMB KEBABS

Lamb and chicken are combined in many Moghul recipes. Here minced chicken and lamb are flavoured with mint, Kashmiri *garam masala* and a suggestion of nutmeg. Traditionally cooked in a *tandoor* oven, the kebabs can also be oven-baked or grilled.

Serve as a starter with a refreshing *raita* or mint chutney (p.207) or both with one of the breads. A squeeze of lemon over the kebabs will enhance their flavour.

Before shaping the kebabs, cover and refrigerate the mixture for about 1 hour or longer if convenient. This will consolidate the texture and make forming the kebabs easier. It will also help if fingers and palms are moistened when rolling the kebabs.

Pre-heat the oven to 190°C/375°F/gas mark 5 for about 10-15 minutes before cooking the kebabs.

3 tbsp fresh mint leaves
1 tsp roughly chopped garlic
1 tsp roughly chopped fresh ginger
1 tbsp lime or lemon juice

Blend the mint leaves, garlic, ginger and lime or lemon juice in a food-processor until smooth. Set aside.

375 g/³/4 lb finely minced skinned chicken breast
375 g/ ³/4 lb finely minced lean lamb
1 tsp salt
2 tsp Kashmiri garam masala
1 tsp chilli powder
¹/2 tsp nutmeg powder
1 beaten egg

Put the minced chicken and meat into a bowl with the blended mixture, the salt, Kashmiri *garam masala*, chilli and nutmeg powder and beaten egg. Knead well to combine all the ingredients. Cover and refrigerate for 1 hour or longer so that the mixture becomes firm.

For a starter or first course, divide the mixture into 8 portions. Moisten your fingers, so the mixture forms more easily, and form into sausage or patty shapes.

Ghee for greasing the baking tray

Place on a greased baking tray and bake for 10 minutes on one side; turn over and bake for about 7 minutes.

Wedges of lemon and tomato

Serve with wedges of tomato and lemon to be squeezed over the kebabs to complement the flavours of mint chutney.

GAME

The Moghul courts were obsessed with hunting. Tiger-hunting was a favourite sport of emperors and princes, and Jahangir started hunting as a young boy – his memoirs record that he shot a total of 17,167 animals, including 86 tigers. Some animals were hunted by other beasts or birds and keepers led chained and hooded leopards and cheetahs trained to hunt deer. Hunts were occasions on which the emperor could display his skills as a marksman and gain credit with his soldiers, and hunting was organised like a military campaign. Proud falconers with hooded hawks were drummed ahead to lead the hunting party and soldiers acted as beaters. On one hunt, 50,000 men surrounded an area some 60 miles in diameter and marched in a circle, closing in over a period of a month, driving all the animals to a central area into which the emperor charged for the first kill. No wonder hunting scenes abound in Moghul miniature painting. The Moghul court, setting out on caparisoned horses and elephants, provided the artists with a most impressive and colourful sight.

Palace chefs, of course, were part of the hunting encampment, waiting to create dishes of edible quarry from the chase. Always plentiful, the game was sometimes varied and unpredictable and on other occasions more seasonable and regularly available. Whether venison, hare, quail, wild duck or partridge, the royal party would, no doubt, have awaited in eager anticipation for some delectable game dishes prepared in Moghul style.

Batair Korma

ॐ

QUAILS IN A SPICY SAUCE

Game birds were a favourite food on Moghul tables. Quails were considered a great delicacy, the prize of a good shoot in a short season, much enjoyed by the *nawabs* of Avadh (Oudh). After the shoot royal kitchens became a hive of activity with the plucking, dressing and cooking of the birds for the numerous guests who eagerly anticipated the food to come.

Here, quails are sautéed in an aromatic sauce. Cardamom seeds are available from Indian shops. If unavailable, bruise several pods, remove the seeds and discard the outer skin. Serve the quails with one of the breads and a grape *raita* (p.205) and remember to provide your guests with finger bowls.

3 tbsp ghee
2 finely chopped onions
1/2 tsp finely chopped garlic
2 tsp grated fresh ginger
1 1/2 tsp cardamom seeds
4 cloves
5 cm/2 inch cinnamon stick
1/2 tsp turmeric powder
2 tsp coriander powder
2 tsp cumin powder
1 tsp chilli powder

Heat the *ghee* in a wide heavy-bottomed saucepan. Add the onions, garlic and ginger and stir-fry until the onions start to change colour. Add the cardamom seeds, cloves and cinnamon and stir-fry for 2 minutes to release their aromas before adding the turmeric, coriander, cumin and chilli. Reduce the heat and stir and simmer for 2 minutes. If the mixture is inclined to stick, add a little water and stir.

1 tsp salt
1/2 tsp ground black pepper
3 tomatoes, skin removed and puréed
1 tbsp finely chopped fresh coriander leaves
1/2 tsp saffron threads, steeped for 15 minutes in 1 tbsp hot milk
8-10 dressed quails

Add the salt, pepper, puréed tomatoes, chopped coriander leaves and saffron threads in milk and simmer for 3 minutes. Place the quails in the pan and turn several times to coat them well. Cover and simmer for 3 minutes; turn the quails and continue to simmer for a further 3 minutes. Quail flesh becomes hard if overcooked; to check whether it is cooked, prick the thigh – the juice should run pale pink to clear. Gently lift the quails out onto a plate and continue preparing the sauce.

1 cup lightly whisked yoghurt
1 tsp garam masala

Gradually stir the yoghurt into the sauce and add the *garam masala*; stir and simmer for 2 minutes. Put the quails back into the sauce and again coat them well.

Cover and simmer gently until the sauce thickens and the quails are cooked. Discard the cinnamon stick.

Carefully transfer the quails to a shallow serving platter and pour the remaining sauce over them.

Batak Kashmiri

DUCK STUFFED WITH WALNUTS AND CHERRIES

This is a Kashmiri dish of early summer when the cherries are ripe. The duck is stuffed with walnuts, spices and cherries and basted with the aromatic *akhni* or stock. I first tasted it at an elaborate picnic beneath the plane trees of the Shalimar gardens at Srinagar.

You will need a thick-bottomed saucepan for the *akhni* and a thick-bottomed casserole or baking dish, with a lid, which can be used in the oven as well as on the hot-plate.

Pre-heat the oven to 230°C/450°F/gas mark 8 for about 15 minutes before cooking the duck.

For the akhni:
1 finely chopped large onion
1 tsp mustard seeds
2 tsp crushed coriander seeds
2 tsp coriander powder
1 tbsp grated fresh ginger
1 tsp finely chopped garlic
1 tsp bruised cumin seeds
1 tsp bruised fennel seeds
3 bruised cardamoms
1/2 tsp salt
1/2 tsp ground black pepper
2 1/2 cups water

Put all the ingredients for the *akhni* in a thick-bottomed saucepan, bring to the boil and simmer for 20 minutes. Strain the *akhni* into a bowl and set aside. Discard the solids.

For the duck:

*A duck weighing about
2 kg/4 lb
2 tbsp melted ghee
2 tsp Kasmiri garam masala*

Wash the duck, pat it dry with kitchen paper and prick the skin all over with a fork. Place the duck in a thick-bottomed casserole. Dribble the melted *ghee* over the duck and sprinkle it with *garam masala*. Set aside and prepare the stuffing.

Pre-heat the oven to 230°C/450°F/gas mark 8.

For the stuffing:

*2 finely chopped onions
1 tbsp ghee
112 g/4 oz pitted ripe
cherries
Yolks of 2 hard-boiled eggs,
mashed; use the whites as
garnish
125 g/4 oz shelled walnuts,
blanched, skinned and finely
chopped
3 tbsp lightly whisked
yoghurt
1 tsp salt
1 tsp ground black pepper
2 fresh green chillies, seeds
discarded, finely chopped
2 tsp finely chopped fresh
ginger
2 cloves finely chopped
garlic
3 drops rose essence*

Brown the onions in the *ghee* in a frying pan, then put them aside to cool. Finely chop the pitted cherries, then transfer them to a sieve over a bowl. Press them with the back of a spoon so that the juice is collected in the bowl. Keep the juice aside until needed for the sauce. Add the onions and *ghee* (now cool) and all the other ingredients for the stuffing with the cherry pulp. Mix well. Fill the cavity of the duck with this mixture. Place the casserole, uncovered, in the oven for 20-25 minutes to brown the duck.

Pour out all the duck fat from the casserole, then reduce the heat to 160°C/320°F/gas mark 3 and pour the *akhni* over the duck, put the lid on the casserole and bake for 50 minutes. Uncover, baste well with the *akhni*, cover again and continue baking for a further 50 minutes. Then test if the duck is cooked by piercing the thickest part of the thigh; the juice should run clear.

When the duck is cooked, remove it from the casserole and cut it into serving portions. Arrange these on a platter and cover them with foil to keep them warm.

For the sauce:

*The juice of the cherries
1 tbsp lime or lemon juice*

To make the sauce, based on the cooking liquid that is left in the casserole, start by boiling the liquid on a high heat until it is reduced by half. Add the cherry juice and lime or lemon juice to the remaining liquid and adjust the seasoning. The sauce may be poured over the duck or served separately.

For the garnish:

*Whites of the 2
hard-boiled eggs
8 cherries*

Serve hot, with plain boiled rice or potatoes. Garnish with rings of the whites of the hard-boiled eggs and halved and pitted cherries.

Khargosh Dahi Korma

ঽ

BRAISED RABBIT OR HARE

Babur's daughter, Princess Gulbadan (Rose-Body), records Babur's fondness for hare, and she may well have enjoyed this dish. Pieces of rabbit or hare are first marinated and then braised gently in a sauce aromatic with whole spices and tinged with essence of roses. Serve with plain basmati rice and a tomato, onion and ginger relish (p.209).

The cooking times recommended may need to be adjusted according to the thickness of the flesh.

Allow 2 hours for marination.

For the marinade:
2 tsp coriander powder
2 tsp cumin powder
1 tsp turmeric powder
1/2 tsp chilli powder
4 cups lightly whisked yoghurt
1 kg/2 lb rabbit, dressed, cleaned and jointed into serving-sized pieces

Mix the coriander, cumin, turmeric and chilli into a bowl with the yoghurt. Put the rabbit pieces into this mixture and coat them well. Set aside and marinate for 2 hours.

For the paste:
3 roughly chopped large onions
2 tsp roughly chopped fresh ginger
2 tsp roughly chopped garlic
2 fresh green chillies, seeds discarded
1 tbsp poppy seeds
3 tbsp water

Put the onions, ginger, garlic, chillies, poppy seeds and water into a food-processor, blend to a smooth paste and set aside.

For the sauce:
5 tbsp ghee
4 cloves

Heat the *ghee* in a heavy-bottomed saucepan. Add the cloves, cinnamon stick and cardamom pods and fry for a few seconds to release their aromas. Add the blended

*2.5 cm/1 inch cinnamon
stick
2 large brown cardamom
pods, bruised*

paste and fry for 5 minutes, then stir in the rabbit pieces and the marinade. Bring to the boil, then reduce the heat, cover and simmer gently for 1 hour. Check from time to time that liquid has not been fully absorbed. If this happens, add a little water. The pieces should be quite moist and sitting in a thick sauce.

*1 tsp salt
2 tbsp finely chopped fresh
coriander leaves
1/4 tsp saffron threads,
steeped for 15 minutes in
1 tbsp hot milk
3 ripe tomatoes, puréed*

Add the salt, coriander leaves, saffron threads in milk and tomato purée. Simmer gently for 15 minutes. Cook until tender and discard the cinnamon stick and the cardamom pods.

*1 tsp garam masala
2 drops rose essence
1 tbsp fresh coriander leaves*

Just before serving, add the *garam masala* and drops of rose essence and simmer for a further 5 minutes. Serve with a scattering of fresh coriander leaves.

Khargosh Padishah

&

JULIENNE OF RABBIT IN A SPICY GARLIC SAUCE

Rabbit pieces are cooked in a stock with cardamom and peppercorns, then cut into julienne strips and laced with garlic, tinged with flavours of nutmeg, mace and mint and finally cooked in a sauce thickened with a paste of cashew nuts. Rajput warriors cherished the hunt and Moghul courts embellished the meats to create delicacies for grand dining. Serve with *naan* (pp.191-2) or *besan roti* (p.198) and cucumber *raita* (p.202) and cashew nut chutney (p.209).

*1 kg/2 lb rabbit, dressed,
cleaned and jointed
Sufficient water to cover the
rabbit pieces generously*

Place the rabbit pieces in a heavy-bottomed saucepan with sufficient water to cover them. Add the cardamom, salt and peppercorns and simmer until the meat is tender and begins to pull away from the bone. Remove the rabbit pieces and allow to cool. Discard the stock.

2 large brown cardamom
pods, bruised
$1/2$ tsp salt
6 cracked peppercorns

When cool, pull the meat off the bones and cut into julienne strips. Set aside.

5 tbsp ghee
2 tsp dry-roasted cumin
seeds
4 finely sliced large onions
1 tbsp finely chopped garlic
2 tsp grated fresh ginger
2 tsp cumin powder
2 tsp coriander powder
1 tsp chilli powder
1 tsp turmeric powder
1 tsp salt
1 tbsp finely chopped fresh
mint leaves
2 cups lightly whisked
yoghurt

Heat the *ghee* in a heavy-bottomed saucepan. Add the dry-roasted cumin seeds and fry for few seconds to release their aroma. Add and fry the sliced onions, garlic and ginger until the onions start to change colour. Add the cumin, coriander, chilli and turmeric; stir-fry for about 4 minutes until the oil starts to separate out. Add the salt, chopped mint leaves and yoghurt. Reduce the heat, stir to mix and simmer gently for about 3 minutes.

20 raw cashew nuts
4 tbsp water
$1/4$ tsp saffron threads,
steeped for 15 minutes in
1 tbsp hot milk
$1/2$ tsp cardamom powder
$1/4$ tsp nutmeg powder
$1/4$ tsp mace powder
2 tsp honey
1 tsp garam masala

Blend the cashew nuts and water to a smooth paste in a food-processor and add to the simmering mixture. Stir in the shredded rabbit meat, saffron threads in milk, cardamom powder, nutmeg and mace. Cover and simmer gently for 5 minutes. Add the honey and *garam masala*. Simmer for 2 minutes. Excess oil should start to rise to the top; skim off any surplus oil before removing to the serving dish.

1 tbsp finely chopped mint
leaves

Scatter the surface with finely chopped mint leaves.

Akbari Hiran Kebabs

&

MINCED VENISON KEBABS

Artists at the Moghul courts captured the vigour and the enjoyment of the hunt in beautiful miniature paintings, and court chronicles recorded hunt scenes in great detail. The prize would be handed over to the royal kitchen, where, I hope, royal chefs got equal enjoyment in preparing the quarry.

No doubt these kebabs of finely minced venison kneaded with a paste of onion, garlic, ginger and spices, filled with almonds, raisins and mint before frying, were a delicacy enjoyed by all after the hunt. Serve them with a tangy mint *raita* (p.203).

Allow 1 hour for soaking the yellow split peas to soften them before cooking and another hour for refrigerating the mince mixture for it to become firm. The kebabs will be more easily formed if you moisten your hands during the rolling process.

For the mince:
100 g/4 oz channa dal (yellow split peas); rinse, cover with water, leave for 1 hour
500 g/1 lb finely minced lean venison
1 cup water
1 tsp salt

Drain the split peas after soaking for 1 hour and put them into a heavy-bottomed saucepan with the minced venison, water and salt.

1 roughly chopped onion
2 tsp roughly chopped fresh ginger
1 tsp roughly chopped garlic
2 tbsp lime or lemon juice

Blend the onion, ginger, garlic and lime or lemon juice to a smooth paste in a food-processor and mix with the venison and split pea mixture.

5 black peppercorns
1 tsp cumin seeds
1/2 tsp cardamom seeds
2.5 cm/1 inch cinnamon stick
2 tsp coriander seeds
2 dried red chillies
1 tbsp blanched almonds

Coarse-grind the peppercorns, cumin, cardamom, cinnamon, coriander, chillies and almonds in a spice-mill or coffee-grinder and stir into the mince to mix well. Bring to the boil, reduce the heat, cover and simmer gently until all the moisture has evaporated and the mince is cooked. Allow to cool.

1 finely chopped medium onion
1 finely chopped fresh green chilli
1 tbsp finely chopped fresh coriander leaves
2 tbsp chick-pea flour

Add the finely chopped onion, chilli and coriander leaves with the chick-pea flour to the cooked and cooled mince mixture. Knead for about 5 minutes to obtain a smooth texture. Cover and refrigerate for 1 hour for the mixture to become firm, or leave refrigerated overnight if convenient.

For the kebabs:
1 lightly beaten egg
1 tbsp lightly whisked yoghurt

Remove the mince mixture from the refrigerator and knead the egg and yoghurt into it.

Slivered almonds
Seedless raisins
Finely chopped fresh mint leaves

Divide the kebab mixture into 8 portions for larger kebabs or into 16 portions for snacks. Moisten your hands, form each portion into a ball, make a depression in the centre and fill with slivered almond, raisin and chopped mint. Pinch together to close the depression, roll into a ball or sausage shape, or flatten gently between your palms to form a round flat patty.

Ghee or vegetable oil for shallow-frying

Heat the oil in a heavy-bottomed frying pan and fry the kebabs gently over a medium heat, turning a couple of times until they become an even brown. Too much oil can cause the kebabs to split. Remove and drain on absorbent paper. Serve hot.

FISH

When the Emperor Babur recorded that, 'The flesh of Hindustan fish is very savoury,' he did not elaborate further and so leaves us guessing whether his comment was intended as a general one or whether he had tasted a particular species of fish.

In the seventh century AD the Chinese traveller Xuan Zang expressed his amazement at the many species of fish available from both the lakes and rivers and from the oceans. He spent sixteen years travelling in India and doubtless had the opportunity to sample fish from the vast rivers, the countless streams, lakes, ponds and thousands of miles of coastal waters.

I was not prepared to challenge a Bengali who was, typically, fanatical about fish and claimed that over 2,000 varieties of edible fish and shellfish are available from the inland and ocean waters of the subcontinent. It is not easy to relate species of fish found in Indian waters with those caught around Britain or North America, and matters are made more confusing by the many regional languages that are spoken in India. Comparisons have, however, been drawn to the cold-water fish common to those different seas; Dover sole has been likened to pomfret, shad to hilsa, halibut to seer, cod to sangara. I have, unless a particular substitute is specified, suggested firm white-fleshed fish, leaving the choice subject to availability.

When it is necessary to use frozen prawns or shrimps, allow them to thaw before proceeding with the recipe. If they are pre-cooked and frozen, allow them to thaw first and when the sauce is nearing completion take it off the heat and leave the thawed prawns in the sauce for about 10 minutes before continuing; they should only require to be heated through.

Begum Kofta

🐟

FISH BALLS IN A TOMATO AND YOGHURT SAUCE

Spicy fish balls, crunchy with crushed almonds, are deep-fried and then coated with a creamy tomato and yoghurt sauce flavoured with saffron. These make a delicious starter; as part of a main meal, serve them on a shallow dish surrounded by white rice. Dot the rice with green peas and garnish the fish balls with coriander leaves and golden slivered almonds.

For the sauce:
3 tbsp ghee
1 large brown cardamom pod, bruised
1 finely sliced large onion
1 tbsp grated fresh ginger

Heat the *ghee* in a heavy-bottomed saucepan. Add the cardamom, onion, ginger and stir-fry until the onion starts to change colour.

$1/2$ tsp turmeric powder
2 tsp cumin powder
$1/2$ tsp chilli powder
1 tsp garam masala

Stir in the turmeric, cumin, chilli and *garam masala*, lower the heat and fry for 3 minutes or until the *ghee* starts to separate out. If the mixture is inclined to stick, add a couple of tablespoons of water.

3 large ripe tomatoes; remove skin and purée
$1/4$ tsp saffron threads, steeped for 15 minutes in 1 tbsp hot milk
$1/2$ tsp salt
8 tbsp yoghurt lightly whisked with 2 tbsp water

Add the puréed tomatoes, saffron threads steeped in milk and salt; stir and simmer for 3 minutes. Gradually add the lightly whisked yoghurt and water. Stir gently and simmer for a further 5 minutes. Squeeze any remaining seeds from the cardamom pod into the sauce and discard the skin. Set aside.

For the fish:
500 g/1 lb white-fleshed fish fillets; wash and pat dry
1 large brown cardamom pod, bruised
1 cup milk
1 large potato; diced, cooked and cooled

Bring the milk and cardamom pod to the boil in a heavy-bottomed frying or poaching pan. Poach the fillets for 6 minutes, turning once during this time. Drain and transfer the fish to a bowl. Discard the cardamom pod. When cool, add the diced potatoes to the fish.

1/4 tsp turmeric powder
1/4 tsp cumin powder
1/2 cup warm milk
1 thick slice bread,
preferably a day old

Add the turmeric and cumin powder to the milk and steep the bread for 15 minutes. Squeeze out any excess moisture and add to the fish and potato mixture.

1 roughly chopped onion
1 tsp roughly chopped fresh
ginger
1 large fresh green chilli,
seeds discarded
1 tbsp water

Blend the onion, ginger, chilli and water to a smooth paste in a food-processor.

1/2 cup finely chopped
coriander leaves
1/4 tsp ground black pepper
1/4 tsp salt
1/2 tsp dry-roasted cumin
seeds
2 tbsp coarsely crushed
roasted almonds
1 tbsp chick-pea flour
1 beaten egg
Oil for deep-frying

Stir the blended onion paste into the fish mixture, add the chopped coriander leaves, black pepper, salt, dry-roasted cumin seeds, crushed almonds, chick-pea flour and beaten egg and knead well together. I do this with my fingers and can feel all the ingredients integrating with the fish, but you may prefer to use a fork or potato masher.

Moisten your fingers and palms and form walnut-sized balls. Heat the vegetable oil in a small heavy-bottomed saucepan until it sizzles. Reduce the heat, then drop in the fish balls, a few at a time; turn them frequently and fry to an even golden brown. Drain on absorbent paper.

For the garnish:
1 tbsp fresh coriander leaves
1 tbsp roasted slivered
almonds

Put the *koftas* into a dish. Reheat the sauce if necessary and pour over the *koftas*. Sprinkle with fresh coriander leaves and a scattering of golden slivered almonds.

Dahi Machhi

🐟

FISH FILLETS IN A SPICY YOGHURT SAUCE

Fillets of fish are first rubbed with spices and lemon juice and then marinated in a paste of onion, ginger, chilli, fresh coriander and yoghurt and finally simmered in a saffron sauce sweetened with raisins. Serve with diced potatoes in *masala* (p.143), plain rice and cucumber and tomato *raita* (p.203).

For the fish:
750 g/1½ lb firm white-
fleshed fish fillets
½ tsp turmeric powder
½ tsp salt
1 tsp chilli powder
1 tsp cumin powder
2 tbsp lime or lemon juice

Cut the fish into large pieces; wash and pat them dry. Mix the turmeric, salt, chilli and cumin powder into the lime or lemon juice and then sprinkle and rub the juice all over the fish pieces. Set aside for 15 minutes.

For the marinade:
1 roughly chopped large
onion
2 tsp roughly chopped fresh
ginger
1 roughly chopped fresh
green chilli
2 tbsp fresh coriander leaves
2 tbsp water
½ cup yoghurt
2 tbsp water

Blend the onion, ginger, chilli, coriander leaves and water to a smooth paste in a food-processor. Lightly whisk the yoghurt and water together. Combine with the blended paste and pour over the fish pieces, making sure all the pieces are well coated. Marinate for 30 minutes, turning the pieces occasionally. Shake any excess marinade from the fish and set aside. Reserve the marinade.

3 tbsp ghee
1 finely sliced medium onion
1½ tbsp seedless raisins
1 tsp garam masala
1 tsp salt
1 tbsp finely chopped fresh
coriander leaves
¼ tsp saffron threads,
steeped for 15 minutes in
1 tbsp hot milk
2 tbsp green peas

Heat the *ghee* in a heavy-bottomed saucepan and fry the onion to a light golden colour. Add the raisins and fry for 1 minute. Stir in the *garam masala*, salt, fresh coriander leaves and saffron threads steeped in milk. Add the marinade, bring to the boil, lower the heat and simmer for 4 minutes. Add the fish pieces and continue on a gentle simmer until the fish is cooked; the cooking time will depend on the thickness of the fish pieces. Serve with a sprinkling of lightly cooked green peas.

Tamatar Machhi

FISH FILLETS IN A TOMATO SAUCE

The fish fillets are first rubbed with spices, honey and lemon juice, then immersed in a tomato and yoghurt sauce lightly flavoured with cinnamon and cardamom. The fish pieces in sauce are coated with a frothy egg topping and baked to a golden brown. Try it as a supper dish with one of the breads and a relish of tomato, onion and ginger (p.209).

You will need a shallow baking tray large enough to take the fish pieces in a single layer. Pre-heat the oven to 190°C/375°F/gas mark 5 for 15 minutes.

750 g/1¹/₂ lb thick, firm white-fleshed fish fillets *¹/₂ tsp turmeric powder* *1 tsp cumin powder* *¹/₄ tsp chilli powder* *¹/₂ tsp salt* *1¹/₂ tsp ground black pepper* *2 tsp honey* *2 tbsp lime or lemon juice*	Cut the fish into large pieces; wash and pat them dry. Mix the turmeric, cumin, chilli, salt, pepper and honey together with the lime or lemon juice and rub over the fish pieces. Set aside for 15 minutes.
4 medium, ripe tomatoes; blanch, peel and purée *4 cloves* *2.5 cm/1 inch cinnamon stick* *1 large brown cardamom pod, bruised* *¹/₂ tsp salt* *1¹/₂ tsp cornflour, mixed to pouring consistency with 2 tbsp water* *1 cup yoghurt* *¹/₂ cup water*	Put the puréed tomatoes into a wide heavy-bottomed saucepan, add the cloves, cinnamon stick, cardamom pod and salt and bring to the boil. Remove from the heat and stir in the cornflour paste; return to the heat and simmer for 3 minutes. Lightly whisk together the yoghurt and water and gradually stir into the sauce and continue simmering for a further 4 minutes. Add the fish pieces and any juices that may have collected; then gently stir and turn to coat the fish well. Simmer for 5 minutes to seal. Set aside and allow to cool. Discard the cinnamon stick and cardamom pod.
2 tbsp ghee *2 finely sliced large onions* *2 tsp grated fresh ginger*	Heat the *ghee* in a heavy-bottomed frying pan, add the onion and ginger and fry until the onions start to change colour.

2 coarsely ground small
dried red chillies
2 tsp coarsely ground
dry-roasted cumin seeds
1 tsp coarsely ground
dry-roasted coriander seeds
1 tsp garam masala
2 tbsp chopped fresh
coriander leaves

Add the chillies, cumin, coriander seeds, *garam masala* and fresh coriander leaves. Stir and fry for 2 minutes. Scatter half of this mixture into a shallow baking tray, one large enough to take the fish pieces in a single layer.

Pre-heat the oven to 190°C/375°F/gas mark 5 for 15 minutes.

Gently remove the fish pieces from the now cooled sauce (and reserve the sauce) and place the fish in a single layer in the baking tray on top of the onion and spice mixture. Scatter the remainder of the onion and spice mixture on top of the fish pieces.

3 eggs

Sieve and strain the cold tomato-based sauce into a bowl. Beat one egg and whisk into the sauce. Pour the sauce over the fish pieces. Separate the whites of the 2 remaining eggs and whisk to form white peaks. Beat the 2 yolks separately, then gently fold into the stiff egg whites and spread over the top of the sauce-covered fish pieces. Bake in the middle of the pre-heated oven for about 20 minutes or until most of the moisture is absorbed and the topping is a light golden brown.

Tandoori Machhi

ॐ

WHOLE FISH RUBBED WITH A MASALA PASTE

This recipe is traditional *tandoori*-style in the preparation and marination, but not in the cooking. A *tandoor* is a type of clay oven heated by embers of charcoal. You will, however, find the flavours are still delicious when cooked over a barbecue or under a grill. It will be easier to turn the fish if a long skewer is passed through from head to tail. A flat fish such as flounder or Dover sole would be suitable.

Serve with mint chutney (p.207), grape *raita* (p.205) and one of the breads.

Allow about 3 hours for marination time and do not forget to pre-heat the grill or barbecue before cooking the fish.

For the fish:
1 kg/2 lb whole fish
1 tsp salt
2 tbsp lime or lemon juice

Ask your fishmonger to clean, scale and, if you prefer, to remove the head of the fish; wash and pat it dry, including the cavity. Cut 3 deep diagonal slits across the fleshy part on each side. Mix the salt and lime or lemon juice together and sprinkle and rub over the fish and into the slits and cavity. Set aside for 20 minutes.

For the marinade:
2 tsp roughly chopped fresh ginger
2 tsp roughly chopped garlic
2 fresh red chillies, seeds discarded
2 tbsp lime or lemon juice

Blend the ginger, garlic, chillies and lime or lemon juice to a smooth paste in a food-processor.

$1/2$ tsp light-coloured cumin seeds
$1/2$ tsp black cumin seeds
1 tsp coriander seeds

Grind the cumin and coriander seeds in a spice-mill or coffee-grinder and combine into the paste.

1 tsp salt
$1/2$ tsp ground black pepper
1 tsp garam masala
$1/2$ tsp nutmeg powder
$1/4$ tsp mace powder
2 tbsp vegetable oil
A few drops of cochineal or red food colouring (optional)

Add the salt, pepper, *garam masala*, nutmeg, mace, vegetable oil and food colouring to the spiced paste mixture. Rub this marinade over the fish and into the diagonal slits and the cavity and set aside to marinate for 3 hours.

2 tbsp melted ghee

Brush a long skewer with melted *ghee* and pass it through the fish lengthways from head to tail. Brush the fish with melted *ghee* and cook over a barbecue or under a pre-heated grill, turning occasionally until the fish is cooked. The cooking time will be determined by the thickness of the fish.

2 onions cut into rings
1 tomato cut into rings
1 lemon cut into wedges

Serve on a flat platter, garnished with onion and tomato rings and wedges of lemon.

Jahangiri Jhinga

PRAWNS IN A CHILLI AND TOMATO SAUCE

The taste belies the simplicity of preparation for these succulent prawns in a smooth sauce. The size of the prawns will determine the cooking time; they must be lightly cooked so that they crunch to the bite before the palate is seduced by the flavours of the sauce. Easy to prepare, this dish makes an excellent starter or can be served as a supper dish served with one of the breads. It is equally as good as a main dish, with rice and vegetables. I often serve it as a starter encircled by plain rice and accompanied by banana *raita* (p.205). If frozen raw prawns are used, allow them to thaw properly before proceeding. If using pre-cooked frozen prawns, they should be thawed and immersed in the cooked sauce for a few minutes before being heated through.

750 g/1½ lb medium-sized raw prawns
½ tsp salt
1 tsp turmeric
1 tbsp lime or lemon juice

Shell the prawns and devein them by cutting a shallow slit along the outer curve and lifting or scraping out the gritty vein. Lightly rinse the prawns. Mix together the salt, turmeric and the lime or lemon juice and sprinkle over the prawns.

3 tbsp ghee
1 tbsp oil
2 finely chopped large onions
1 tbsp grated fresh ginger
1 tsp finely chopped garlic
2 finely chopped fresh green chillies, seeds discarded
½ tsp turmeric powder
1 tsp cumin powder
¼ tsp chilli powder
¼ tsp ground black pepper
¼ tsp grated nutmeg

Heat the *ghee* and oil in a heavy-bottomed saucepan and fry the onion, ginger and garlic until the onion starts to change colour. Add the green chillies, turmeric, cumin and chilli powder, ground black pepper and grated nutmeg. Reduce the heat and simmer, stirring constantly, until the oil begins to separate out.

4 ripe tomatoes, blanched, peeled and puréed
4 tbsp lightly whisked yoghurt
1 tsp salt
½ tsp dry-roasted cumin seeds

Add the puréed tomatoes and continue simmering and stirring for 2 minutes. Gradually stir in the yoghurt, salt and dry-roasted cumin seeds. Simmer for a further 3 minutes.

1 tsp garam masala
1 tbsp lime or lemon juice
*1 tbsp finely chopped fresh
coriander leaves*

Stir in the prawns and simmer for 2 minutes. If you are using pre-cooked prawns, remove the sauce from the heat and steep the prawns in the sauce for about 10 minutes before heating through. Add the *garam masala*, lime or lemon juice and fresh coriander leaves.

Simmer for a further 3 minutes or until the prawns become pink or the pre-cooked prawns are heated through.

Masala Machhi

SPICED AND BAKED WHOLE FISH

Salted lemon juice is first sprinkled over the fish and rubbed into the cavity to break down the membranes so that the flesh flakes easily on cooking. A gingery tomato-based sauce is prepared and spooned into diagonal cuts and into the cavity of the whole fish, which is then baked in the oven. If convenient, use a dish suitable for both cooking and serving the fish. The cooking time will be determined by testing that the thickest part of the flesh is no longer opaque and parts easily from the bone. Flounder or Dover sole would be suitable as a choice of fish.

Serve with one of the bean or potato dishes.

Pre-heat the oven to 175°C/350°F/gas mark 4 for about 15 minutes.

*1 kg/2 lb whole fish, scaled
and cleaned*
3 tbsp lime or lemon juice
1 tsp salt

Wash the fish and pat it dry with kitchen paper. Make 2 deep diagonal cuts in the fleshy part on both sides of the fish. Mix the lime or lemon juice and salt together and rub into the cuts and cavity. Sprinkle the remainder all over the fish and set aside for 20 minutes.

3 tbsp vegetable oil
2 finely sliced large onions

Heat the oil in a heavy-bottomed saucepan, add the onions and fry to a golden brown. Remove with a slotted spoon and drain on absorbent paper. Set aside, leaving the remaining oil in the saucepan.

1½ tbsp roughly chopped
fresh ginger
1 tsp roughly chopped garlic
1 roughly chopped large
fresh red chilli, seeds
discarded
1 tbsp roughly chopped fresh
coriander leaves
2 tsp dry-roasted coriander
seeds
1 tsp dry-roasted cumin
seeds
½ tsp black mustard seeds
½ tsp fennel seeds
1 tbsp vegetable oil
3 tbsp lime or lemon juice

Blend the ginger, garlic, chilli, coriander leaves, dry-roasted coriander and cumin seeds, the mustard and fennel seeds, the vegetable oil and the lime or lemon juice to a smooth paste in a food-processor. Heat the remaining oil in the saucepan, add the blended paste and stir and fry for about 4 minutes or until the oil starts to separate out.

½ cup water
3 finely chopped large ripe
tomatoes

Add and stir in the water and chopped tomatoes. Reduce the heat and simmer for 3 minutes.

1 lightly whisked cup
yoghurt
1 tsp salt

Gradually add the yoghurt and salt and simmer until the sauce begins to thicken. Stir in the golden onion slices. Allow to cool.

Pre-heat the oven to 175°C/350°F/gas mark 4. Place the fish in a baking dish.

When the sauce is cool, spoon one third of it into the cavity of the fish. Spread the remainder over the rest of the fish and into the diagonal cuts. Cover the dish with foil and bake in the middle of the oven for about 30 minutes or until the fish is cooked. Test that fish is cooked through at the thickest section.

2 tomatoes, cut into rings
Cucumber

Serve with rings of tomato and unpeeled cucumber.

Zenana Machhi Korma Hyderabadi

Fish Fillets in a Nut Sauce

Palace chefs in Hyderabad liked their dishes to be praised by the ladies of the *zenana*. This fish in a spiced and nutty sauce has a tangy taste of lemon juice and yoghurt and was a favourite among the dozen or so dishes presented to the ladies for their midday meal, served with plain rice and lightly spiced cauliflower and potato (p.159) or spicy new potatoes (pp.144-5) or both.

750 g/1¹/₂ lb firm white-fleshed fish fillets
¹/₂ tsp salt
¹/₂ tsp ground black pepper
¹/₂ tsp turmeric powder
2 tbsp lime or lemon juice

Cut the fish into fairly large pieces, wash and pat it dry. Mix the salt, pepper and turmeric with the lime or lemon juice and sprinkle over and rub into the fish pieces. Set aside for 10 minutes.

4 tbsp vegetable oil

Heat the vegetable oil until sizzling in a heavy-bottomed frying pan. Slide the fish pieces into the hot oil, turning and frying them until they are sealed. Drain on absorbent paper and set aside, leaving the remaining oil in the frying pan.

1 roughly chopped large onion
2 tsp roughly chopped fresh ginger
¹/₂ tsp roughly chopped garlic
2 roughly chopped fresh red chillies
20 blanched almonds
1 tbsp white poppy seeds or sesame seeds
2 tbsp lime or lemon juice
2 tbsp water

Blend the onion, ginger, garlic, chillies, almonds, poppy seeds, lemon juice and water to a smooth paste in a food-processor.

3 tbsp ghee

Add the *ghee* to the oil remaining in the frying pan and, when hot, add the paste, stirring and frying the mixture for about 4 minutes.

1/2 tsp turmeric powder
2 tsp coriander powder
1 tsp cumin powder
1 tsp garam masala

Add the turmeric, coriander, cumin and *garam masala* and continue to stir-fry for about 2 minutes.

1 cup water
1 1/2 cups lightly whisked yoghurt
1 tsp salt
1/4 tsp saffron threads, steeped for 15 minutes in 1 tbsp hot milk
2 tbsp chopped fresh coriander leaves

Add the water, continue cooking and stirring until the oil starts to separate out. Reduce the heat and gradually add the yoghurt, salt and saffron threads in milk and simmer gently for 3 minutes. Add the fresh coriander leaves. Place the fish pieces in the sauce and coat them well. Cover and simmer gently. Turn the pieces after about 2 minutes and continue cooking until the fish pieces are cooked.

Eggs

Eggs are a popular ingredient for main courses in India today. They are considerably kinder on the budget than meat, chicken or fish and they provide a high protein food enriched with iron and vitamins A and B$_{12}$.

It is interesting to note that there have been periods in India's culinary history when eggs were prohibited as a food. They were, however, obviously approved of in the fifth century BC, as an early text records that Buddha enjoined 'the taking of food made out of rice, barley and wheat ... eggs and others, which are full of soul qualities but devoid of faults'. The Parsis, who fled to India over 1,200 years ago when Islam was established in Iran, have always enjoyed eggs cooked in various ways, but in the tenth century a traveller from Baghdad, visiting the Gangetic region of West Bengal on the eve of occupation by the Muslim Amir of Ghazni, noted the prohibition against 'the eating of cow flesh, tame poultry and all eggs among the people'.

Certainly there is evidence that the Muslim kings and aristocracy in India from the twelfth century enjoyed egg dishes, and we know from the Moghul biographer Abul Fazl that eggs were favoured by the Moghul court in many dishes which combined meat and eggs. *Nargisi kofta* (pp.131-2) is one such exotic Moghul presentation.

Eggs, cooked in the Moghul style, on their own or combined with meat or vegetables and immersed in delicate sauces are both substantial and appetising and, of course, particularly acceptable when lighter meals are desired.

Nargisi Kofta

ᥦᏭ

EGGS ENCASED IN MINCED LAMB

Whole hard-boiled eggs are shelled and encased in a thick layer of delicately spiced, finely minced lamb. They are then deep-fried to a golden brown and simmered in a gingery tomato sauce. *Nargisi koftas* can be served, without the sauce, after the deep-frying stage with slices of tomato and cucumber and a cucumber *raita* (p.202). They can also be eaten cold, and are not unlike scotch eggs with the addition of chilli and spices.

Nargisi koftas are a contrast of colour, flavour and texture. When served they are cut in half to reveal the golden brown outer crust and the lighter inner casing, which contrasts with the pure white and the golden yolk of the egg. No wonder the Moghuls gave this dish the evocative name of 'Narcissus'.

For the koftas:
2 tsp roughly chopped garlic
1 tbsp roughly chopped fresh ginger
2 roughly chopped fresh green chillies, seeds discarded
2 tbsp fresh mint leaves
2 tbsp fresh coriander leaves
2 tbsp lime or lemon juice

Blend the garlic, ginger, chillies, mint, coriander leaves and lime or lemon juice to a smooth paste in a food-processor. Set aside.

1 tsp cardamom seeds
4 cloves
5 cm/2 inch cinnamon stick
6 black peppercorns

Grind the cardamom seeds, cloves, cinnamon stick and peppercorns together in a spice-mill or coffee-grinder.

500 g/1 lb finely minced lean lamb
1 tsp cumin powder
1 tsp coriander powder
1/2 tsp chilli powder
2 1/2 tbsp chick-pea flour
1 tsp salt
1/2 cup water

Put the minced meat, blended paste, ground spices, cumin, coriander and chilli powders, chick-pea flour and salt into a mixing bowl. Mix all together and knead well to integrate all the flavours into the meat. Put the meat mixture in a heavy-bottomed saucepan, add the water and mix together. Bring to the boil, reduce the heat, cover and simmer for about 20 minutes, stirring occasionally. If the mixture is inclined to stick to the bottom of the pan, add a little water. The mixture should be fairly dry by the end of the cooking time. Allow to cool.

2 tbsp chick-pea flour
1 lightly beaten egg
4 hard-boiled eggs

Put the cooled mixture through a fine mincer to break the granules, but do not allow it to become a paste. Add the chick-pea flour and the lightly beaten egg and knead the meat mixture until it becomes smooth. Divide into four portions. Moisten your fingers and palms and form a casing of the meat mixture round each of the shelled hard-boiled eggs, retaining the oval egg shape. Refrigerate for about 1 hour so the mixture becomes firm.

Vegetable oil for deep-frying

Heat the vegetable oil in a heavy-bottomed saucepan. Reduce the heat and deep-fry the *nargisi koftas* until golden brown. Remove with a slotted spoon and drain on absorbent paper. Set aside.

For the sauce:
2¹/₂ tbsp ghee
2 tbsp vegetable oil
3 finely chopped onions
2 tbsp grated fresh ginger
2 tsp finely chopped garlic
1 finely chopped fresh red chilli, seeds discarded
1 tsp turmeric powder
¹/₂ tsp chilli powder
2 tbsp finely chopped fresh coriander leaves
1 tbsp finely chopped mint leaves
2 tsp garam masala
salt to taste

Heat the *ghee* and oil in a heavy-bottomed saucepan. Fry the onions for a couple of seconds, add the ginger, garlic and chilli and continue frying until the onions start to change colour. Reduce the heat, add the turmeric, chilli, chopped coriander, mint leaves, *garam masala* and salt and stir-fry for 2 minutes.

4 large, well-ripened tomatoes, puréed
1 cup lightly whisked yoghurt

Add the puréed tomatoes, stir and simmer for 3 minutes. Gradually add and stir in the yoghurt and simmer for a further 4 minutes. Slip the whole *koftas* into the sauce and turn to coat; simmer for a couple of minutes to heat through. Remove the *koftas* to a shallow serving dish with a slotted spoon. Cut each in half, pour the sauce over and serve.

Ande Korma

𝕫𝕒

EGGS IN A NUTTY SAUCE

Eggs are popular in most parts of India. They make a substantial meal and hard-boiled eggs are introduced into a variety of sauces. In this dish, hard-boiled egg halves are steeped in a spicy, aromatic nut-based sauce with fennel seeds which add a lingering flavour.

2 roughly chopped medium onions
2 tsp roughly chopped fresh ginger
2 tsp roughly chopped garlic
2 roughly chopped large fresh green chillies
2 tbsp roughly chopped fresh coriander leaves
2 tbsp yoghurt

Blend the onions, ginger, garlic, chillies, coriander leaves and yoghurt to a smooth paste in a food-processor. Set aside.

2 tbsp ghee
1 tbsp vegetable oil
3 small, light-coloured cardamom pods, bruised
1 tsp fennel seeds

Heat the *ghee* and vegetable oil in a heavy-bottomed saucepan. Fry the cardamom and fennel seeds for a few seconds to release their aromas into the oil. Add the blended paste and fry on a medium heat for about 4 minutes.

1 tsp turmeric powder
3 tsp coriander powder
2 tsp cumin powder
1/4 tsp cardamom powder
1/4 tsp nutmeg powder
1/2 tsp ground black pepper

Stir in the turmeric, coriander, cumin, cardamom, nutmeg and pepper, reduce the heat and stir and simmer for 3 minutes.

10 blanched almonds
1 tbsp white poppy seeds
10 cashew nuts
2 tbsp yoghurt

Blend the almonds, poppy seeds, cashew nuts and yoghurt to a smooth paste and stir into the mixture. Stir-fry for 3 minutes or until oil starts to separate out. If the paste is inclined to stick, add a little water.

3 ripe tomatoes, blanched and puréed *1 tsp salt*	Add the puréed tomatoes and salt, stir and simmer for 2 minutes.
1/2 cup yoghurt, lightly whisked *1/4 tsp saffron threads, steeped for 15 minutes in 1 tbsp hot milk* *1 tbsp finely chopped fresh coriander leaves*	Gradually stir in the yoghurt, saffron threads in milk and the coriander leaves. Stir and simmer gently for 5 minutes.
4 hard-boiled eggs *2 tsp garam masala*	Cut the shelled eggs lengthways into halves or quarters. Place the egg pieces, yolk side up, in a shallow serving dish and pour the sauce over. Sprinkle with *garam masala*.

Palak Ande

❧

EGGS IN A SPINACH PURÉE

This is a nutritious dish of puréed spinach added to a lightly spiced sauce with mustard seeds. Somewhat similar to the classic European recipe eggs florentine, here the eggs are first hard-boiled and egg circles are layered into the spinach mixture. Before serving, mustard seeds are fried in hot *ghee* and poured over the surface. Served in a glass dish, the layered colours look most attractive. Complement this with a pulse dish.

6 hard-boiled eggs	Cut the shelled eggs into circles and divide into 2 or 3 portions according to the size of serving dish. Set aside.
2 tbsp ghee *1 tsp cumin seeds* *1/2 tsp dark mustard seeds* *1 finely chopped small onion* *2 tsp grated fresh ginger* *1 tsp finely chopped garlic* *1 finely chopped fresh green chilli*	Heat the *ghee* in a heavy-bottomed saucepan, add the cumin and mustard seeds and sizzle for a few seconds; if your saucepan is shallow, some of the mustard seeds will pop out. Add the onion, ginger, garlic, chilli and fresh coriander leaves and fry for 4 minutes. Reduce the heat and gradually stir in the yoghurt and salt. Simmer for 2 minutes. Leave to sit in the saucepan until the spinach is puréed.

*2 tbsp finely chopped fresh
coriander leaves
3 tbsp lightly whisked
yoghurt
1 tsp salt*

*500 g/1 lb spinach leaves
1/2 cup water
1/4 tsp salt*

Wash the spinach well to free it of grit. Pack it into a saucepan, add the water and salt. Cover the pan and cook over a high heat until the leaves are wilted; this will take about 2-3 minutes. Drain and purée the spinach and add it to the mixture in the saucepan. Bring to the boil and remove from the heat.

Divide the mixture into 2 or 3 portions according to the size of your serving dish. Spoon one portion into the serving dish and layer with a portion of egg circles. Repeat once or twice.

*1 tsp ghee
1 tsp dark mustard seeds*

Immediately before serving, heat the *ghee* in a small frying pan and fry the mustard seeds until they begin to pop. Scatter over the top layer of egg circles.

Keema Ande

EGGS AND MINCED LAMB

This recipe makes an ideal brunch or light supper dish. Eggs are laid into a bed of spiced lemon-flavoured mince and briefly baked. Serve with *naan* (pp.191-2) or *paratha* (pp.193-4) and a *raita* and chutney.

Use a small, shallow, oven-proof baking dish, preferably with a cover, to take layer of mince about 3 cm/1½ inch deep. Serve in the same dish.

Pre-heat the oven to 175°C/350°F/gas mark 4 for about 15 minutes.

*500 g/1 lb finely minced
lean lamb
1 tbsp lime or lemon juice*

Mix the lime or lemon juice into the mince and set aside.

3 tbsp ghee
4 cloves
5 cm/2 inch cinnamon stick
2 large brown cardamom
pods, bruised
8 peppercorns
1 tsp cumin seeds
2 finely chopped onions
2 tsp finely chopped fresh
ginger
1 tsp finely chopped garlic

Heat the *ghee* in a heavy-bottomed saucepan. Add the cloves, cinnamon, cardamom pod, peppercorns and cumin seeds and sizzle for few seconds to release their aromas. Add the onion, ginger and garlic and stir-fry until the onion starts to change colour.

1 tsp turmeric powder
1/2 tsp chilli powder
2 tsp coriander powder
1 tsp garam masala

Reduce the heat, add the turmeric, chilli, coriander and *garam masala* and continue to stir and fry for 3 minutes or until the oil starts to separate out.

2 tbsp lime or lemon juice
1 tsp salt
2 tomatoes, blanched, peeled
and puréed

Gradually combine the mince into this mixture. I do this with a fork, pressing the mince granules against the sides of the pan to keep it from forming lumps. Stir-fry until the mince turns a light brown, add the lime or lemon juice and salt and simmer on a low heat for 10 minutes, stirring from time to time. Most of the liquid should be absorbed but the mixture should be moist. Discard the cinnamon stick and cardamom pods. Stir in the tomato purée and transfer to a shallow oven-proof baking dish.

Pre-heat the oven to 180°C/350°F/gas mark 4.

4 eggs
1/2 cup cooked peas

Make four shallow depressions in the mixture with the back of a spoon and break an egg into each. Cover the dish and bake in a pre-heated oven for about 20 minutes or until the eggs are sealed. Scatter the surface with cooked green peas.

Ande Bakla

❧

EGGS WITH BEANS

Whole, hard-boiled eggs are first fried to a golden brown, then halved and added to a nutty textured sauce with dry-roasted cumin and sesame seeds. Cooked green beans are folded into the sauce to add both nutrition and a contrast of colour.

500 g/ 1 lb green beans; string and cut into pieces
1 1/2 cups water
1/2 tsp salt

Bring the water to a rapid boil, add the beans and salt and cook for 3 minutes. Drain and set aside.

3 tbsp ghee
2 light-coloured cardamom pods, bruised
4 hard-boiled eggs

Heat the *ghee* in a heavy-bottomed saucepan. Add the bruised cardamom pods and sizzle for a couple of seconds to release their aromas. Put the whole shelled eggs into the hot *ghee* and roll round and fry to a golden brown. Remove to absorbent paper.

2 finely chopped medium onions
1 tbsp grated fresh ginger
2 tsp finely chopped garlic
1 finely chopped fresh red chilli, seeds discarded
1 tsp dry-roasted cumin seeds
1 tbsp dry-roasted sesame seeds
1 tsp turmeric powder
2 tsp coriander powder
1/2 tsp chilli powder
2 tsp garam masala
1 tsp salt
1 1/2 cups water

Using the *ghee* remaining in the saucepan, and adding more if necessary, stir-fry the onion, ginger, garlic and chilli until the onion starts to change colour. Add the cumin and sesame seeds and fry for a few seconds. Stir in the turmeric, coriander, chilli powder, *garam masala* and salt; stir-fry for 4 minutes or until the *ghee* starts to separate out. Add and stir in the water and simmer for 3 minutes, stirring to prevent sticking. Discard the cardamom pods.

Halve the eggs and add them to the sauce, yolk sides up. Spoon the sauce to coat the eggs and simmer for 3 minutes. Lift the eggs out carefully with a slotted spoon and place them in a shallow serving dish. Add the beans to the sauce and heat them through, then spoon the beans and sauce over the egg halves.

1 tbsp dry-roasted sesame seeds

Serve with a sprinkling of dry-roasted sesame seeds.

Bhagmati Ande Hyderabadi

EGGS WITH TOMATO AND MUSHROOM

When Prince Quli Qutub of Golconda married his favourite concubine, Bhagmati, he named a city Bhagnagar after her. He renamed her Hyder Mahal when he became King and he named the city Hyderabad in 1587. We can only muse on the probability of the dish having been a favourite of the concubine for whom Hyderabad was named.

The whites of eggs are beaten to form peaks and are spread over a thick almond-flavoured tomato and mushroom sauce, the yolks are laid on top of the egg whites and baked until sealed. Serve this light and appetising dish with one of the breads and a tomato, onion and ginger relish (p.209).

Pre-heat the oven to 175°C/350°F/gas mark 4 for about 15 minutes.

3 tbsp ghee
1 tsp cumin seeds
1/2 tsp black mustard seeds
3 halved and finely sliced onions
1 tbsp finely chopped fresh ginger
1 tsp finely chopped garlic
1 finely chopped large fresh green chilli, seeds discarded

Heat the *ghee* in a heavy-bottomed saucepan, add the cumin and mustard seeds and fry for a few seconds until they splutter and pop. Add the onions, ginger, garlic and chilli and stir-fry until the onions start to change colour.

3 large ripe tomatoes, blanched, peeled and puréed
1 tsp salt
1/2 tsp ground, black pepper
10 finely ground blanched almonds
10 finely ground cashew nuts
250 g / 8 oz mushrooms
3 tbsp cream
1 tbsp finely chopped coriander leaves

Stir in the puréed tomatoes. Reduce the heat and simmer until the sauce becomes fairly thick. Add the salt, pepper, ground almonds and cashew nuts and simmer for 2 minutes. Sliver the mushrooms, add them to the mixture and simmer for 1 minute; gently stir in the cream and continue simmering for 3 minutes. Stir in the coriander leaves and transfer to a shallow baking dish.

Pre-heat the oven to 175°C/350°F/gas mark 4.

8 small eggs, allowing 2 per person

Separate the egg yolks from the whites and keep the yolks individually separate. Beat the egg whites until they form peaks. Spread over the mixture in the baking dish. Very carefully slide the yolks to nestle, spaced apart, on top of the beaten whites.

1 tsp garam masala
1/2 tsp chilli powder

Sprinkle the *garam masala* and chilli powder over the yolks and bake on the middle shelf of the pre-heated oven for about 15 minutes or until the yolks are sealed.

VEGETABLES

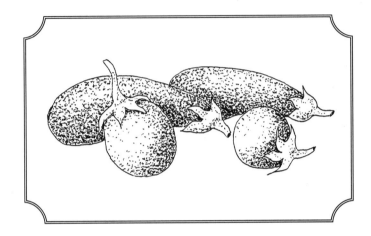

In 1526, when Babur proclaimed himself Emperor of Hindustan, there was no lack of variety of vegetables grown there, although it is difficult to determine when some of those vegetables were introduced into the subcontinent. Before the arrival of the Moghuls layer upon layer of invasions had taken place, satrapies had been established which were eventually absorbed into the culture, and many developed into Hindu kingdoms. Each wave of invaders introduced some aspects of its own religion, culture, clothing, cuisine and food items. Visitors to the kingdoms, including travellers, emissaries, traders and, later, missionaries have left records remarking on the wide-spread practice of vegetarianism and commenting on the profusion of vegetables grown in the various regions. Buddhist and Jain texts make mention of many vegetables, including spinach, mustard, lotus roots, cucumber, yams, radish, gourds, bread-fruit, aubergines, leeks and garlic.

Akbar brought horticulturalists from Persia to introduce different varieties of fruit and vegetables and to improve the strains of those already available. Cooks in the imperial kitchens were able to embrace the profusion of vegetables available to them and created dishes which combined other ingredients or other vegetables – as many as nine in the dish created for Akbar's nine courtiers (pp.145-6).

The cooking of vegetables can be classified into 'dry' or 'wet' styles. The style is deemed dry when the vegetables are added to cooked spices and cooking is completed without the addition of liquid. The style is wet when the vegetables are cooked in a purée or sauce.

Hindus had been moving towards becoming vegetarians from the fifth century BC, beginning with the preaching of *ahimsa* or non-killing of animals for food by Buddha. Recent statistics estimate that 30 per cent of India's population are strict vegetarians; their numbers run into hundreds of millions.

Many of the Moghul emperors abstained from eating meat on certain days and on those days the Hindu cooks in the vegetarian sections of the kitchens would, no doubt, have revelled in being able to innovate and present vegetable dishes to please the emperor's palate. We know from Abul Fazl's list that there were favoured vegetable-only dishes. He also mentions Akbar's particular liking for the lightly spiced spinach dish *saag moghlai* (p.151).

Niramish

🕭

Mixed Vegetables

This colourful, lightly spiced dish of mixed vegetables with a lemony flavour can be prepared very quickly, which makes it a favourite accompanying dish to some of the richer recipes and those that take more time to prepare.

750 g/1¹/₂ lb mixed vegetables	Prepare the vegetables as necessary by peeling and dicing harder vegetables such as carrots and potatoes or separating florets of cauliflower or broccoli and shelling peas.
2 tbsp vegetable oil *1 finely chopped medium onion* *2 tsp grated fresh ginger* *1 tsp finely chopped garlic* *¹/₂ tsp salt* *1 tsp turmeric powder* *¹/₂ tsp chilli powder* *1¹/₂ cups water* *6 tbsp lime or lemon juice* *1 tbsp finely chopped fresh coriander leaves* *1 tsp garam masala*	Heat the oil in a heavy-bottomed saucepan. Sauté the onion, ginger and garlic until soft. Add the salt, turmeric and chilli powder and continue frying for about 1 minute. Add the harder diced vegetables first, together with 1 cup of water. Cover the saucepan and par-boil. Stir occasionally to prevent sticking; if this does happen, add a little more water and stir. When the harder vegetables are par-boiled, stir in the softer vegetables with half a cup of water, the lime or lemon juice, coriander leaves and *garam masala*; cover and simmer for about 5 minutes or until the vegetables are cooked to your liking.

Gobi Kaju

CAULIFLOWER WITH CRUNCHY NUTS

Cauliflower is steamed and then lightly grilled and garnished with a mixture of spiced seeds and nuts. This nourishing recipe is easy to prepare and goes well with most other dishes. I often serve it with lamb chops in a tomato sauce (pp.73-4).

1 small cauliflower divided into 4 portions

Wash the cauliflower and trim off the thick stem, then steam the florets to a firm nutty texture.

1 tbsp ghee
1/4 tsp chilli powder
1/2 tsp garam masala
2 tsp cumin seeds
2 tsp sunflower seeds
2 tsp sesame seeds
1 tbsp roughly chopped unsalted cashew nuts

While the cauliflower is steaming, heat the *ghee* in a small frying pan, add the chilli powder, *garam masala*, cumin, sunflower and sesame seeds and the cashew nuts. Stir-fry until the cashews start to turn light brown. Remove from the heat. Set aside.

Pre-heat the grill to medium.

1 1/2 tbsp butter
1 tsp ground black pepper

Place the steamed cauliflower portions on a greased baking or grilling tray. Smear with the butter, sprinkle with the ground black pepper and place under the grill to bring top to a light golden-brown. Remove to a serving platter and sprinkle with the mixture of seeds and nuts.

Aloo Haldi Bhaji

੨ॐ

Diced Potatoes in Masala

Whole potatoes are first cooked in their skins, then peeled, diced and tossed in a lightly spiced stir-fried *masala*. The potatoes become flecked with cumin and mustard seeds and take on a golden hue from the turmeric in the *masala*. Variations of this recipe are prepared, with love, all over India. Try it. It is so easy and will become a favourite accompaniment to many other dishes. Although it may seem an extra chore to first cook and then peel the potatoes, this does result in a nice floury texture.

Crispy-fried onions are available in containers from Indian shops.

500 g/1 lb potatoes, washed but unpeeled
Hot water to cover the potatoes
1/2 cup cooked peas

Cover the washed potatoes with hot water and cook them in their skins; test with a skewer to make sure they are cooked through but firm. Drain and allow to cool. When cool, peel the skins and dice into 1 cm/1/2 inch pieces, add the cooked peas and set aside.

2 tbsp ghee
1 finely sliced large onion
2 tsp finely chopped fresh ginger
1 tsp large black mustard seeds
1/2 tsp light-coloured cumin seeds
1 tsp turmeric powder
salt to taste
2 tbsp lime or lemon juice

Heat the *ghee* in a heavy-bottomed saucepan. Fry the onion and ginger until the onion becomes soft and translucent. Add the mustard and cumin seeds, the turmeric and salt, fry for a few seconds then add the lime or lemon juice and allow to simmer briefly to absorb the flavours. Remove from the heat.

2 tbsp finely chopped fresh coriander leaves
1 small fresh green chilli, snipped into fine circles

Toss in the diced potatoes, the chopped coriander and chilli and gently coat the potatoes by turning with a fork a few times. Too much turning will break the potato. If some break, don't worry, this is not a disaster and the taste will not be affected.

A few coriander leaves or crispy-fried onion

Serve garnished with fresh coriander leaves or crispy brown onions.

Dum Aloo

🍃

SPICY NEW POTATOES

New potatoes are par-boiled in their skins, pricked all over and then simmered in a sauce flavoured with nuts, spices and saffron. Potato dishes are popular and this is a unique way of preparing them to present a fragrant spiciness which permeates through the new potatoes. I first tasted this version when staying on a houseboat in Kashmir.

For the potatoes:
500 g/1 lb new potatoes
Hot water to cover the potatoes

3 tbsp ghee

For the paste:
1 roughly chopped onion
2 tsp roughly chopped fresh ginger
1 roughly chopped large fresh green chilli
2 tsp white poppy seeds
1 tbsp blanched almonds
1/2 tbsp unsalted cashew nuts
1/2 tsp cardamom seeds
1 tsp light colour cumin seeds
1/2 cup loosely packed fresh coriander leaves
1 tsp Kashmiri garam masala
1 tsp coriander powder
1/4 tsp nutmeg powder
1/4 tsp mace powder
1 tsp salt

Wash the potatoes and put them into a saucepan with enough hot water to cover; bring to the boil and par-boil for 8 minutes. Drain and prick lightly into the potatoes on all sides with a fine skewer. Set aside.

Heat the *ghee* in a heavy-bottomed saucepan, add the potatoes and stir-fry very lightly for about 3 minutes. Remove with a slotted spoon and set aside. Leave the remaining *ghee* in the saucepan.

Blend the onion, ginger, chilli, poppy seeds, almonds, cashew nuts, cardamom, cumin, coriander leaves, *garam masala*, coriander, nutmeg and mace powders, salt, lime or lemon juice and water in a food-processor until smooth.

Re-heat the *ghee* remaining in the pan, add the blended paste and stir-fry for 4 minutes. Add a little water if the mixture is inclined to stick.

3 tbsp lime or lemon juice
4 tbsp water

¹/4 tsp saffron threads,
steeped for 15 minutes in
1 tbsp hot milk
1 cup lightly whisked
yoghurt

Add the saffron threads in milk and the yoghurt and simmer for 2 minutes. Add the potatoes and simmer for about 6 minutes or until the potatoes are firm but cooked through. Test by sticking with a skewer.

1 tsp dry-roasted light
cumin seeds

Remove to a serving platter and scatter with the dry-roasted cumin seeds.

Birbal Sabzi Navrattan

❧

NINE VEGETABLES

Akbar's court was full of talented men. Nine of the most distinguished, one of whom was Birbal, the philosopher wit, came to be known as the nine jewels of the empire, the *navrattan*.

To prepare this jewel-coloured dish, use nine varieties of vegetables with a variety of colours and flavours such as peas, beans, carrots, potato, turnip, pumpkin, tomato, cauliflower florets and broccoli. The vegetables will, in varying degrees, subtly take on the flavours of the nuts, coconut, honey and saffron.

750 g/1¹/2 lb mixed vegetables

Peel and dice the vegetables and par-boil any that are hard-textured such as carrot, potato and turnip. Set aside.

¹/2 cup desiccated coconut,
steeped for 30 minutes in
1 cup hot milk

Push the steeped coconut through a sieve to extract liquid; discard the pulp and reserve the liquid.

1 tbsp blanched almonds
2 tbsp poppy seeds
1 tbsp cashew nuts
2 tbsp lime or lemon juice

Blend the almonds, poppy seeds, cashew nuts and lime or lemon juice to a smooth paste in a food-processor. Set aside.

3 tbsp ghee
4 cloves
2.5 cm/1 inch cinnamon stick
4 light-coloured cardamom pods, bruised
2 halved and finely sliced onions
1 tbsp grated fresh ginger

Heat the *ghee* in a heavy-bottomed saucepan, add the cloves, cinnamon stick and cardamom pods and fry for a few seconds to release their aromas. Add the onions and ginger and fry until the onions start to change colour.

1/2 tsp chilli powder
1/2 tsp Kashmiri garam masala
1/2 tsp ground black pepper

Mix in the blended nut paste and fry for 2 minutes. Stir in the chilli powder, *garam masala* and pepper and fry for a further 3 minutes. If the mixture is inclined to stick, add a little water.

2 large ripe tomatoes, blanched and puréed
1 tsp salt

Add the puréed tomatoes and salt and reduce the heat. Gradually pour in the extracted coconut liquid and simmer for 3 minutes.

1 cup lightly whisked yoghurt
2 tsp honey
1/4 tsp saffron threads, steeped for 15 minutes in 1 tbsp hot milk

Add the vegetables and cover and simmer for 5 minutes, stirring occasionally. Add the yoghurt and the honey and simmer for 3 minutes. Stir in the saffron threads and milk and simmer for a further 2 minutes.

The vegetables should be cooked to a firm texture. Discard the cinnamon stick and cardamom pods before serving.

Baghare Baigan

AUBERGINES WITH TAMARIND

This is a speciality of *chowki* dinners in Hyderabad. *Chowki* is actually the name of the low square wooden tables at which the meal is served. Each table seats four people; it is first covered with a white tablecloth, which is overlaid with a square of red cloth on which the food is served. A *chowki* dinner is a sumptuous affair, with course following course. Though many of the dishes date from Moghul times, this style of entertaining originated in the days of the Bahmani kings of Hyderabad in the fifteenth century and continues today in many *nawabi* households.

Bagare is the Hindi culinary term for tempering when flavours and aromas are released into hot oil. Herbs and spices are added rapidly to smoking hot oil or *ghee* and poured while sizzling over the dish just before serving.

This tangy *baghare baigan* is one of the accompaniments to a main course. It should be made with *brinjal,* the small finger-shaped aubergines which are sold in Indian grocers and some oriental shops. It is tamarind which gives this dish its sour-sweet flavour. Tamarind concentrate, sold in jars, may be used for convenience, but I prefer to use the liquid extracted from tamarind pulp, which results in a less tart flavour.

For the paste:
1 roughly chopped large onion
2 tsp roughly chopped garlic
1 tbsp dry-roasted sesame seeds
1 tbsp dry-roasted coriander seeds
1/2 tsp dry-roasted cumin seeds
1/4 tsp turmeric powder
4 tbsp water
3 tbsp vegetable oil

Dry-roast the sesame, coriander and cumin seeds by putting them in a small wok or frying pan on a medium heat and stirring them continuously for 1 minute or until they begin to change colour; it is important not to let the seeds burn. Then turn off the heat but continue stirring for 1 more minute. Transfer the seeds immediately onto a small plate.

Put all the ingredients for the paste in a food-processor and blend until smooth. Transfer the paste to a bowl and set aside.

To be added during the cooking:
2 dried red chillies
2 tbsp desiccated coconut, dry-roasted until golden
1/2 tsp salt

Dry-roast the chillies and desiccated coconut as for the seeds above for 1 minute only, stirring all the time. Transfer these straight away to a mortar, add the salt and crush the chillies with the pestle to mix them well with the coconut and the salt. Set aside.

450 g/1 lb brinjals
1/2 cup vegetable oil

Remove the stems, wash the aubergines and dry them well with kitchen paper. Heat the vegetable oil in a heavy-bottomed frying pan and fry the aubergines for about 30 seconds only, on a high heat, turning them often.

After 30 seconds reduce the heat and continue frying and turning the aubergines until their purple skins turn brown. Remove the aubergines with a slotted spoon and let them drain in a colander. When they are cool enough to handle, cut each one, from the base towards the stem end, into halves or quarters, taking care not to cut the stem end right through. Discard the oil.

1/2 tsp turmeric powder
2 tsp brown sugar
2 tbsp tamarind pulp,
steeped for 15 minutes in
3 tbsp boiling water, then
pushed through a sieve to
extract 2 tbsp tamarind
liquid
1 cup water

Put the paste into a small saucepan and bring it to the boil. When it boils, reduce the heat and simmer, stirring often, for 8 minutes so that the onion is cooked. Stir in the previously prepared mixture of dried red chillies, roasted coconut and salt, the turmeric and the sugar. Continue simmering for 2 minutes and then add the tamarind liquid extract plus one cup of water.

Increase the heat to bring the liquid once more to the boil, then reduce it again and simmer for 5 minutes. Add the aubergines and continue to simmer for 2 more minutes. Remove to a serving dish and add garnish.

For the bagare or garnish:
1 tbsp ghee
10 curry leaves (optional)
1 tsp mustard seeds

To garnish, heat the *ghee* in small frying pan almost to smoking point, remove from the heat and add the curry leaves (if used) and the mustard seeds. As soon as the seeds begin to pop, pour the mixture over the aubergines.

Serve hot with any suitable main course dish.

Tamatar Kut

PURÉED TOMATOES WITH TAMARIND

I have enjoyed many epicurean meals in Hyderabad and very rarely has this aromatic dish of puréed tomatoes not accompanied one of the main courses. The final addition of a tempering of garlic and spices fried in smoking hot oil lifts this tomato purée to a taste sensation you will love.

Tamarind is sold either in pulp form or concentrate. If using concentrate, follow the instructions to obtain 3 tablespoons of diluted juice.

3 tbsp tamarind pulp
4 tbsp boiling water

Steep the tamarind pulp in boiling water for 15 minutes and then push it through a fine sieve to extract 3 tablespoons of juice. Set aside.

1 kg/2 lb finely chopped
ripe tomatoes
1 cup water
1 tsp salt
³/4 tsp chilli powder
¹/2 tsp turmeric powder
1 tbsp whole coriander
seeds, dry-roasted and
crushed
2 tsp light-coloured cumin
seeds, dry-roasted and
crushed
1 tbsp grated fresh ginger
1 tsp finely chopped garlic
10 curry leaves

Put the chopped tomatoes, water, salt, chilli powder, turmeric powder, dry-roasted crushed coriander and cumin seeds, ginger, garlic, curry leaves and the tamarind juice into a heavy-bottomed saucepan. Bring to the boil, reduce the heat and simmer for about 5 minutes.

Strain the sauce through a sieve into a bowl, pushing the purée through with the back of a wooden spoon. Discard the solids.

2 tbsp chick-pea flour,
dry-roasted until it starts to
change colour
¹/2 cup hot water

Gradually add the hot water to the dry-roasted chick-pea flour to make a thickening agent. Add this mixture to the tomato purée and return to a heavy-bottomed saucepan and stir and simmer over a low heat for about 3 minutes to thicken the purée, which should be smooth and thick, but not stodgy. Remove to a serving dish.

2 tbsp ghee
¹/2 tsp mustard seeds
¹/2 tsp cumin seeds
2 garlic cloves cut into
quarters
2 dried red chillies broken
into pieces
10 curry leaves

Before serving, heat the *ghee* in a small frying pan until it is smoking hot, then add the mustard and cumin seeds, garlic, dried red chilli and the curry leaves. As soon as the garlic begins to change colour, but not darken, pour over and mix into the tomato purée.

Dahi Makkai

LIGHTLY SPICED CORN KERNELS

Corn has been part of India's culinary repertoire since the Portuguese introduced it in the sixteenth century. Here corn kernels are simmered in a lightly spiced yoghurt sauce. Serve it as an accompanying vegetable to the marinated leg of lamb (pp.74-6). The quantities given here are intended for a dish that will accompany a main meal. The chilli flowers are a colourful decoration and it has been known for them to be eaten and enjoyed.

3 tbsp ghee
4 light-coloured cardamom pods, bruised
2 cups sweetcorn kernels; if using canned corn, drain and discard the liquid

Heat the *ghee* in a heavy-bottomed saucepan. Add the bruised cardamom pods and fry for a few seconds to release their aroma. Add the corn kernels and fry for about 1 minute. Remove with a slotted spoon to drain on absorbent paper. Discard the skins of the cardamom pods.

2 finely chopped onions
1 tbsp grated fresh ginger
1/2 tsp finely chopped garlic
1 finely chopped fresh green chilli, seeds discarded
3/4 tsp turmeric powder
1 1/2 tsp cumin powder
1/4 tsp chilli powder

Add the onions, ginger, garlic and fresh green chilli to the remaining *ghee* and stir-fry until the onion starts to change colour. Add the turmeric, cumin and chilli powder and fry for 2 minutes. Add a little water to the mixture if it is inclined to stick.

1 1/2 cups yoghurt
1/2 cup water
1 tsp salt
1/2 tsp sugar

Lightly whisk together the yoghurt, water, salt and sugar and gradually stir into the mixture. Reduce the heat and simmer for 3 minutes. Stir in the corn kernels and simmer gently for another 10 minutes, stirring occasionally.

1 tsp garam masala
2 tbsp chopped fresh coriander leaves

Add the *garam masala* and fresh coriander leaves and simmer for 1 minute. Remove to a serving dish and decorate with chilli flowers.

2 fresh green chillies

To make chilli flowers, hold the fresh chillies at the stalk end and, with sharp scissors, make as many cuts as possible along the length, from the pointed end to the stalk. Put the chillies into a bowl of iced water to open out.

Saag Moghlai

🌿

LIGHTLY SPICED SPINACH

Spinach is a favourite combination with meat, eggs, vegetables or *dal* in many Moghul recipes. Here is spinach without a partner, lightly spiced and cooked in the Moghul style. It is a dish that is cooked easily and quickly and is best prepared just before serving.

2 tbsp ghee
2 light-coloured cardamom pods, bruised
1/2 tsp fennel seeds
1/2 tsp cumin seeds
1/2 tsp mustard seeds
1 finely chopped onion
1 tbsp grated fresh ginger
1 finely chopped large fresh red chilli, seeds discarded

Heat the *ghee* in a large heavy-bottomed saucepan. Add the cardamom pods, fennel, cumin and mustard seeds; fry for a few seconds to release their aromas. Add the onion, grated ginger and chilli and stir-fry until the onion starts to change colour.

1 kg/2 lb fresh spinach leaves; rinse well and chop roughly
1 tsp salt
1/2 tsp Kashmiri garam masala
1/2 tbsp blanched and slivered almonds

Put the spinach leaves in the saucepan and pack them down. Cover the pan and simmer on a low heat for a couple of minutes. As soon as the spinach starts to wilt, add the salt, *garam masala* and the slivered almonds and mix well into the spinach.

2 tbsp cream

Gently fold and stir in the cream. Heat through and serve immediately.

Chukandar Dalna

BEETROOT AND POTATOES

This combination of beetroot and pink-hued potato encircled with green peas is delicate in flavour and makes an interesting variation of texture and colour. Make it to accompany chicken in almond sauce (pp.91-2) and serve with plain white rice or a choice of breads. It is a dish that can be served cold and is ideal as part of a picnic or with barbecued meats.

Make sure that you reserve the liquid from the cooked beetroot as you will need it to cook the potatoes.

---

750 g/1¹/₂ lb peeled beetroot

Peel and cook the beetroot in sufficient liquid to reserve 1¹/₂ cups after cooking. Dice the beetroot and set aside.

1 tbsp ghee
2 tbsp vegetable oil
2 small light-coloured cardamom pods, bruised
¹/₂ tsp fennel seeds
1 finely chopped large onion
2 tsp grated fresh ginger
¹/₂ tsp chilli powder
2 diced medium potatoes
1 tsp salt, or to taste

Heat the *ghee* and oil in a heavy-bottomed saucepan, add the cardamom and fennel seeds and fry for a few seconds to release their aromas. Add the onion and ginger and stir-fry until onions are transparent. Add the chilli powder, diced potatoes and salt. Stir and fry the potatoes for 2 minutes. Add the reserved beetroot liquid, reduce the heat and cook until the potato is cooked but firm. Strain and discard any excess liquid.

1 tsp Kashmiri garam masala

Add the cooked and diced beetroot, sprinkle with *garam masala* and mix gently. Cover and simmer for 2-3 minutes.

¹/₂ cup cooked green peas

Remove to a serving dish and sprinkle with green peas.

Same Bhaji

ॐ

Beans with Sesame Seeds

The addition of sesame seeds to lightly cooked green beans results in a pleasing combination of taste and texture. Use French, runner, Chinese or flageolet green beans. This is a dish that will add interest to any meal and goes particularly well with egg dishes. Serve it hot or cold as a salad with barbecues.

500 g/1 lb green beans	Top, tail and remove the stringy parts down the side of the beans, as required. Cut into short lengths, wash and set aside.
2 tbsp vegetable oil *1/2 tsp black mustard seeds* *2 finely chopped medium onions* *2.5 cm/1 inch piece fresh ginger cut into julienne strips* *1/2 tsp finely chopped garlic* *1 finely chopped large fresh red chilli, seeds discarded*	Heat the oil in a heavy-bottomed saucepan and fry the mustard seeds until they splutter and pop. Add the onion, ginger garlic and chilli and stir-fry until the onion starts to change colour.
1 tsp salt *1 tbsp sesame seeds* *1 tbsp lime or lemon juice* *1/2 cup water*	Add the beans, salt and sesame seeds. Mix well, reduce the heat, add the lime or lemon juice and water, cover and simmer until the beans are lightly cooked and crisp.

Band Gobi Mattar

❦

CUMIN-FLAVOURED CABBAGE AND PEAS

This combination of cumin-flavoured cabbage and peas scattered with peppercorns will soon become a favourite. Pepper was a highly prized spice and used to be known as 'black gold' because of its export-earning capacity. The chilli was a welcome introduction in the sixteenth century as an alternative medium of heat. A *bagare* or tempering of spices is poured over the surface of the completed dish.

3 tbsp vegetable oil
1 tsp light-coloured cumin seeds
$1/2$ tsp black cumin seeds
$1/2$ tsp black mustard seeds
20 black peppercorns

Heat the vegetable oil in a heavy-bottomed saucepan. Add both varieties of cumin seeds, mustard seeds and peppercorns and fry for a few seconds until the mustard seeds begin to pop and splutter.

1 tsp turmeric powder
$1^1/2$ tsp cumin powder
1 tbsp finely chopped fresh coriander leaves
3 tbsp lime or lemon juice
1 tsp salt
1 tsp honey
500 g/1 lb cabbage, cored and cut into shreds
125 g/4 oz shelled green peas
$1/2$ cup water

Add the turmeric, cumin, fresh coriander leaves, lime or lemon juice, salt and honey. Stir in the shredded cabbage and simmer for 5 minutes. Add the shelled green peas and the water. Reduce the heat, cover and simmer for about 2 minutes.

3 tbsp lightly whisked yoghurt

Stir in the yoghurt, cover and simmer for 3 minutes or until the cabbage is cooked to your liking. Remove to a serving dish.

1 tbsp ghee
$1/2$ tsp light cumin seeds
$1/4$ tsp black cumin seeds
$1/2$ tsp mustard seed

Immediately before serving, heat the *ghee* to smoking in a small frying pan. Remove from the heat and toss the cumin and mustard seeds into the hot *ghee* and pour over the surface of the cabbage and peas.

Shahi Khumb

Lightly Spiced Mushrooms

Mushrooms are a great favourite in Kashmir, where they grow profusely on the forested mountain slopes. Kashmiri mushrooms are similar in taste to French morels and a generous addition of coriander leaves complements and further enhances their flavour. Kashmiri onions have a flavour not dissimilar to that of shallots, but onions can be substituted if shallots are not available.

2 roughly chopped shallots
2 tsp roughly chopped fresh ginger
1 large fresh green chilli, seeds discarded
1 tbsp blanched almonds
2 tbsp lime or lemon juice

Blend the shallots, ginger, chilli, almonds and lime or lemon juice to a smooth paste in a food-processor. Set aside.

3 tbsp ghee
4 cloves
2.5 cm/1 inch cinnamon stick

Heat the *ghee* in a heavy-bottomed saucepan, add the cloves and cinnamon stick and fry for a few seconds to release their aromas. Add the blended paste and stir-fry for 3 minutes.

1 tsp coriander powder
1/2 tsp chilli powder
1/4 tsp mace powder
1 tsp salt
750 g/1 1/2 lb mushrooms; washed, cleaned and sliced
3/4 cup chopped coriander leaves

Reduce the heat and mix in the coriander powder, chilli, mace and salt and cook for 2 minutes. If the mixture is inclined to stick, add a little water. Add the mushrooms and coriander leaves and stir into the mixture. Continue frying until the mushrooms begin to change colour.

1 cup yoghurt
1/4 cup water

Lightly whisk the water and yoghurt together and gradually add to the mixture. Simmer gently for about 15 minutes or until the mushrooms are tender. Discard the cinnamon stick.

2 tsp finely chopped fresh ginger

Scatter the chopped fresh ginger over the surface and serve.

Sabzi Kofta

&

VEGETABLE BALLS SIMMERED IN A SPICY SAUCE

Delicately spiced vegetable *koftas*, the size of walnuts, are deep-fried until golden brown then simmered in a creamy sauce. They are delicious with lightly spiced spinach (p.151) and ballooned *chapatis* (pp.195-6). I sometimes dispense with the sauce and serve the *koftas* with a cucumber *raita* (p.202) as a starter. They are also popular as a snack served with drinks.

For the koftas:
250 g/8 oz unpeeled potatoes
250 g/8 oz peeled and diced carrots
125 g/4 oz peas
1 finely chopped fresh green chilli, seeds discarded
1/2 tsp salt
2 tbsp chick-pea flour; add more to bind if required
1 beaten egg

To obtain a full-flavoured stock, cook the unpeeled potatoes, the carrots and the peas successively in the same water; reserve 1 cup of the stock and set aside. When the potatoes have cooled, remove their skins.

Put the cooled potatoes, carrots and peas in a bowl. Add the finely chopped chilli, salt, chick-pea flour and beaten egg and mash together. Moisten your fingers and form the mixture into walnut-size balls. Set aside.

Oil for deep-frying

Heat the oil for deep-frying in a heavy-bottomed pan. Reduce the heat and gently fry the *koftas* a few at a time to a golden brown. Remove to absorbent paper.

For the sauce:
3 cloves
2.5 cm/1 inch cinnamon stick

Strain the oil through a sieve into a bowl to get rid of any solids. Return 2 1/2 tablespoons of the oil to the saucepan and heat. Add the cloves and cinnamon and fry for a few seconds to release their aromas.

2 finely chopped medium onions
2 tsp grated fresh ginger
1/2 tsp finely chopped garlic
1/2 tsp turmeric powder
1/2 tsp chilli powder
1 tsp coriander powder
1 tsp cumin powder

Add the onion, ginger and garlic and stir-fry until the onions are a light golden colour. Add the turmeric, chilli, coriander and cumin powder and stir-fry for 2 minutes. If the mixture is inclined to stick, add a little of the reserved vegetable stock.

3 puréed ripe tomatoes
1 tbsp finely chopped fresh
coriander leaves
1/2 tsp salt
1 cup vegetable stock
(reserved from cooking the
vegetables)

Reduce the heat, add the puréed tomatoes, fresh coriander leaves and salt and simmer for 2 minutes. Add the reserved vegetable stock and simmer for a further 3 minutes. Discard the cinnamon stick.

3 tbsp yoghurt, lightly
whisked
1/4 tsp saffron threads,
steeped for 15 minutes in
1 tbsp hot milk

Gradually add the yoghurt, saffron threads and milk. Add the *koftas* and simmer for 5 minutes, turning them once gently during this time. Remove to a serving dish and pour the sauce over the *koftas*.

Moghlai Aloo Saag

POTATOES WITH SPINACH

Here spinach is combined with potatoes in the Moghul style. This can be served as part of a vegetarian meal with one of the breads, or it is a dish that goes equally well with meat dishes and rice.

Make sure that the potatoes are almost cooked before adding the spinach. The spinach does not take long to cook, and overcooking will cause it to lose some of its colour, although the flavour is not impaired.

4 tbsp vegetable oil
1 finely chopped small onion
5 cm/2 inch piece fresh
ginger cut into strips
1 fresh green chilli chopped
into fine rings
1/2 tsp cumin seeds
1/2 tsp black mustard seeds
1/2 tsp fennel seeds
A pinch of asafoetida
(optional)

Heat the oil in a heavy-bottomed saucepan. Add the onion, ginger and fresh green chilli and stir-fry for 2 minutes. Mix in the cumin seeds, mustard seeds, fennel seeds, asafoetida, salt, turmeric and lime or lemon juice.

Now add the diced potatoes with a little water and continue cooking until they are par-boiled; this should take about 10 minutes. If the mixture is inclined to stick, add a little water. Stir in the spinach, cover and continue cooking for about 5 minutes. Check that the potatoes are cooked.

1 tsp salt
1 tsp turmeric
1 tbsp lime or lemon juice
1 cup peeled potatoes, diced fairly small
500 g/1 lb roughly chopped spinach

1 or 2 hard-boiled eggs
1 tsp garam masala

Remove to a serving dish, garnish with rings of hard-boiled egg and sprinkle with *garam masala*.

Shalgum Bhurta

TURNIPS FOLDED INTO A SPICY TOMATO PURÉE

This is a dish for cold winter months in Kashmir. I was served this on a visit to Gul Marg (the Meadow of Flowers) at an altitude of some 2,600 metres with the threat of frost in the clear air suffused with bright sunlight. Turnips cooked separately and mashed smooth are folded into a spicy tomato-based sauce. They are delicious scooped up with a ballooned *chapati* (pp.195-6).

375 g/³/4 lb young turnips

Peel and slice the turnips. Steam them until very tender, then mash and set aside.

3 tbsp ghee
1 tsp cumin seeds
¹/2 tsp fennel seeds
¹/2 tsp black mustard seeds

Heat the *ghee* in a heavy-bottomed saucepan. When it is sizzling, add the cumin, fennel and mustard seeds and fry for a few seconds. They will splutter and pop and release their aromas into the *ghee*.

1 finely chopped large onion
2 tsp grated fresh ginger
2 finely chopped fresh green chillies, seeds discarded
1 tsp coriander powder
1 tsp Kashmiri garam masala
A pinch of asafoetida (optional)

Add the onion and ginger and fry until the onion starts to change colour. Add the chillies, coriander powder, *garam masala*, asafoetida, sugar, salt and pepper and cook for 3 minutes.

Stir in the puréed tomatoes, reduce the heat and simmer for 5 minutes. Fold in the steamed mashed turnips and heat through gently.

¹/₂ tsp sugar
¹/₂ tsp salt
¹/₄ tsp ground black pepper
2 large tomatoes, peeled and
puréed

Fresh coriander leaves

Serve in a circular bowl and decorate with whole coriander leaves.

Phool Gobi Aloo Bhaji

CAULIFLOWER AND POTATO

Cauliflower florets are combined with tiny cubes of potato with a subtle bite which comes from mustard seed and chilli powder and both black and white cumin seeds.

2 tbsp ghee
1¹/₂ tsp white cumin seeds
¹/₄ tsp black cumin seeds
¹/₂ tsp black mustard seeds
1 large potato peeled and cut
into small cubes
1 tsp salt
1 tsp chilli powder
1 tsp turmeric powder
1 tsp coriander powder
1 small to medium cauli-
flower split into florets
3 tbsp lightly whisked
yoghurt

Heat the *ghee*, add the cumin and mustard seeds and fry for a few seconds to release their aromas. Add the potato cubes and stir-fry for about five minutes; depending on the size of the pan a little more *ghee* may need to be added. Add the salt, chilli, turmeric, coriander and the cauliflower florets; stir to mix in all the ingredients. Mix in the yoghurt and simmer until the vegetables are almost cooked, stirring from time to time to prevent sticking. If the mixture becomes too dry, add a couple of tablespoons of water.

1 tsp garam masala
1 tbsp chopped fresh
coriander leaves

A few minutes before completion add the *garam masala* and the coriander leaves.

PULSES

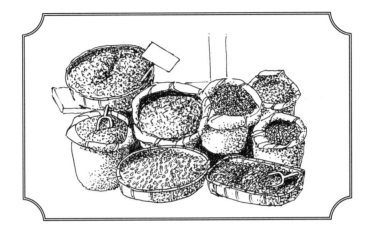

In English, 'pulse' is the general term for the dried edible seeds of peas, beans and lentils. In Hindi the generic term is *dal*. Strictly speaking, the word *dal* should apply to split pulses of any kind, but in fact the term has become gradually accepted to include whole dried peas and beans; *rajma dal* (pp.163-4), for example, uses whole red kidney beans.

Dal is an important part of meals in India and most meals will include at least one *dal* dish and often other dishes using a combination of pulses with vegetables or meats. Pulses are highly rated as a source of protein, particularly by vegetarians. Moghul emperors and the *nawabs* of Lucknow were extremely fond of *dal* dishes. In Lucknow one highly regarded chef in a *nawabi* household, employed only to innovate and prepare dishes of *dal*, downed tools and walked off the job because the king continued to talk rather than eating immediately the meal was served.

Pulses should always be picked over for dirt and grit and rinsed in several changes of water. Some of the beans require lengthy soaking to soften them. Soaking will reduce the cooking time, while the use of a pressure-cooker can reduce the cooking time by about two-thirds. When soaking the beans for long periods, store in a cool place or refrigerate to prevent fermentation. Lentils and split peas will not require lengthy soaking and they will cook more quickly. In most *dal* recipes, a pinch of asafoetida is added to counteract flatulence and to make the *dal* more digestible.

Maharani Panch Rattan

🍃

FIVE VARIETIES OF PULSES

Royal ladies called this the dish of five jewels. Five different types of pulses are simmered gently and the spices and seasonings are cooked separately. The pulses are mashed and then folded into the spice mixture and heated through so that the flavours are mingled. This is delicious served with chicken in a buttery tomato sauce (pp.86-7) and any of the breads or plain rice.

Allow about 3 hours to soak the pulses, although most of those used in this recipe require just 1 hour's soaking, so that they will soften and swell. This helps to cut down the cooking time and also ensures that they will cook through and be easily digested.

3 tbsp channa dal
3 tbsp masoor dal
3 tbsp mung dal
3 tbsp toor dal
3 tbsp urad dal
8 cups water
2 tsp salt
1 tsp turmeric
2 tsp coriander powder
¹/₂ tsp chilli powder
A pinch of asafoetida

Pick over the pulses to remove any grit, then rinse well. Cover the pulses, except the *masoor dal*, with water and soak the *channa dal* for 3 hours and all the others for 1 hour.

Drain and discard the liquid in which the lentils have been soaking. Put the lentils and the 8 cups of water into a heavy-bottomed saucepan with the salt, turmeric, coriander powder, chilli powder and asafoetida; stir to mix. Bring to the boil, reduce the heat and simmer gently for 1 hour, stirring the mixture from time to time to prevent sticking. Drain off most of the liquid. Use the back of a wooden spoon to mash the lentils roughly against the sides of the pan. Set aside.

2 tbsp ghee
1¹/₂ tsp black cumin seeds
2 finely sliced medium onions
1 tsp finely chopped garlic
2 tsp grated fresh ginger
1 tsp cumin powder
1 tsp fennel powder
2 firm, ripe tomatoes, cut into wedges
2 tbsp lightly whisked yoghurt

Heat the *ghee* in another saucepan and fry the black cumin seeds for a few seconds. Add the onion, garlic and ginger and fry gently for about 3 minutes. Add the cumin and fennel powder and fry for 1 minute. Stir in the tomato, yoghurt, chopped coriander leaves and *garam masala* and simmer for 4 minutes.

*2 tbsp roughly chopped fresh
coriander leaves
1 tsp garam masala
Extra whole coriander leaves
for the garnish*

Gently fold in the lentil mixture and continue to simmer until the mixture is heated through. Serve immediately, garnished with a sprinkling of coriander leaves.

Khatti Toor Dal Tarka

SWEET AND SOUR LENTILS

This piquant dish comes from Lucknow. Translated it means 'tempered sour lentils'; the tempering process is when the seasonings are spluttered in hot *ghee* and poured over just before serving. The sweet and sour flavour comes from the tamarind. Tamarind pulp and concentrate can be purchased from Indian shops and some other stores.

The *dal* can be prepared ahead and re-heated. Do, however, check the purée consistency of the *dal*, as it is inclined to thicken further with keeping. When re-heating, stir in as many tablespoons of hot water as are necessary to bring the mixture to the desired texture. The tempering of seasoned *ghee* must be prepared and added just before serving. Sweet and sour lentils can be served as a side dish to main courses or on their own with one of the breads.

*1¹/2 cups toor dal
Cold water to cover*

Pick over the lentils to remove any grit. Rinse well and soak the lentils for 3-4 hours. Drain and discard the liquid.

*A pinch of asafoetida
¹/2 tsp turmeric powder
1 tsp salt
4-6 cups hot water*

Put the drained lentils into a heavy-bottomed saucepan with the asafoetida, turmeric and salt. Pour over 4 cups of water and mix well together. Simmer for about 40 minutes, stirring frequently to keep the mixture from sticking. Add more water if required.

*2 tbsp tamarind pulp
4 tbsp boiling water*

Prepare the tamarind juice while the lentils are cooking. Steep the tamarind pulp in the hot water for 15 minutes, then push it through a sieve to extract 2 tablespoons of tamarind juice. Set aside.

When the lentils are cooked and can be roughly

mashed against the sides of the saucepan with the back of a wooden spoon, add the tamarind juice and simmer for about 5 minutes while mashing the lentils. Turn the mixture into a serving bowl and prepare the tempering when ready to serve.

2 tbsp ghee
1 tsp black cumin seeds
3 roughly crushed dried red chillies

Heat the *ghee* to the point of spluttering in a small frying pan, add the cumin seeds and the dried chilli pieces and stir-fry for about 10 seconds. Pour immediately over the top of the *dal* in the serving dish.

Rajma Dal

RED KIDNEY BEANS IN A MASALA SAUCE

A famous Delhi poet wrote, 'The world is the body and Delhi is its soul.' Old-timers from Delhi claim this dish of red kidney beans as their own, and add that it is a great source of energy. 'It feeds the soul,' they claim. Serve as part of a vegetarian meal or to accompany one of the meat dishes.

The red kidney beans need to be soaked for about 6 hours or overnight in plenty of water. They will soften and swell during this process.

8 cups cold water
1^1/2 cups red kidney beans

Rinse the beans and soak them for 6 hours or overnight if convenient. Drain them of the water in which they have been soaking.

8^1/2 cups cold water
1^1/2 tsp turmeric
^{1}/2 tsp chilli powder
1 tsp salt
A pinch of asafoetida

Put the drained beans into a heavy-bottomed saucepan and add 8^1/2 cups of water, turmeric, chilli powder, salt and a pinch of asafoetida. Bring to the boil, reduce the heat and cover the saucepan. Allow the mixture to simmer gently for about 2 hours or until the beans are cooked and tender but still whole. Drain into a colander over a deep bowl and reserve one cup of the liquid.

2 roughly chopped onions
1 tbsp roughly chopped fresh ginger

Blend the onions, ginger, garlic and chilli to a paste in a food-processor. Set aside.

1 tsp roughly chopped garlic
1 roughly chopped fresh
green chilli

1 tbsp ghee
1 tbsp vegetable oil
1 tsp cumin seeds
1/4 tsp black mustard seeds

While the beans are cooking, heat the *ghee* and oil in another saucepan and fry the cumin and mustard seeds for a few seconds until they begin to splutter. Add the onion paste. Reduce the heat and continue frying and stirring until the onion mixture begins to change colour.

2 tsp coriander powder
1 tsp cumin powder
1 tsp garam masala
4 puréed ripe tomatoes
2 tbsp yoghurt
1/2 tsp salt
2 tbsp finely chopped fresh
coriander leaves

Add the coriander, cumin and *garam masala*, mix well and fry for 4 minutes, stirring to prevent sticking. Add the tomatoes and simmer for about 2 minutes. Gently stir in the yoghurt and salt and cook for 5 minutes or until most of the liquid is evaporated. Now add the beans, the chopped coriander leaves and the cup of the reserved liquid to the mixture. Stir and bring to the boil. Reduce the heat and simmer gently with the cover on for 5 minutes.

Lobia

BLACK-EYED BEANS IN A YOGHURT SAUCE

This highly nutritious recipe finds great favour with vegetarians, but it will also complement most meat or chicken dishes. The beans are first simmered with flavourings of garlic and cardamom and, when cooked, they are added to a stir-fry mixture of blended onion, ginger, garlic and chilli and flavoured with spices made moist by yoghurt. Serve with ballooned *chapatis* (pp.195-6) or *paratha* (pp.193-4) and one of the egg dishes.

Allow at least 4-6 hours to soak the beans. *Cinnamomum cassia* leaves (often incorrectly referred to as Indian bay leaf) are not always easily available. Omit altogether if you cannot find them.

1 1/2 cups lobia (black-eyed
beans)

Cover the beans well with water and soak for 4-6 hours or overnight if convenient.

2 cassia leaves
1 tsp finely chopped garlic
1 tsp turmeric powder
2 large brown cardamom
pods, bruised
1 tsp salt
A pinch of asafoetida
Cold water sufficient to
cover the beans

Drain off the liquid in which the beans have been soaking and put them into a heavy-bottomed saucepan with the *cassia* leaves, garlic, turmeric, cardamom pods, salt and asafoetida. Cover well with cold water and bring to the boil. Put a lid on the saucepan and simmer for about 40 minutes or until the beans are tender. Do not allow them to dry out. When the beans are tender, drain into a sieve or colander over a bowl and reserve 1 cup of the liquid. Discard the cardamom pods and *cassia* leaves (if used) and set the beans aside.

2 roughly chopped onions
3 tsp roughly chopped
fresh ginger
2 tsp roughly chopped garlic
2 dried red chillies, seeds
discarded

Blend the onions, ginger, garlic and chillies to a paste in a food-processor and set aside.

1 tbsp ghee
1 tbsp oil
1 tsp cumin seeds
1/2 tsp dark mustard seeds

Heat the *ghee* and oil in a heavy-bottomed saucepan and add the cumin and mustard seeds and fry for a few seconds until they begin to splutter. Add the blended onion paste and continue frying until the onion starts to change colour.

1/2 tsp black pepper
6 tbsp lightly whisked
yoghurt
1 tsp garam masala
2 tbsp roughly chopped fresh
coriander leaves

Add the freshly ground black pepper, yoghurt and the reserved cup of liquid; stir and simmer for 3 minutes. Add the beans and simmer for 5 minutes. Just before completion, stir in the *garam masala* and chopped coriander leaves.

Palak Tamatar Dal

SPINACH WITH MUNG BEANS

This is a wholesome combination of *mung* beans with spinach and tomato and can be a complete meal in itself. It can be served with rice dishes or any of the breads or, for non-vegetarians, with a choice of meat or chicken from the Moghul kitchen. The chopped tops of spring onions, while providing a garnish will also add another dimension of taste to the dish.

500 g/1 lb fresh spinach leaves *2 tbsp water*	Roughly chop and rinse the spinach well to free it of grit, put it into a saucepan, sprinkle with water and cook lightly to wilt. Set aside.
1 cup small whole green mung beans (moong sabat)	Pick the *mung* beans over for stones or grit and rinse in several changes of water. Cover with water and leave to soften for 30 minutes.
4 cups hot water *1/2 tsp turmeric powder* *1 tsp salt* *Pinch of asafoetida* *1/2 cup lightly whisked yoghurt*	Drain the *mung* beans and put them into a heavy-bottomed saucepan with the hot water, turmeric, salt and asafoetida. Simmer slowly until the beans become soft but retain their round shape; this could take up to 1 hour. Add the chopped spinach leaves, mix well and continue cooking for about 5 minutes, stirring occasionally to make sure the mixture is not sticking. Add the whisked yoghurt, stir and simmer for about 4 minutes. Remove from the heat but leave in the saucepan.
1 tbsp ghee *2 tbsp vegetable oil* *1 tbsp cumin seeds* *1 finely chopped large onion* *2 tsp grated fresh ginger* *1/4 tsp black ground pepper* *2 fresh green chillies, seeds discarded, sliced into fine strips* *2 ripe, medium tomatoes, chopped* *1 tsp garam masala*	Heat the *ghee* and oil in another saucepan, add the cumin seeds and fry for a few seconds to release their aroma. Add the onion and ginger and continue stir-frying until the onion changes to a light gold colour. Add the black pepper, chilli slices and chopped tomato. Reduce the heat and simmer until the oil starts to separate, which should take about 5 minutes. Add the *garam masala*.
Spring onions	Remove to a serving dish and garnish with circles of finely chopped green spring onion tops.

Dal Nawabi

❧

BLACK GRAM BEANS WITH NUTS AND RAISINS

Cooks in courtly kitchens knew the importance of including *dal* dishes in daily banquets, especially on days preceding and following fasts. The variety of lentils and beans available were combined in many guises with subtle additions of spices making each dish a speciality. Almonds and pistachio nuts give a crunchy texture and the raisins a touch of sweetness in this dish from Avadh (the old Muslim kingdom of Oudh). Serve with lamb with spinach and tomato (p.77) and a rice dish.

1½ cups urad dal

Pick over the lentils for grit or stones, wash well in several rinses of water, cover with water and soak for 30 minutes. Drain and discard the liquid.

½ tsp turmeric powder
a pinch of asafoetida
3 cups hot water

Put the soaked and drained lentils, the turmeric, asafoetida and the hot water into a heavy-bottomed saucepan. Bring to the boil, reduce the heat and simmer gently until the *dal* is soft and most of the liquid absorbed. Stir occasionally to prevent sticking, adding a little more water if necessary. Remove from the heat and set aside.

2 tbsp ghee
2 tsp grated fresh ginger
1 tsp coriander powder
½ tsp cumin powder
1 tsp garam masala
½ tsp chilli powder
1 tsp salt
2 ripe, medium tomatoes,
skinned and puréed
½ tbsp finely chopped mint
leaves
1 tbsp finely chopped fresh
coriander leaves
1 cup lightly whisked
yoghurt

In another saucepan heat the *ghee* and stir-fry the ginger for about 1 minute. Add the coriander, cumin, *garam masala*, chilli powder and salt and stir-fry for 2 minutes. Add the puréed tomatoes, mint and coriander leaves and simmer gently for about 3 minutes. Stir the yoghurt and saffron threads in milk into the mixture and bring to the boil. Mix in the *dal* and simmer for about 3 minutes – the consistency should be fairly thick. Remove from the heat.

*¹/2 tsp saffron threads,
steeped for 15 minutes in
1 tbsp hot milk*

*1 tbsp ghee
1 tbsp slivered blanched
almonds
1 tbsp blanched and
chopped pistachio nuts
1 tbsp raisins*

Fry the nuts and raisins in the *ghee* until the nuts begin to change colour and the raisins begin to puff up. Fold into the *dal* mixture and serve.

RICE

The character of Islamic Turko-Persian *pilaus* and *biryanis* underwent a dramatic change in the Moghul kitchen with the addition of ginger, pepper, saffron and other ingredients. Cooks created dishes like the nine-ingredient rice *navrattan* (pp.180-1) and *shah jahani biryani*, rose-scented *biryani* with chicken (pp.184-6). The rice dishes became more elaborate as independent kingdoms were established and the nobility demanded yet more unusual and delectable presentations. They were obeyed and today we have *moti pilau jahanara* with meatballs coated in silver on a bed of rice (pp.182-4).

Although many of the recipes that follow appear to be lengthy, do try them. You will soon become quite an expert by following the stages of preparation and will get great satisfaction when you present the aromatic dishes, many of which are almost a meal in themselves, at table.

A visit to a rice-seller's stall at one of the markets in big cities such as Delhi, Bombay (now Mumbai), Calcutta or Bangalore is quite an education. Dozens of varieties of rice are stacked in mounds in individual baskets or packed in open-topped bags. Before buying, shoppers will feel, smell and discuss the harvesting time and the age of their favourite grain – only then will they make a decision to purchase.

There are several methods of cooking rice. The result should yield fluffy, separate grains. The rice should be soft but firm; a good test is to squeeze a few grains between your fingers. Before cooking, rice should be picked over for stones and grit and washed in several changes of water. Plain boiled rice is cooked in large amounts of boiling water. After the rice is added the water is kept on a rolling boil for 10-12 minutes; it is then strained and often finished off in a pre-heated oven for 10 minutes.

The absorption method, for which a heavy-bottomed saucepan with a close-fitting lid is essential, is very popular. Rice is cooked on a low heat in a minimum amount of liquid. After the cooking time a tea-towel is placed over the saucepan and the cover replaced – this absorbs the moisture created by the remaining steam. With this method the bottom of the saucepan often becomes encrusted with a layer of rice. Stand the saucepan on a wet tea-towel or in a shallow dish with water to release the crust of rice. Some recipes call for rice to be soaked and then allowed to dry before being cooked. This relaxes the rice. The grains absorb moisture and this results in the grains remaining separate. There is a general rule of thumb for quantities when cooking rice by the absorption method: use 1 cup of rice and 2 cups of liquid, adding 1½ cups of liquid for each additional cup of rice.

Long-grain rice of the basmati type is used in these recipes. It is a fragrant rice with a nutty flavour. One cup of uncooked long-grain rice makes approximately three cups of cooked rice.

Degi Biryani

‰

BIRYANI WITH LAMB CHOPS AND POTATOES

Lamb chops and cubes of lamb take on flavours of garlic, ginger, yoghurt and chilli before being layered on rice to become fragrant with cardamom, cinnamon and cloves.

This *biryani* is from the lavish courts of the *nawabs* of Lucknow and, although it is of some complexity, it almost pales into insignificance in comparison with many of the Moghul and *nawabi pilaus* and *biryanis* that follow. Use it as an initiation into cooking the more elaborate rice dishes.

The chops need to be marinated for about 6 hours. If convenient, this stage can be carried out the day before and the chops left to marinate overnight in the refrigerator. With an ingredient such as *ghee*, which is required at 4 separate points in this recipe, amounts are specified in the list of ingredients and again in the instructions to avoid confusion.

Traditionally, the saucepan is covered and sealed with dough so that the steam is contained and the aromas and flavours are trapped. Use a seal of foil crimped around the rim of the saucepan and the cover.

The oven will need to be pre-heated to 160°C/325°F/gas mark 3 for about 20 minutes.

1 tsp roughly chopped garlic
*3 tsp roughly chopped fresh
ginger*
1 fresh red chilli
1 cup yoghurt
1½ tsp salt
6-8 small lamb chops
250 g/8 oz cubed lean lamb

Blend the garlic, ginger, chilli, yoghurt and salt to a smooth paste in a food-processor and rub over the chops and cubes of meat. Allow to marinate for 4-6 hours. If convenient, turn the chops in the marinade from time to time.

1½ cups basmati rice
1½ tsp salt
4 cups boiling water

Rinse the rice until the water runs clear, then cover with water and leave to soak for 10 minutes. Drain. Boil the water in a heavy-bottomed saucepan, stir in the rice and salt and parboil for 3 minutes. Drain. Divide into 2 portions and set aside.

As the stages of cooking proceed, portions of the cooked ingredients will be divided into two. The reason for this will become evident once the layering of the ingredients with the rice begins.

2 tbsp oil
2 tbsp ghee
*1 large potato, peeled and
cut into small cubes*
½ tsp turmeric

Dry the saucepan and heat the oil and the *ghee*, add the turmeric and lightly fry the potato cubes. Remove with a slotted spoon and drain on absorbent paper; set aside in 2 portions.

1 finely sliced large onion

Re-heat the remaining *ghee* and fry the onion until it becomes light brown. Divide into 2 portions and set aside.

1 tbsp ghee
12 peppercorns
*2 fresh red chillies, slit in
halves, seeds discarded*
*4 small, light-coloured
cardamoms, bruised*
4 cloves
*5 cm/2 inch cinnamon stick,
broken in two*
2 cassia leaves

Heat the tablespoon of *ghee* and stir-fry the peppercorns, chillies, cardamom, cloves, cinnamon and *cassia* leaves for 1 minute. Remove with a slotted spoon, divide into 2 portions and set aside.

*1 cup lightly whisked
yoghurt*
½ tbsp melted ghee

Combine the yoghurt and the melted *ghee* and divide into 2 portions. Set aside.

2 tbsp ghee
2 finely sliced onions

Heat the 2 tablespoons of *ghee* in a heavy-bottomed saucepan or casserole dish suitable for both hot-plate and oven. Remove from the heat and line the base by putting the finely sliced raw onion into the melted *ghee*. From all the divided portions above, prepare two layers of ingredients to go into the casserole in the following manner.

Lay half of the par-boiled rice on top of the raw onion; then sprinkle on top of the rice half the par-fried cubed potato, half the fried onion, three of the chops and half of the cubes of lamb, with half the marinade, and roughly half of the lightly fried peppercorns, chilli, cardamom, cloves, cinnamon and *cassia* leaves.

Dribble half the combined yoghurt and melted *ghee* over this; repeat this process of layering with the other half portions of ingredients. Ensure that the lid is tightly fitted by crimping foil round the rim so that all the steam, aroma and flavours are contained. Place in the oven which has been pre-heated to 200°C/350°F/gas mark 4, lower the temperature to 160°C/325°F/gas mark 3 and cook for 50 minutes. Turn out onto a large serving dish. Discard the cinnamon, cardamom pods and *cassia* leaves and bring the lamb chops to the top.

Varak (silver leaf)

To garnish, flutter a couple of sheets of *varak* over the surface.

Zaffrani Pilau

SAFFRON-FLAVOURED PILAU

Raisin-studded rice, with flavours of onion, ginger, garlic and spices and the perfume of saffron threads, is aromatic and makes an attractive dish surrounded by golden-centred eggs. Serve with apricot-flavoured lamb (pp.62-3) and a carrot *raita* (p.206).

A tea-towel placed under the lid of the saucepan at the final stages of cooking absorbs the final steam and prevents the moisture from dripping back into the rice.

Allow 1 hour for soaking and draining the rice.

1½ cups basmati or long-grain rice

Rinse the rice until the water runs clear; cover with cold water and soak for 30 minutes; drain and allow to dry for a further 30 minutes. Set aside.

3 tbsp ghee
4 small light-coloured cardamom pods, bruised
5 cm/2 inch cinnamon stick
½ tsp cumin seeds
6 cloves
2 finely chopped medium onions
2 tsp grated fresh ginger
1 tsp finely chopped garlic

Heat the *ghee* in a heavy-bottomed saucepan. Add the cardamom, cinnamon, cumin and cloves and stir-fry for a few seconds to release their aromas. Add the onions, ginger and garlic and stir-fry for about 2 minutes or until the onion starts to change colour.

2 tbsp seedless raisins
2 cups milk
½ cup water
1½ tsp salt
½ tsp saffron threads, steeped for 15 minutes in 1 tbsp warm milk

Add the drained rice and continue stirring to coat the grains. Add the raisins, milk, water, salt and saffron threads in milk; stir well while bringing to the boil.

Cover the saucepan with a well-fitting lid. Reduce the heat to low and cook for 15 minutes. Remove the cover and gently fork right through, lifting and loosening the rice. The liquid should be absorbed. Place a tea-towel over the saucepan, replace the lid and cook on a low heat for another 3 minutes. Leave to rest for at least 10 minutes, then fork through gently once again. Discard the cinnamon stick.

4 hard-boiled eggs

Fork the rice gently to a mound in the centre of a shallow platter surrounded with the halved or quartered eggs.

Khichdi Alamgiri

🐚

KEDGEREE WITH MINCE, MUNG DAL AND RICE

All the Moghul emperors loved the combination of pulses with rice, *khichri* or *khichdi*. If the emperor favoured any dish specialist cooks would out-do each other to improve the dish until it attained royal approval. This dish of Aurangzeb's time combines minced lamb with rice and *mung dal* and was given the royal title of *Alamgiri*, 'Seizer of the Universe'. *Khichri* is also known as *khichdi*, the Hindi word for the mixture of *dals* and rice. *Khichri* is considered a meal in itself, served with accompanying *raita*. You will need a dish suitable for the oven with a close-fitting cover.

Allow 1 hour for soaking and draining the rice.

For the mince:
2 roughly chopped medium onions
2 tsp roughly chopped fresh ginger
1 tsp roughly chopped garlic
1 tsp chilli powder
2 tbsp lime or lemon juice

Blend the onions, ginger, garlic, chilli powder and lime or lemon juice to a smooth paste in a food-processor. Set aside.

1 tbsp dry-roasted coriander seeds
1 tsp black cumin seeds
1/4 tsp cardamom seeds

Coarse-grind the coriander, cumin and cardamom seeds in a spice-mill or coffee-grinder. Set aside.

2 tbsp ghee

Heat the *ghee* in a heavy-bottomed saucepan. Stir-fry the blended paste for 3 minutes. Add the ground spices and stir-fry for another 4 minutes.

250 g/8 oz finely minced lean lamb
1/4 tsp nutmeg powder
1 tsp garam masala
1 tsp salt
2 tbsp roughly chopped fresh mint leaves
3 tbsp lightly whisked yoghurt

Add the minced meat, stir and mash the meat with back of a spoon as it starts to cook to prevent lumps from forming. Add the nutmeg powder, *garam masala*, salt, mint leaves and yoghurt. Reduce the heat, cover and simmer until the mince is cooked and the liquid absorbed. Divide into 2 portions and set aside.

Pre-heat the oven to 180°C/350°F/gas mark 4 for about 15 minutes.

For the rice:
1½ cups basmati rice

Rinse the rice until the water runs clear; then cover it with water and soak it for 30 minutes. Drain and set aside for a further 30 minutes.

¾ cup mung dal
(split green gram)

Rinse the *mung dal* well, drain and set aside.

3 tbsp ghee
4 cloves
2 large dark cardamom
pods, bruised
2 finely chopped onions
1 tsp grated fresh ginger
½ tsp finely chopped garlic
1 finely chopped fresh green
chilli, seeds discarded

Heat the 3 tablespoons of *ghee* in a heavy-bottomed saucepan. Add the cloves and cardamom pods and fry for a few seconds to release their aromas. Add the onion, ginger, garlic and chilli and stir-fry until the onion becomes a pale golden colour.

1½ tsp salt
3½ cups water
3 drops kewra (screwpine)
essence

Add the drained rice and *mung dal* and stir-fry until well coated. Stir in the salt, water and *kewra* essence. Bring to the boil, cover with a well-fitting lid, reduce the heat and simmer for 10 minutes. Most of the liquid should be absorbed. Gently lift and fork through the *dal* and rice. Divide the mixture into 2 portions.

Spoon into and spread as far as possible 1 portion of the minced meat mixture in a utensil with a cover, suitable for the oven. Layer 1 portion of the rice mixture over the mince, then spread the remaining meat mixture over that layer of rice and finally put the remaining rice over the top.

3½ tbsp ghee
2 finely sliced onions
½ cup hot milk

Heat the 3½ tablespoons of *ghee* and fry the onion until it is quite brown. Scatter the fried onions and remaining *ghee* over the rice and sprinkle with the hot milk. Cover with a tight-fitting lid and crimp foil round the rim to seal and prevent steam from escaping. Bake in the pre-heated oven for 15-20 minutes. Turn the oven off and leave for a further 10 minutes, after which the moisture should be fully absorbed.

Fork through gently before serving and discard the cardamom pods.

Jeera Pilau

CUMIN-FLAVOURED PILAU

The flavouring of cumin comes from both seeds and powder and it also gives the rice a light brown tinge in this aromatic *pilau* dish which is made yet more aromatic with cloves and cinnamon. Easy to prepare, it is a *pilau* that will complement most other dishes. Serve it with quails in a spicy sauce (pp.110-1) and a cucumber *raita* (p.202).

A tea-towel placed between the saucepan and the lid at the final stages will absorb steam and prevent drops of moisture from dripping back into the rice grains.

Allow 1 hour for soaking and draining the rice.

1¹/₂ cups basmati or long-grain rice

Rinse the rice until the water runs clear; cover it with water and soak for 30 minutes; drain and set aside for a further 30 minutes.

3 tbsp ghee
1 tsp cumin seeds
6 cloves
5 cm/2 inch cinnamon stick
2 finely chopped medium onions
2 tsp grated fresh ginger
1 tsp finely chopped garlic

Heat the *ghee* in a heavy-bottomed saucepan. Add the cumin seeds, cloves and cinnamon stick and fry for a few seconds to release their aromas. Add the onion, ginger and garlic and stir-fry until the onions start to turn to a golden colour.

2 tsp cumin powder
2 tsp salt
2 tbsp raisins
2³/₄ cups water

Stir in the cumin powder, salt, raisins and drained rice and stir-fry for 2 minutes. If the mixture is inclined to stick, add a couple of tablespoons of water. Stir well to coat the rice. Add the water and mix well. Bring to the boil. Cover with a close-fitting lid, reduce the heat and cook for 15 minutes. Remove the cover – and watch out for rising hot steam. Gently fork right through, lifting and loosening the rice.

2 tbsp lightly cooked peas

Place a tea-towel over the saucepan and replace the lid. Cook on a low heat for 3 minutes. Remove from the heat and leave undisturbed for 10 minutes. Fork through gently once again. Discard the cinnamon stick and serve with a scattering of lightly cooked peas.

Khichri Nurjahan

৯

KEDGEREE WITH AROMATIC RICE AND MUNG DAL

Akbar started the Moghul's craze for *khichri*, and variations on the theme were a regular feature of Moghul meals. It is said that Jahangir's wife Nurjahan was the power behind the throne and if, being named after her, this was her favourite *khichri*, cooks at the palace would have taken great care to please the empress in preparing a dish which she particularly enjoyed.

This variation of rice and *dal* is a great favourite with vegetarians. Split *mung* beans are first dry-roasted to give them a nutty flavour before being par-boiled with rice and spices on top of the stove and then baked in the oven. *Khichri* dishes are quite filling and are traditionally served with a *raita* and chutney. A combination of chopped cucumber and tomato with yoghurt with a sprinkling of chilli powder or black pepper will complement this *khichri* perfectly.

You will need a heavy-bottomed saucepan or a casserole suitable for both hot-plate and oven.

Pre-heat the oven to 160°C/325°F/gas mark 3 for about 15 minutes.

1¹/2 cups basmati or long-grain rice	Rinse the rice until the water runs clear and set aside.
1¹/2 cups mung dal (split mung beans)	Rinse the *mung dal*, then spread it on a kitchen towel to dry. Heat a heavy-bottomed pan and dry-roast the beans until they turn light brown and give off a nutty aroma. Keep the beans moving in the pan with a wooden spoon to prevent them from burning. Set aside.
3 tbsp vegetable oil *8 cloves* *3 light-coloured cardamom pods, bruised* *3 large brown cardamom pods, bruised* *5.5 cms/2¹/2 inch cinnamon stick* *2 finely chopped onions* *1 tbsp grated fresh ginger*	Heat the vegetable oil in a heavy-bottomed saucepan. Add the cloves, cardamom pods and cinnamon and stir-fry for a few seconds to release their aromas. Add the onion, ginger and garlic and continue stir-frying. When the onion starts to change colour, add the turmeric, chilli, coriander, cumin, salt and sugar and fry for about 1 minute before adding and stirring in the rice and roasted *mung dal*.

1 tsp finely chopped garlic
1/2 tsp turmeric powder
1/2 tsp chilli powder
2 tsp coriander powder
2 tsp cumin powder
3 tsp salt
1 tsp sugar

1 cup yoghurt
3 cups hot water
1/2 tsp saffron threads,
steeped for 15 minutes in
1 tbsp hot milk

Add the yoghurt, water and saffron threads in milk and mix well until it starts to boil. Then cover it with a tight-fitting lid, reduce the heat and simmer for 15 minutes.

1 tbsp ghee
1 tbsp slivered blanched
almonds

While the mixture is simmering, heat the *ghee* in a small frying pan and toss in the slivered almonds and stir-fry until they begin to change colour. Lift the cover off the cooking rice and dribble the *ghee* and scatter the almonds over the *khichri* and fork through gently. Replace the cover and put the pan in the pre-heated oven for 15 minutes.

After 15 minutes, turn the oven off, remove the cover and allow the *khichri* to stand in the hot oven for about 5 minutes. Fork through gently. Discard the cinnamon stick and cardamom pods.

Mutanjan
❧

SWEET AND SOUR LAMB WITH RICE

This sour-sweet, hot and aromatic dish is one that was popular with Akbar and his courtiers. Cubes of lamb are rubbed with lemon juice, garlic and ginger and first simmered with spices and then cooked in a syrup of sugar, honey and lemon juice before being combined with rice flavoured with rose essence and saffron.

Garnish, if you wish, with a scattering of roasted slivered almonds and lightly cooked peas and serve with tamarind-flavoured tomato purée (pp.148-9) or a spinach dish.

Allow 1 hour for soaking and draining the rice; the meat can be marinating at the same time.

1¹/₂ cups basmati or long-grain rice

Rinse the rice until the water runs clear. Cover with cold water and soak for 30 minutes, then drain and set aside for 30 minutes.

500 g/1 lb lean lamb cut into 2.5 cm/1 inch cubes
1 tbsp lime or lemon juice
¹/₂ tsp salt
3 tsp grated fresh ginger
¹/₂ tsp finely chopped garlic

Mix the lime or lemon juice, salt, ginger and garlic together and rub into the meat cubes. Set aside for 1 hour.

1 roughly chopped onion
3 tsp lightly crushed coriander seeds
5 cm/2 inch cinnamon stick
2 large brown cardamoms, bruised
1¹/₂ cups water
¹/₂ tsp salt

When the cubes of meat have marinated, put them into a heavy-bottomed saucepan with the onion, coriander seeds, cinnamon, cardamom, water and salt. Bring to the boil, reduce the heat, cover and simmer until the meat is tender, stirring occasionally to prevent sticking. Remove the meat with a slotted spoon and set aside.

1¹/₂ tbsp sugar
1 tsp honey
4 tbsp lime or lemon juice

Strain the remaining sauce into a bowl and discard the solids, then return the sauce to the saucepan. Add the sugar, honey and lemon juice to the sauce, bring to the boil, reduce the heat and simmer until the sugar is dissolved. Stir in the cooked meat cubes and continue to simmer for about 2 minutes. Remove from the heat and set aside.

6 cups boiling water
¹/₂ tsp salt
1 tbsp lime or lemon juice
2 tbsp ghee
4 cloves
6 peppercorns
3 small, light-coloured cardamoms, bruised
1 tsp fennel seeds

Meanwhile, put the boiling water in another heavy-bottomed saucepan and keep it on a rolling boil, add the salt and lime or lemon juice, stir in the drained rice and par-boil for 5 minutes. Drain well in a colander. Rinse and dry the saucepan and return to the stove. Heat the *ghee*, add the cloves, peppercorns, cardamoms and fennel seeds and stir-fry for a few seconds to release their aromas.

1½ tbsp blanched and slivered almonds
½ tsp saffron threads, steeped for 15 minutes in 1 tbsp hot milk
3 drops rose essence

Add the meat mixture and stir in the par-boiled rice, slivered almonds, saffron threads in milk and rose essence. Reduce the heat to low, cover the saucepan with a tight-fitting lid and simmer for 12 minutes. Remove the cover and fork through, lifting the rice grains gently. The liquid should be absorbed. Place a tea-towel over the saucepan and replace the lid; leave undisturbed for 10 minutes.

1 tbsp roasted almonds
1 tbsp lightly cooked peas

Discard the cardamom pods. Transfer to a serving dish and garnish with the roasted almonds and cooked peas.

Navrattan

🍃

NINE JEWELS: PILAU WITH VEGETABLES AND NUTS

The Emperor's nine jewels were Akbar's most brilliant courtiers. Having built the palatial city of Fatephur Sikri, he gathered around him there the most talented men and women of his empire. The nine jewels were all men, but they included Hindus as well as Muslims: the Raja Bhagwandas of Amber; the musician Tansen; the general Raja Man Singh; Todarmal, who became Akbar's chief minister and a great financial reformer; Birbal and Mullah Dopiaza, wise philosophers and witty raconteurs; Abdul Rahim Khan-e-Khanan, translator of manuscripts, and, perhaps the most attractive of all to us, the brothers Abdul Fazl and Faizi. Abdul Fazl was a statesman who wrote a vivid biography of the emperor, while Faizi was a poet who on his deathbed bequeathed to Akbar his library of 4,600 books, all bound and comprehensively catalogued. This dish was devised to honour these favoured courtiers.

2 cups basmati or long-grain rice

Rinse the rice until the water runs clear, cover it with water and soak for 30 minutes; then drain and set aside.

3 tbsp ghee
5 cm/2 inch cinnamon stick
4 cloves

Heat the *ghee* in a heavy-bottomed saucepan and add the cinnamon, cloves, cardamom, cumin seeds and peppercorns. Fry these a few seconds to release their

4 small, light-coloured
cardamom pods, bruised
$1/2$ tsp black cumin seeds
8 black peppercorns
2 finely chopped onions
2 tsp grated fresh ginger
1 tsp finely chopped garlic
1 finely chopped fresh green
chilli, seeds discarded

aromas. Stir in the onion, ginger, garlic and chilli and fry them until the onions start to change colour.

8 small cauliflower florets
1 diced carrot
$1/4$ cup shelled peas
$1/2$ cup French beans,
chopped into short lengths
1 small diced potato or
turnip
1 tbsp seedless raisins

Add the vegetable pieces and raisins. Stir-fry for 2 minutes. Add the drained rice and stir for 2 more minutes.

$1^1/2$ tsp salt
$2^1/2$ cups water
1 cup yoghurt
$1/4$ tsp saffron threads,
steeped for 15 minutes in
1 tbsp hot milk

Lightly whisk together the salt, water and yoghurt and add this to the rice mixture with the saffron threads and milk. Bring the mixture back to the boil and stir with a wooden spoon so that everything is well mixed. Reduce the heat, cover with a tight-fitting lid and cook on a low heat for 20 minutes. Then remove from the heat, take off the lid and gently fork through the rice. Place a tea-towel over the saucepan, replace the lid and leave undisturbed for 10 minutes.

$1/2$ cup vegetable oil
$1/2$ tbsp raw cashew nuts
$1/2$ tbsp blanched almonds
$1/2$ tbsp unsalted pistachio
nuts
8 cherry tomatoes
2 tbsp lightly cooked peas
2 hard-boiled eggs

To make the garnish, first heat the oil in a small frying pan, add the nuts and fry, stirring constantly until the nuts are cooked. This will take 2-3 minutes. Drain them in a colander and discard the oil.

To serve, turn the rice mixture onto a serving platter. Discard the cinnamon stick. Dot the surface with cherry tomatoes, peas and slices of hard-boiled egg. Sprinkle with nuts immediately before serving the *pilau* hot to accompany meat or vegetarian dishes.

Moti Pilau Jahanara

❧

AROMATIC PILAU WITH MEATBALLS

Aurangzeb wrested the throne from Shah Jahan and imprisoned him in the exquisite Jasmine Tower at Agra. Princess Jahanara shared her father Jahan's captivity as his nurse and companion until the day he died. Aurangzeb had the highest respect for Jahanara and gave her the title *Salubat-uz-Zaman*, 'Mistress of the Age' and no doubt Princess Jahanara enjoyed this *pilau* with meatballs. This dish will be more flavoursome if cooked with *yakhni*, aromatic meat stock (p.33), but hot water can be used in place of the stock. It can be made ahead of time and gently reheated.

Moti means pearl. I first saw this pretty dish as part of a wedding banquet at Agra. The tiny meatballs had all been covered in *varak* (silver leaf) and they twinkled out like silvery pearls in the bed of fragrant rice which was surrounded by bright red rose petals.

There is no need to wrap all the meatballs in silver. I usually reserve about 20 after the cooking stage and allow them to cool. When the rice is ready to be served, lay one sheet of silver with its backing sheet on a flat work surface and gently roll the meat balls across. Repeat with more sheets of silver until the meatballs are coated or speckled with silver. You may prefer to flutter a couple of sheets of silver tissue onto the rice.

For the meatballs:

1 roughly chopped medium onion
1 tsp roughly chopped fresh ginger
1/2 tsp roughly chopped garlic
1 fresh green chilli, seeds discarded
1 tbsp lime or lemon juice
1 tbsp roughly chopped fresh coriander leaves
1 tbsp roughly chopped fresh mint leaves

Blend the onion, ginger, garlic, chilli, lime or lemon juice, coriander leaves and the mint leaves to a smooth paste in a food-processor.

500 g/1 lb finely minced lean lamb
2 tsp garam masala

Put the mince and the blended paste into a bowl and mix well to combine all the ingredients. Add the *garam masala*, salt, pepper, chick-pea flour, whisked egg and

1/2 tsp salt
1/2 tsp ground black pepper
2 tbsp chick-pea flour
1 lightly whisked egg
1 tsp ghee

1 teaspoon of *ghee* and knead in. Form tiny balls slightly larger than peas.

2 tbsp ghee
5 cm/2 inch cinnamon stick
3 cloves
4 tbsp yoghurt
3 tbsp water

Heat the 2 tablespoons of *ghee* in a heavy-bottomed saucepan, add the cinnamon and cloves and fry for a few seconds to release their aromas. Lightly whisk together the yoghurt and water, add to the frying spices and bring them to the boil. Reduce the heat, then gently add the meatballs and simmer for about 4 minutes or until the meat juices have combined into the sauce and the meatballs are cooked. Roll the meatballs over by gently shaking the saucepan from side to side while they are cooking.

Carefully remove the cooked meatballs from the sauce and set aside. Reserve the remaining sauce and set aside to cool.

For the pilau:
1 1/2 cups basmati or long-grain rice

Rinse the rice until the water runs clear, cover it with water and soak for 30 minutes. Drain and set aside.

2 tbsp ghee
2.5 cms/1 inch cinnamon stick
4 cloves
2 large brown cardamom pods, bruised
1 finely chopped medium onion
2 tsp grated fresh ginger
1/2 tsp finely chopped garlic
1 tsp turmeric powder
1/2 tsp chilli powder

Heat the *ghee* in a heavy-bottomed saucepan. Add the cinnamon, cloves, cardamoms and fry for a few seconds to release their aromas. Add the onion, ginger and garlic and fry until the onion turns a pale gold; then stir in the turmeric and chilli powder.

2 1/2 tsp salt
2 tbsp seedless raisins
1/4 tsp saffron threads, steeped for 15 minutes in 1 tbsp hot milk

Add the drained rice, salt, raisins, saffron threads in milk and stir in the stock or hot water and 2-3 tablespoons of the sauce from cooking the meatballs. Keep about 20 of the meatballs aside if they are to be covered in silver leaf. Add the remaining meatballs. Stir carefully.

2³/4 cups hot stock or
hot water
Sauce reserved from cooking
the meatballs

Bring to the boil, reduce the heat, cover with a well-fitting lid and cook for 15 minutes. Remove the lid. The liquid should be absorbed.

Fork through, lifting the rice gently. Put a tea-towel over saucepan to absorb steam and moisture. Replace the lid and leave undisturbed for 10 minutes. Discard the cinnamon stick and cardamom pods.

For the garnish:
Silver coated meatballs
Rose petals
Lightly cooked green peas

To serve, mound the rice in the centre of a serving platter and surround with rose petals. Place a lightly cooked pea in the centre of each rose petal. Scatter the rice with silver-coated or speckled meatballs.

Shah Jahani Biryani

🍵

ROSE-SCENTED BIRYANI WITH CHICKEN

It is fitting that this superb *biryani* was named after the emperor whose reign saw magnificent ostentation in extravagant architectural creations at Lahore, Agra and Shahjahanabad (Delhi); in the dazzling, jewel-encrusted Peacock Throne, which displayed some of the wealth of the royal treasury; in his love of being surrounded by fine things such as his drinking cup of white nephrite jade exquisitely carved and monogrammed *Sahib-i-qiran-i-sani*, 'Second Lord of the (Auspicious) Conjunction', which can be seen at the Victoria and Albert Museum in London.

One of the joys of this elaborate-looking dish is that it can be cooked ahead and gently reheated. If prepared in separate stages with the ingredients assembled on individual trays to represent the stages of cooking, you will breeze through and be able to present this majestic *biryani* before your guests with great aplomb.

You will need two heavy-bottomed saucepans with close-fitting lids and a casserole dish with a tight-fitting lid.

When the chicken is under way, start the rice stage to speed things along.

Allow 1 hour for the rice to soak and drain.

For the chicken:

*2 roughly chopped medium
onions*
*2 tsp roughly chopped fresh
ginger*
1 tsp roughly chopped garlic
2 tbsp blanched almonds
1 tbsp white poppy seeds
3 tbsp water

Blend the onions, ginger, garlic, almonds, poppy seeds and water to a smooth paste in a food-processor and set aside.

5 tbsp ghee
1 tsp fennel seeds
*2.5 cm/1 inch cinnamon
stick*
4 cloves

Heat the *ghee* in a heavy-bottomed saucepan. Add the fennel seeds, cinnamon and cloves and fry for a few seconds to release their aromas. Add the blended paste and stir-fry over a medium heat for about 4 minutes, when the oil should start to separate out.

1/4 tsp cardamom powder
1 tsp cumin powder
1 tsp coriander powder
1 tsp chilli powder
1/4 tsp nutmeg powder
1/4 tsp mace powder
1 tsp garam masala

Stir in the cardamom, cumin, coriander, chilli, nutmeg, mace and *garam masala*. If the mixture is inclined to stick, add a little water and keep stirring.

*375 g/12 oz skinned chicken
breast or thigh fillets, cut
into large bite-sized pieces.*
1 1/2 tsp salt
1 tbsp seedless raisins
*3 tbsp lightly whisked
yoghurt*
*1/4 tsp saffron threads,
steeped for 15 minutes in
1 tbsp hot milk*

Add the chicken pieces, salt and raisins; stir to coat the chicken pieces. Cover and simmer gently for 15 minutes, stirring occasionally. Stir in the yoghurt and simmer until the moisture is absorbed. Sprinkle with saffron threads and milk. Discard the cinnamon stick and set aside.

Pre-heat the oven for 15 minutes to 160°C/325°F/ gas mark 3.

For the aromatic rice:

*1 1/2 cups basmati or
long-grain rice*

Rinse the rice until the water runs clear. Cover it with water and soak for 30 minutes, then drain and set aside for 30 minutes to dry.

2 cups water
2 tsp salt
*2.5 cm/1 inch cinnamon
stick*

Put the drained rice in a heavy-bottomed saucepan with the water, salt, cinnamon, cardamom, cloves and the rose essence. Bring to the boil on a high heat. Cover with a close-fitting lid, reduce to a low heat and simmer

3 small light-coloured cardamom pods, bruised
2 cloves
3 drops rose essence

for 8 minutes. The rice will be not quite cooked, but most of the liquid will be absorbed. Fork through gently and discard the cinnamon stick and cardamom pods.

2¹/₂ tbsp melted ghee
3 tbsp pouring cream
¹/₄ tsp saffron threads, steeped for 15 minutes in 1 tbsp hot milk

Grease a heavy-bottomed oven-proof casserole with about half a tablespoon of the melted *ghee*. Arrange alternate even layers of rice and the chicken mixture. (The number of layers will depend on the size of the casserole; I have assumed 2 layers here.)

Start with a layer of rice, then evenly distributed chicken pieces; dribble each layer with cream, melted *ghee* and sprinkle with saffron threads in milk and repeat for as many layers as the dish will accommodate. Cover with a close-fitting lid and crimp foil round the edge to seal and to trap the steam.

Bake in the pre-heated oven for 20 minutes. Fork through and gently mound onto a serving platter.

For the garnish:
1 tbsp ghee
1 tbsp blanched and slivered almonds
1 tbsp unsalted pistachio nuts
1 tbsp unsalted cashew nuts

Heat the *ghee* in a frying pan and toss and fry the nuts to a golden colour.

Rose petals
Varak (silver leaf)

Surround the edge of the rice with rose petals and sprinkle mixed nuts over the surface. Flutter a few sheets of edible silver leaf onto the rice.

Khichri

৯৯

KEDGEREE WITH SPICED LENTILS AND RICE

Khichri was prepared in vast quantities when great armies were on the move. Lentils and rice complement each other, not only in taste and texture but also in proteins and carbohydrates. Cooked together, they provide an attractive and nourishing dish. In Moghul kitchens *khichri* was often elaborated with meat, chicken or vegetables and more than one type of lentil would be cooked with the rice.

After fasting throughout the daylight hours in the month of Ramadan, Akbar would often call for *khichri* to be prepared in the simplest possible manner. No doubt the result was very similar to the *khichri* that had been introduced to the palace at Fatehpur Sikri by the Parsi priests from Gujarat. *Khichri* makes a substantial meal served with one of the sauce-based egg dishes accompanied by a *raita* and a chutney.

1¹/2 cups basmati or long-grain rice
³/4 cup masoor dal (orange or red split lentils)

Wash and drain the rice and *dal* separately and set aside.

3 tbsp ghee
1 tsp cumin seeds
4 cloves
2.5 cm/1 inch cinnamon stick
2 finely sliced medium onions
1 tsp grated fresh ginger
¹/2 tsp finely chopped garlic

Heat the *ghee* in a heavy-bottomed saucepan. Add the cumin seeds, cloves and cinnamon and fry for a few seconds to release their aromas. Add the onions, ginger and garlic and fry until the onions start to change colour. Add the rice and the lentils and stir until the grains of rice and lentils are well coated.

3¹/2 cups hot water
1¹/2 tsp salt
1 tsp garam masala
2 tbsp lime or lemon juice

Add the hot water, salt, *garam masala* and lime or lemon juice. Bring the liquid to the boil, reduce the heat to low, cover the pan with a close-fitting lid and simmer for 20 minutes. Remove from the heat. Lift the lid carefully – beware of rising steam. Gently lift and fork through the mixture. Cover the saucepan with a tea-towel, replace the lid and leave undisturbed for 10 minutes. The towel will absorb any excess moisture. Discard the cinnamon stick. Serve hot.

Gulrukh Zarda

ORANGE-FLAVOURED SWEET PILAU

Babur loved his gardens and flowers, particularly roses. He gave his wives and daughters names such as Gulbadan (Princess Rosebody), Gulrang (Rose-Coloured Princess), Gulchira (Rosy-Cheeked Princess) and Gulrukh (Rose-Faced Princess), for whom this dish is named.

This sweet rice dish, flavoured with orange, rose essence and saffron, is popular on Muslim feast days and is a must for wedding celebrations. It is a filling and fitting follow-on if serving kebabs or *tandoori* as a light main course with a bread. Golden-hued rice is dotted with contrasting currants or sultanas and further flavoured with nuts and saffron.

If pistachio nuts are not available, substitute cashews or walnuts. Steep the currants or sultanas for about 10 minutes to soften.

2 cups basmati or long-grain rice	Rinse the rice until the water runs clear, then cover with water and soak for 30 minutes. Drain and set aside to dry.
2 tbsp currants or sultanas	Steep the currants or sultanas for 10 minutes in hot water. Drain and set aside.
4 tbsp ghee *6 cloves* *6 cardamoms* *5 cm/2 inch cinnamon stick* *³/4 tsp turmeric powder* *1 tsp salt* *2³/4 cups hot water*	Heat the *ghee* in a heavy-bottomed saucepan, add the cloves, cardamom and cinnamon and fry for a few seconds to release aromas. Stir in the turmeric powder and salt, then add the drained rice and stir-fry for 2 minutes. Pour the hot water over the rice and mix, bring to the boil, reduce the heat, cover and simmer for about 5 minutes, after which much of the moisture will be absorbed and the rice par-boiled. Remove from the heat.
³/4 cup sugar *¹/2 tsp saffron threads, steeped for 15 minutes in 1 tbsp hot milk* *1 tbsp blanched and slivered almonds*	Add the sugar, saffron threads steeped in milk, almonds, pistachios, currants, nutmeg powder, grated orange rind, orange juice and the *kewra* or rose essence to the rice mixture and fold in gently to mix well.

1 tbsp blanched and lightly
crushed pistachio nuts
1/2 tsp nutmeg powder
1 tbsp orange rind, finely
grated
2 tbsp orange juice
3 drops kewra (screwpine)
or rose essence

1/2 cup milk

Return to the heat, add the milk, cover the saucepan and simmer for about 6 minutes. The rice should have a moist appearance, but most of the moisture should have been absorbed. Fork through gently and discard the cinnamon stick.

Place a cloth over the saucepan and replace the cover. Leave undisturbed for 15 minutes. If prepared ahead, re-heat gently in a moderate oven for about 10 minutes before serving.

1 tbsp ghee
2 tbsp slivered almonds or
cashew nuts

Heat the *ghee* in a small frying pan and fry the nuts until they are deep golden in colour.

Whipped cream to swirl in
centre
Rose petals

Mound the rice onto a serving platter and sprinkle with golden fried nuts, swirl some whipped cream onto the rice and top with rose petals.

BREADS

*R*oti has become a generic name for unleavened bread in India. A great variety of flat breads are prepared under individual names such as *chapati, puri, phulka* and *paratha*. They are mostly made from whole wheat flour called *atta* in which the kernel of the wheat is ground to yield a fine flour which contains all the nutrients of the bran and the grain.

Some breads are made with a mixture of wheatflour and cornflour, some with plain white flour and some are made from a chick-pea flour called *besan*. *Naans* are usually leavened breads made with white flour and baked in a *tandoor* oven.

The leavened breads like *naan*, cooked in the *tandoor*-type oven, were introduced into north-west India from Central Asia. The *paratha*, popular on restaurant menus today, evolved in the Moghul kitchen from the *puri*; *ghee* was added in between layers of dough during the rolling process in order to create the layered effect. It did not stop there; innovative cooks experimented with stuffings of spiced minced meat or vegetables (p.196-7), and sometimes spinach and spices would be kneaded into the dough before rolling. Other *parathas* have a dominant flavour like cardamom (pp.193-4).

The kneading and the resting of the dough is the key to the texture of Indian breads – the more kneading, the lighter the texture, while the resting of the dough allows the glutens to relax. If the dough is refrigerated for any length of time, bring it back to room temperature before kneading again.

The breads are often dry-cooked or very lightly fried on a *tawa*, the Indian version of a griddle, which is a slightly concave iron plate that retains heat well. Some *rotis,* other than *naans*, are also cooked in a *tandoor* oven.

Naan

LEAVENED BREAD

Naan, the Persian for bread, is a flat, teardrop-shaped, leavened bread and is similar to Middle Eastern breads. Variations of *naan* are traditionally served with *tandoori* dishes. When cooked in the *tandoor* clay oven, the shaped dough is smacked against the concave walls of the oven and miraculously stays there until lifted off with a prong to emerge puffed up with bubbles of golden brown spots. Watching the experts is a fascinating experience as they slap the dough from palm to palm to form a double hand-span sized circle which is pulled down at one end to form the shape of a teardrop.

Allow about 3 hours for the preparation and resting of the dough. The quantities given here will make 6 *naans*.

A very hot oven is pre-heated for about 15 minutes at 230°C/450°F/gas mark 8 and reduced to 180°C/350°F/gas mark 4 to bake the *naans*.

4 cups plain flour 1/2 tsp salt 1/4 tsp bicarbonate of soda (baking soda) 1 tsp baking powder	Sift the flour into a bowl and stir in the salt, bicarbonate of soda and baking powder.
3/4 cup water 1 egg 2 tsp sugar 1/2 cup yoghurt 3 tbsp milk	In another bowl whisk together the water, egg, sugar, yoghurt and milk. Gradually add to the flour and mix to a dough. Knead for about 10 minutes to a soft smooth dough or until it comes away clean from the sides of the bowl; add a little extra water if necessary. Cover with a damp cloth and leave for 30 minutes.
1 tbsp peanut oil	After half an hour add the peanut oil and knead on a work surface for 10 minutes with a pressing and pushing movement, using the heel of your hand as you fold the dough over itself. Cover with a damp cloth and leave for 2 hours. Divide the dough and roll into 6 equal balls on a floured board. Give them a bang with the palm of your hand to flatten them slightly, then leave for 3 minutes.

4 tsp melted ghee
*1 tbsp poppy seeds or black
cumin seeds (optional)*

Smear a couple of drops of the melted *ghee* over your palms and with a firm clapping movement slap the dough from hand to hand until it spreads and flops over the hand. Hold one end and give the other end a few gentle tugs to elongate into a teardrop shape. If desired, sprinkle one surface with a few poppy seeds or black cumin seeds and press down gently. The dough can be rolled to a 13 cm/5 inch circle and then pulled at one edge to elongate.

Place the *naans* on lightly greased baking trays and put into the pre-heated oven. Reduce the heat to 180°C/350°F/gas mark 4 and bake for 8-10 minutes. Remove from the oven and brush with melted *ghee*. If you have a separate grill, the *naans* can be pushed under a pre-heated grill for a couple of seconds to brown the puffy spots.

It is best to serve the *naans* as they emerge from the oven or to have some foil to hand and stack and wrap them in foil to keep warm for a short time.

Begum Puris

MILK-FLAVOURED PURIS

Puris are disks of unleavened dough which puff up when fried. They are made on high days and holidays and, indeed, daily in many households across India. Generally made from a simple water-based dough, like the *chapati,* the Moghul version has been embellished. Milk is used instead of water and a hint of rose essence added to the hot oil gives the *puris* an exotic lift. Rose essence is highly concentrated and only a minute quantity is needed. The *puris* will eventually deflate. Serve with potatoes in *masala* (p.143) or with any of the vegetable dishes.

Allow 1 hour for the dough to rest. The quantities given here will make about 16 *puris*.

2 sifted cups atta flour
2 sifted cups plain white
flour
$^1/_2$ tsp salt
$^1/_2$ tsp baking powder
1 cup milk at room
temperature
1 tbsp ghee

Put the sifted *atta* and white flour in a bowl and stir in the salt and baking powder. Make a well and gradually mix in the milk to make a dough. Add the *ghee* and knead for 10 minutes or longer – the more kneading the lighter the dough. Cover with a damp cloth and leave to rest for 1 hour.

Extra flour for dusting

Divide the dough into 16 portions and roll into balls. Dust the pastry board and rolling pin with flour, give the balls a light bang with the palm of your hand to flatten them and roll out to rounds of approximately 10 cm/4 inches.

Vegetable oil for deep-frying
2-3 drops rose essence

Heat the oil to smoking point or until a haze appears off the oil in a wok or deep-fryer. Add the drops of rose essence to the oil and fry the *puris* one at a time.

As each *puri* is dropped into the hot oil, hold it down very gently with a spatula so that it is just covered in hot oil. Release almost immediately and the *puri* should puff up and rise. Turn over to fry the other side; the *puris* should be light gold in colour. The frying process for each will only take seconds. Remove to a plate or dish lined with absorbent kitchen paper. Serve as soon as possible.

Moghlai Parathas

CARDAMOM-FLAVOURED PARATHAS

The *nawabi* city of Lucknow is famous for many dishes. These fine-textured flaky *parathas* are made with plain flour delicately flavoured with cardamom. They make a satisfying meal served with *shami kebabs* (pp.78-9) and mint chutney (p.207). Chefs in the days of the *nawabs* would use as much *ghee* as the dough would hold to make each layer of the *paratha* tissue-thin.

Allow 1 hour for the dough to rest. The quantities given here will make 8 *parathas*.

2 sifted cups plain flour
1 tsp salt
¹/4 tsp cardamom powder
1 tbsp melted ghee
¹/2 cup milk, at room
temperature, diluted with
¹/4 cup water, also at room
temperature

Extra flour for dusting
4 tbsp melted ghee

3 tbsp ghee for shallow-
frying

Mix the sifted flour into a bowl and stir in the salt and cardamom powder. Rub in the tablespoon of melted *ghee* and gradually add as much as is required of the cup of diluted milk to mix to a dough consistency. Knead on a work surface for about 15 minutes. Return to the bowl and cover with a moistened cloth. Leave at room temperature for 1 hour. Divide into 8 portions and roll into balls; cover with a moistened cloth.

Lightly dust the rolling surface and rolling pin with flour. Roll each ball out to a thin circle and smear the surface with 2 teaspoons of the melted *ghee*. Make a radial cut from the centre to the outer edge. Take one cut edge and keep rolling with your finger tips to join the other cut edge in order to make a firmly rolled conical shape.

Moisten your palms with a little melted *ghee*. Pick the cone up at narrow pointed end and stand the base on the palm of one hand. Gently press the narrow point down to the centre of the base. Repeat with all 8 portions and cover with a moist cloth.

Dust the rolling surface and rolling pin and, with minimum pressure, roll each *paratha* out to a thickness of 0.75 cm / ¹/4 inch. Keep the *parathas* covered with a moistened cloth.

Heat 2 teaspoons of the *ghee* in a *tawa* or heavy-bottomed griddle. When the *ghee* is quite hot, fry the *parathas* separately, for about 1 minute on each side, dribbling extra *ghee* round the edges and turning over to shallow-fry each side to a light golden colour. Repeat until all are cooked.

Stack the *parathas* and wrap in foil to keep them warm. Serve as soon as possible. The *parathas* can be re-heated.

Phulka

ε●

BALLOONED CHAPATIS

Phulka means puffed and these *chapati*-type breads are dry-cooked, first on the *tawa* or griddle, and then held over an open flame to balloon out. These golden balloons look very impressive and I once invested in a portable single gas burner just to do this particular job.

The balloon effect can only be achieved over an open flame which causes the *phulka* to swell and fill with steam. The *phulkas* will deflate eventually and in fact, although the effect is achieved, the breads are often deliberately deflated. The ballooning effect of heat lifting a layer of the dough seems to give the *phulkas* a different texture and taste to its companion, the *chapati*; otherwise, the dough-making procedure for both is the same except that *chapatis* are made only from *atta* flour not a mixture of flours.

Allow the time indicated for the dough to rest. The quantities given here will make 10 *phulkas*.

³/4 cup atta flour
³/4 cup plain flour

Sift the *atta* and plain flours together into a deep bowl.

¹/2 tsp salt
³/4 cup water at room temperature
Extra atta flour for dusting

Add the salt to the sifted flour. Make a well in the centre and gradually add the water and mix to a dough. Knead on a work surface for 10-15 minutes to make a soft pliable dough. Cover with a moistened cloth and let the dough rest for 5 minutes; then moisten your fingers and knead for another 3 minutes. Put the dough into the bowl and cover with a moistened cloth and allow to rest at room temperature for 1 hour. It can be left for longer or even overnight, in which case wrap it firmly in foil or plastic and refrigerate.

If the dough has been refrigerated, it will need to rest at room temperature for ¹/2 hour before proceeding. Knead lightly, then divide into 10 portions and roll into balls. Cover with a moistened cloth. Lightly dust the rolling surface and rolling pin with *atta* flour and roll each ball into a circle measuring about 13 cm/5 inches. Cover with a moistened cloth.

Heat the ungreased *tawa* or heavy-bottomed griddle on a medium heat until splashing on a few drops of water makes an instant splutter. Cook the *phulkas* one at a time, in the order in which they were rolled, allowing 1 minute a side or until light-brown bubble spots start appearing on the underside.

3 tbsp melted ghee

Now comes the dramatic part if you are cooking over a gas flame or open fire. Using tongs, lift the *phulka* and place it over the flame for a few seconds until it balloons up. Brush one side with melted *ghee*. You will become quite adept at lifting one *phulka* off the griddle and popping the next one on while holding the cooked *phulka* over the flame. The *phulkas* will deflate fairly quickly.

If a gas flame is not available, a lightly bubbled effect can still be achieved by pressing the cooked side lightly with a spatula or by covering your closed hand with a tea towel and pressing lightly but firmly around the *phulka* with the second joints of your closed fingers as it is cooking.

Aloo Roti

ROTI STUFFED WITH SPICY POTATO

These *rotis* are filled with delicious spicy mashed potato before frying. The potatoes for the filling retain a floury texture when cooked in the skins before peeling. You may prefer to use a cooked and mashed vegetable other than potato. The *rotis* are quite filling and make a good sandwich substitute for lunch served with a beetroot *raita* (p.204) and one of the chutneys. *Roti* is a generic name for unleavened bread.

These quantities will make 8 *rotis*. Allow 1 hour or more resting time for the dough.

250 g/8 oz potatoes
1 finely chopped large onion
1 finely chopped fresh green chilli, seeds discarded
1 tbsp finely chopped fresh coriander leaves
1 tsp cumin powder
1 tsp garam masala
1 tsp salt

Cook the potatoes in their skins, then cool, peel and cut them into large pieces. Add the onion, chilli, coriander leaves, cumin powder, *garam masala* and salt and mash into the potatoes. Set aside.

2 cups sifted atta flour
1/2 tsp salt
1 tbsp ghee
3/4 cup water at room temperature

Put the sifted flour into a bowl with the salt and rub in the *ghee*. Gradually add the water and mix to a dough. Knead to a soft pliable dough on a work surface for 10-15 minutes. Return to the bowl and cover with a moist cloth. Leave to rest for 1 hour or longer.

Knead again with moistened fingers. Divide into 8 portions and roll into balls. Flatten the balls with the palm of your hand and cover with a moistened cloth for 10 minutes.

Extra flour for dusting

Dust the work surface and rolling pin with *atta* flour and roll out the balls to circles about 10 cm/4 inches. Put a spoonful of the spicy potato mixture in the centre. Pull the edges up over the filling and pinch together to make a pouch. Lightly moisten your hands with water or a little *ghee* and gently roll into a ball.

Dust the rolling surface and rolling pin with more flour and gently and lightly roll the *rotis* out to about 13 cm/5 inches.

3 tbsp melted ghee

Heat the griddle, dribble a teaspoon of melted *ghee* over the surface and put a *roti* in the centre. After a few seconds, dribble a few drops of *ghee* round the edge, cook for 1 minute, turn and do the same for the other side. The *rotis* should be golden on both sides and served as soon as possible. If they need to be kept warm for a short while, wrap them individually in foil.

Besan Roti

ن&

CHICK-PEA FLOUR BREAD

These *rotis* are often served as a teatime snack. The chick-pea flour is first dry-roasted to give a subtle, nutty flavour. Dry-roast the flour in a small frying pan over a low heat until it begins to change colour; immediately it starts to change colour, take the pan off the heat to prevent the flour from burning and becoming bitter. The dough is kneaded with chopped onions, chilli and coriander leaves, then rolled into circles and lightly fried.

Allow 1 hour or more for resting the dough. The quantities given here will make 8 *rotis*.

1 cup atta flour
1 cup lightly dry-roasted chick-pea flour
1 tsp salt
1 finely chopped medium onion
1 finely chopped fresh green chilli
1 tbsp finely chopped fresh coriander leaves
1 tbsp melted ghee
Water at room temperature

Extra chick-pea flour for dusting

3 tbsp melted ghee for shallow-frying

Put the *atta* and chick-pea flours into a bowl with the salt, chopped onion, chilli, coriander leaves and the tablespoon of melted *ghee* and mix together well. Gradually add sufficient water to mix to a dough. Knead on a work surface for 10-15 minutes. Return to the bowl and cover with a moist cloth and leave to rest for 1 hour or more if convenient.

After the dough has rested, knead it again with moist hands. Divide into 8 portions and roll into balls. Flatten the balls with the palm of hands. Cover with a moistened cloth and leave for 10 minutes.

Dust the rolling surface and rolling pin with chick-pea flour and roll each ball out to a circle, ensuring that they are not too thin or the onion pieces will pierce through the dough.

Heat the *tawa* or griddle, dribble a little melted *ghee* over it and place a *roti* in the centre. After a few seconds dribble a little melted *ghee* round the edges, cook for 1 minute, turn and do the same for the other side. The *rotis* should be a nice golden brown. It is better to serve the *rotis* immediately, but they can be individually wrapped in foil to keep them warm for a short while.

Qamar-Ud-Din-Kulcha

🐌

HYDERABAD'S LEAVENED BREAD

The flag of the Asaf Jahi dynasty of Hyderabad displays a *kulcha* on a yellow background. Legend tells of a battle-weary and hungry general Qamaruddin (who assumed the viceroyalty of the Deccan in Aurangzeb's time and finally became its independent ruler) being offered some *kulchas* by a holy man. The holy man wrapped seven of them in a yellow cloth and prophesied that the general's dynasty would survive seven generations – and so it came to pass. This tale was told to me by Krishna Reddy as we sat on the verandah at his family home outside Hyderabad and scooped up morsels of Joan Reddy's *raja haleem* (pp.71-3) with pieces of *kulcha*.

This recipe is for plain *kulchas*, but variations can easily be achieved by incorporating finely chopped garlic or mint into the dough.

Allow 3-5 hours for the dough to rise. The quantities given here will make 6-8 *kulchas*. Pre-heat the oven 180°C/350°F/gas mark 4 for about 15 minutes.

1 tsp dried yeast *1 tsp sugar* *1¹/2 cups lukewarm milk*	Sprinkle the yeast and sugar over the milk and allow to froth; this will take about 15 minutes.
4 cups sifted plain flour *1 tsp salt* *1 tbsp melted ghee* *2 tbsp yoghurt*	Add the salt to the sifted flour in a bowl, make a well in the centre and pour in the *ghee*, yoghurt and the frothing milk and yeast mixture and mix to a soft dough. Knead on a work surface to a soft pliable ball. Cover with a moist cloth and leave to rise, for about 5 hours.
Extra flour for dusting	If the dough has been refrigerated, it will need to rest again at room temperature for about 30 minutes before proceeding. Knead again and divide into 6 portions. Dust with flour and flatten out between your palms or roll out to disks about 13 cm/5 inches in diameter.
2 egg yolks	Arrange on a greased baking tray, cover the tray with a moist cloth and leave for 20 minutes. Brush the tops of the *kulchas* with egg yolk and bake in the pre-heated oven for 10-15 minutes.

RAITAS AND CHATNIS

*R*aitas and *chatnis,* pickles and relishes are popular in most Middle Eastern countries, and many of those served in Iran today have been in the culinary repertoire from the days of Shah Tahmasp and earlier. There are many similarities to be found between old Persian recipes and those that follow. I have heard the accompaniments referred to as the 'spurs', the 'whips' and the 'teasers'. They certainly add a tang to tickle the taste buds with their variety of flavours ranging from salt, sour and hot to mild and sweet. *Chatnis* are generally prepared to a purée texture from fresh, uncooked ingredients and flavoured with herbs and spices, and the word 'chutney' is an anglicisation of the Hindi *chatni*. The *chatnis* included in this section bear no resemblance to the preserved sweet and spicy jam-textured concoctions commonly known as chutney.

Preserved pickles, or *achars*, also very popular as accompaniments, are made by marinating and cooking fruits or vegetables. They range in flavour from mild to fiery hot or sour-sweet. The preparation of pickles can be a lengthy process, often requiring strong sunlight to commence the first stage of marination. Inexpensive commercial brands are available from most supermarkets, and I have not included any pickle recipes in this chapter.

Raita acts as a cooling agent and as a digestive and is the name given to a dish with a yoghurt base. The addition of a main ingredient to the yoghurt will cause it to be called by that name; add cucumber and it becomes cucumber *raita*. The variations are endless; tomatoes, onion, mint, radish, potato, spinach, carrot, beetroot, just to name a few. *Raitas* are easy to put together and can be prepared well ahead. The yoghurt is considered an essential balance to a meal and it can also be served without the addition of other ingredients. Cumin seeds, dry-roasted and sometimes crushed, are often sprinkled over the surface of *raitas*. I keep a small amount of each to hand. *Chachumbars* or relishes are made from chopped fruits, vegetables and chillies seasoned with salt and lime or lemon juice.

Baigan Raita

AUBERGINE IN YOGHURT

For this dish, the purple skin of the aubergine is traditionally seared over hot coals. The skin is then peeled off but the smoke which has penetrated into the flesh gives a particular flavour to this *raita*. The barbecue does a good job of this, but for convenience this recipe uses a conventional grill.

Pre-heat the grill to medium.

1 large or 2 small aubergines weighing about 500 g/l lb

Prick the aubergine in a few spots with a fork to prevent it from bursting under the grill and push a skewer through it lengthways to make turning easy. Set aside ready for grilling.

1½ cups lightly whisked yoghurt
½ tsp salt
1 tsp grated fresh ginger
1 finely chopped fresh green chilli
1 finely chopped medium onion
1 tsp dry-roasted and crushed coriander seeds
1 tbsp finely chopped fresh coriander leaves

½ tbsp fresh coriander leaves

Put the yoghurt into a bowl and add the salt, ginger, chilli, onion, dry-roasted crushed coriander seeds and the fresh coriander leaves. Stir to mix well and set aside.

Pre-heat the grill to medium, put the whole aubergine under the grill and keep turning it until the skin becomes dark and wrinkled; this can take up to 15 minutes. The heat must penetrate to cook the flesh inside. Allow to cool, then either peel off the skin and put the flesh in a bowl or cut the aubergine in half and scoop out the flesh from both halves. Discard the skin and mash the flesh.

Add the mashed aubergine to the spiced yoghurt and mix well to combine. Remove to a serving dish or bowl, cover and chill. Garnish with fresh coriander leaves.

Kheere, Nariyal Raita

CUCUMBER AND COCONUT IN YOGHURT

1 medium cucumber — Peel the cucumber and cut it in half lengthways. Discard the seeds by scraping down the seed channel with a spoon. Grate coarsely or chop finely.

2 tbsp desiccated coconut
2 tbsp lime or lemon juice — Steep the coconut in lime or lemon juice for about 20 minutes.

2 finely chopped fresh green chillies, seeds discarded
1/2 tsp salt
1 1/2 cups lightly whisked yoghurt — Mix the grated cucumber, steeped coconut, chopped chillies and the salt into the yoghurt.

2 tsp ghee
1 tsp black mustard seeds
1/2 tsp black cumin seeds — Heat the *ghee* and fry the mustard and cumin seeds until they splutter. Stir into the *raita*, cover and chill.

Kheere Raita

CUCUMBER IN YOGHURT

1 medium cucumber — Peel the cucumber and cut it in half lengthways. Discard the seeds by scraping down the seed channel with a spoon. Grate the flesh of the cucumber.

1/2 tsp salt
1/4 tsp ground black pepper
1 finely chopped small fresh green chilli, seeds discarded
2 cups lightly whisked yoghurt
1/2 tsp chilli powder — Fold the grated cucumber, salt, pepper and chilli into the lightly whisked yoghurt. Sprinkle with chilli powder, cover and chill.

Podina Raita

ﻛﻻ

MINT-FLAVOURED YOGHURT

3 tbsp finely chopped fresh
mint leaves
1 finely chopped medium onion
1 tsp finely chopped fresh
ginger
1 finely chopped small fresh
green chilli, seeds discarded
1/2 tsp salt
1/4 tsp chilli powder
1 1/2 cups lightly whisked
yoghurt

Mix the chopped mint leaves, onion, ginger and chilli together in a bowl. Sprinkle with salt and chilli powder. Add the yoghurt and stir to combine.

A sprig of mint

Garnish with a small sprig of mint, cover and chill.

Kheere, Tamatar Raita

ﻛﻻ

CUCUMBER AND TOMATO IN YOGHURT

1 peeled and diced medium
cucumber
1 finely chopped medium onion
1 finely diced firm medium
tomato
1 tbsp finely chopped fresh
coriander
1 tsp dry-roasted cumin seeds
1/2 tsp salt
1 1/2 cups lightly whisked
yoghurt

Fold the cucumber, onion, tomato, coriander leaves, cumin seeds and salt into the yoghurt.

1/4 tsp chilli powder or
paprika

Sprinkle the surface with chilli powder or paprika, cover and chill.

Chukandar Raita

BEETROOT IN YOGHURT

This beetroot *raita* becomes a lovely shade of pink as the beetroot bleeds into the yoghurt.

2 medium-sized beetroot; cook, peel and cut into small cubes	Put the beetroot cubes into a glass bowl and set aside.
¼ tsp salt *1 tsp sugar* *¼ tsp chilli powder* *1 tsp dry-roasted cumin seeds* *2 cups lightly whisked yoghurt*	Mix the salt, sugar, chilli powder and cumin seeds into the lightly whisked yoghurt. Pour the spiced yoghurt over the beetroot cubes. There will be a gradual bleeding of the beetroot streaking into the yoghurt.
A sprig of mint or a rose petal	Garnish with a sprig of mint or a rose petal, cover and chill.

Palak Raita

SPINACH IN YOGHURT

I often make this spinach *raita* when I am using spinach in another dish. Simply prepare 1 cup of cooked spinach in addition to that required for the main dish.

1 cup cooked and chopped spinach	Set the chopped spinach aside to cool.
1 finely chopped medium onion *1 finely chopped fresh red chilli, seeds discarded* *¼ tsp salt* *2 cups lightly whisked yoghurt*	Combine the cooled, chopped spinach with the onion, chilli and salt. Fold in the yoghurt.

2 tsp ghee
1/2 tsp fennel seeds
1 tsp cumin seeds
1 tsp mustard seeds

Heat the *ghee* in a small frying pan, toss in the fennel, cumin and mustard seeds for a few seconds or until they begin to splutter. Pour over the yoghurt and spinach and fold in. Cover and chill.

Angoor Raita

GRAPES IN YOGHURT

2 tsp honey
1/4 tsp salt
1/4 tsp chilli powder
2 cups lightly whisked yoghurt
40 halved seedless grapes

Mix the honey, salt and chilli powder into the yoghurt and then fold in the grapes.

1/4 tsp grated nutmeg

Sprinkle with grated nutmeg, cover and chill.

Kela Raita

BANANA IN YOGHURT

1 tbsp blanched and crushed almonds
1 tbsp seedless raisins
1/2 tsp salt
1/4 tsp ground black pepper
2 tbsp honey
1/4 tsp crushed cardamom
1 1/2 cups lightly whisked yoghurt
2 large ripe bananas, peeled and cut into thin rounds

Combine the almonds, raisins, salt, pepper, honey and cardamom into the yoghurt, then gently fold in the banana slices.

1/4 tsp grated nutmeg

Sprinkle with nutmeg, cover and chill.

Gajar Raita

🍃

CARROT IN YOGHURT

3 diced and cooked medium
carrots
1¹/₂ cups yoghurt
1 roughly chopped fresh green
chilli, seeds discarded
6 mint leaves
¹/₄ tsp salt
¹/₄ tsp ground black pepper
1 tsp sugar

Put all the ingredients into a food-processor and blend to a purée.

Put into a glass bowl, cover and chill.

Adrak Chatni

🍃

COCONUT AND GINGER CHUTNEY

2 tbsp desiccated coconut
2 tbsp lime or lemon juice

Steep the desiccated coconut in the lime or lemon juice for 15 minutes.

2 tbsp roughly chopped fresh
ginger
¹/₂ cup fresh coriander leaves
1 roughly chopped large fresh
green chilli
¹/₂ tsp salt

Put the ginger, coriander leaves, green chilli, steeped coconut and salt in a food-processor at high speed for 1 minute.

2 tsp ghee
1 tsp black mustard seeds
1 tsp black cumin seeds

Heat the *ghee* in a small frying pan and toss in the mustard and cumin seeds for a couple of seconds until they splutter. Mix into the chutney, cover and chill.

Tamatar Chatni

TOMATO CHUTNEY

2 roughly chopped large ripe tomatoes
1 tbsp sugar
¹/₂ tsp salt
1 tsp garam masala

Put the chopped tomatoes, sugar, salt and *garam masala* into a saucepan.

1 roughly chopped fresh red chilli
1 tsp roughly chopped garlic
2 tsp roughly chopped fresh ginger
2 tbsp lime or lemon juice

Blend the chilli, garlic, ginger and lime or lemon juice to a smooth paste in a food-processor.

Add the paste to the tomato mixture in the saucepan. Bring to the boil, reduce the heat and simmer for 5 minutes. Cool, cover and chill.

Podina Chatni

MINT CHUTNEY

This relish is served with *tandoori*-style and kebab dishes.

1 cup mint leaves
1 roughly chopped medium onion
1 roughly chopped large fresh green chilli
1 tsp roughly chopped fresh ginger
¹/₂ tsp roughly chopped garlic
¹/₂ tsp salt
2 tbsp lime or lemon juice
1 tsp sugar

Blend all the ingredients to a smooth purée in a food-processor. Cover and chill.

Aam Chatni

એ

GREEN MANGO CHUTNEY

4 unripe mangoes
1 cup fresh mint or coriander
leaves
1 tsp dry-roasted cumin seeds
1/2 tsp salt
1/2 tsp chilli powder
2 tbsp sugar

Peel, stone and roughly chop the mangoes. Blend all the ingredients in a food-processor to a smooth purée. Cover and chill.

Hare Dhania Chatni

એ

FRESH CORIANDER CHUTNEY

1 1/2 cups fresh coriander leaves
1 roughly chopped medium
onion
1 tsp roughly chopped fresh
ginger
1 fresh green chilli
2 tbsp lime or lemon juice
1/2 tsp salt
1/4 tsp ground black pepper

Blend the coriander leaves, onion, ginger, chilli and lime or lemon juice, salt and pepper to a smooth purée in a food-processor.

1 tsp dry-roasted cumin seeds

Sprinkle the dry-roasted cumin seeds over the surface, cover and chill.

Kaju Chatni

CASHEW NUT CHUTNEY

1¹/2 cups unsalted cashews
1 small onion, roughly
chopped for blending
1 tsp roughly chopped fresh
ginger
2 tbsp lime or lemon juice
2 tbsp finely chopped mint
leaves
¹/2 tsp salt

Blend all the ingredients to a smooth paste in a food-processor. Cover and chill.

Piaz, Adrak Cachumbar

TOMATO, ONION AND GINGER RELISH

2 finely diced large, firm
tomatoes
1 finely chopped medium
onion
2 tsp finely chopped fresh
ginger
1 finely chopped large fresh
green chilli, seeds discarded
1 tbsp finely chopped fresh
coriander or mint leaves
¹/2 tsp salt

Put the tomato, onion, ginger, chilli, coriander and salt into a bowl and turn gently to mix the colours and flavours.

1 tbsp lime or lemon juice
¹/2 tbsp white wine vinegar
2 tsp sugar

Stir and dissolve the sugar into the vinegar and lime or lemon juice. Trickle over the mixed ingredients, cover and chill.

Gajar, Piaz Cachumbar

CARROT AND ONION RELISH

225 g/8 oz carrots, peeled and cut into julienne strips
1 onion, halved and finely sliced
1 tsp grated fresh ginger
1/2 tsp salt
1/4 tsp ground black pepper
1/4 tsp chilli powder
2 tsp honey, mixed with 2 tbsp lime or lemon juice

Steep the carrot strips in boiling water for 2 minutes and then drain them. Mix with the raw onion, grated ginger, salt, pepper and chilli powder and trickle over the mixture of honey and lime or lemon juice. Cover and chill.

Kache Piaz

RAW ONION RELISH

Tandoori-style dishes and kebabs are usually accompanied by a dish of sliced raw onion rings. This relish is best made with red onions, if these are available.

2 medium onions

Cut the onions into thin rings and separate them; rinse in cold water and drain.

3/4 tsp salt
1/4 tsp chilli powder
2 tbsp lime or lemon juice

Put the drained onion rings on a flat dish, sprinkle with the salt and chilli powder. Trickle over the lime or lemon juice, cover and chill.

Gul Kishmish Chatni

ROSE-SCENTED RAISIN CHUTNEY

100 g/3¹/₂ oz seeded raisins
1 finely chopped large fresh
red chilli, seeds discarded
2 tsp grated fresh ginger
2 tbsp lime or lemon juice
3 drops rose essence
2 tsp salt
1 tsp sugar
2 tsp dry-roasted cumin seeds

Combine and blend the raisins, chilli, ginger, lime or lemon juice, rose essence, salt, sugar and cumin seeds in a food-processor. Put into a small glass bowl and decorate with a rose petal or a sprig of mint.

SWEETMEATS AND DESSERTS

Sweets played an important part in a Moghul meal. The lavish entertainment which began at the Moghul court was continued on an even grander scale by the royalty and aristocracy of the newer courts at Lucknow and Hyderabad. Further extravagant dimensions were given to many dishes as *nawabs* and *nizams* vied with each other for the supremacy of one dish or another. The creative cook became a highly regarded specialist and was often bribed or enticed to leave one position for another. When Lucknowis boasted the best sweetened bread and named it *sheermal* (pp.218-9), Hyderabadis responded with their exotic bread pudding, *shahi tukre* (pp.220-1). *Firnis, kheers* and *halwas* became ever sweeter and richer.

Many of India's dessert dishes are milk-based and very sustaining. Milk or cream is first reduced by a long, slow cooking (and stirring) process on a low heat using a heavy-bottomed saucepan. When the milk or cream becomes a semi-solid mass which tastes like canned evaporated milk, other ingredients such as sugar, nuts, raisins or fruit and flavourings of cardamom, saffron or rose essence are added.

Buffalo milk is often favoured for the making of sweet dishes and it is said that in Moghul times the buffaloes were fed on almonds, pistachio nuts and drops of rose essence.

Sweetmeats and confections are most often professionally made and are consumed in vast quantities at festival times. Guests are invariably offered something to sweeten the mouth on entering a home and gifts of sweetmeats are often exchanged. Most of the desserts, sweetmeats and confections are very sweet and rich with large quantities of sugar and *ghee. Varak*, gossamer fine sheets of pure silver, and occasionally gold, is used extensively in decoration and garnish.

Confectioners and other Indian shops display freshly made sweetmeats and confections, and it is certainly very convenient to be able to buy them ready-made. I have not included recipes for the popular fudge-like confection *barfi* or the powdered-milk dough dumplings, *gulab jamuns*. Although *halwas*, too, are readily available, I have included a recipe for a delicious beetroot and a carrot *halwa*. Do try it, and the other recipes which follow, which are more likely to be prepared in the home, to put a delicious sweet ending to a Moghul meal.

Firni

२॰

ALMOND AND RICE FLOUR PUDDING

This cooling, smooth and creamy dessert, set and served in small terracotta bowls called *shikoras* or *katoris*, is very popular in India. *Firni* is best described as a custard or blancmange type of dessert, with flavours of cardamom, almond, saffron and rose essence. Pistachio nuts may be substituted for almonds.

I often make double the quantity (everyone always seems to want more) and set it in a clear glass bowl, sprinkled with slivered almonds round the edge of the bowl and silver leaf and rose petals in the centre.

4-6 tbsp rice flour
2 tbsp ground almonds (almond meal)
3¹/2 cups full cream milk
A small pinch of saffron threads
4 tbsp caster sugar
¹/2 tsp cardamom powder
5 drops rose essence

Slivered almonds or chopped pistachios
Varak (silver leaf)
Rose petals

Mix the rice flour and ground almonds in a small bowl with a little of the milk to form a smooth paste of thick pouring consistency and set aside. Bring the remainder of the milk with the saffron threads to the boil in a heavy-bottomed saucepan, add the sugar and continue boiling and stirring for a couple of minutes until the sugar has dissolved.

Remove the saucepan from the heat and stir in the rice flour and ground almond mixture; return to the heat and stir and simmer gently to thicken to a custard consistency. Sprinkle in the cardamom powder and add the drops of rose essence and simmer for 1 more minute.

Pour into individual dishes and chill. Decorate with a sprinkling of nuts, a flutter of silver leaf and rose petals just before serving.

Khajoor Halwa

🍃

DATE DESSERT

Chopped dates are simmered in milk until the mixture thickens. It is then sweetened, *ghee* is added and cooking continues until the *ghee* starts to separate out – which is an indication that the mixture can absorb no more *ghee*.

This is strictly for date-lovers and those with a sweet tooth. You may like to think of it as an unusual and quickly made pudding, to be eaten with plenty of whipped cream or as a very sweet topping for plain ice-cream.

250 g/8 oz chopped dates
¹/4 cup milk
2 tbsp sugar
1 tbsp ghee

Put the dates and the milk in a heavy-bottomed saucepan and bring the milk to the boil. Reduce the heat and simmer gently, stirring all the time with a wooden spoon, until the mixture begins to thicken; this will take 7-10 minutes. Add the sugar and mix well. Add the *ghee* and continue stirring and cooking until the *ghee* starts to separate out. Remove the mixture and transfer it to a flat serving dish or individual dishes.

1 tbsp slivered almonds

Sprinkle the almond slivers on the surface and, to make them adhere, press them very lightly with a spatula or the back of a spoon, but do not push them right into the *halwa*.

Refrigerate and serve chilled.

Shahjahani Seviyan Kheer

🍃

SWEET MILKY VERMICELLI

As the month-long fast of Ramadan draws to a close, devout Muslims await the day of the new moon to celebrate the breaking of the fast with the festival of Idd. New clothes and fine jewels are donned, gifts of sweetmeats and good wishes are exchanged. No Idd would pass without the appearance of this easily prepared creamy-textured dessert. The *kheer* may be served hot or cold. If rice vermicelli is not available, substitute durum wheat vermicelli.

Constant stirring is required from start to finish.

2 tbsp ghee
³/4 cup rice vermicelli broken into 5 cm/2 inch pieces
5¹/2 cups milk
1/2 tsp cardamom powder
1/4 tsp nutmeg powder
1/2 cup caster sugar
1 tbsp honey
1¹/2 tbsp seedless raisins
1¹/2 tbsp slivered almonds
1/4 tsp saffron threads, steeped for 15 minutes in 1 tbsp hot milk

Heat the *ghee* in a frying pan, add the broken vermicelli and stir and fry until the vermicelli becomes a golden colour. Remove with a slotted spoon and set aside.

Bring the milk to the boil in a heavy-bottomed saucepan. Reduce the heat. Add the cardamom, nutmeg and the golden threads of vermicelli and stir and cook over a low heat until softish. Add the sugar, honey, raisins, almonds and the saffron threads and milk.

3 drops kewra (screwpine) essence

Keep stirring on a low heat until the mixture thickens to an even consistency. This can take some time. Remove from heat and add the *kewra* essence.

Varak (silver leaf)
2 tbsp crumbled pistachios
Rose petals

Put into serving bowl or individual serving dishes and decorate with flutters of silver leaf, a sprinkling of crushed pistachio nuts and rose petals. Serve warm or chilled.

Balushahi

PASTRIES COATED IN SYRUP AND NUTS

Balushahis, deep-fried pastry circles, are dipped in syrup and coated with crumbly nuts, go particularly well with after-dinner coffee. Almonds and pistachios are used here, but any other unsalted nuts may be substituted.

For the pastry:

250 g/8 oz plain flour
1/4 tsp bicarbonate of soda
A pinch of salt
1/4 tsp cardamom powder
4 tbsp melted ghee
3 tbsp yoghurt
1 1/2 tbsp cold water

Sift the flour into a bowl with the bicarbonate of soda and stir in the salt and cardamom powder. Rub in the *ghee*, mix in the yoghurt and water and knead to a soft dough. Divide the dough into 16 portions and roll into equal-sized balls. Make a depression in the centre with your thumb and then flatten out the circles. The centre should be thinner than the outer rim.

Ghee for deep-frying
2 light-coloured cardamom pods, bruised

Heat the *ghee* for deep-frying in a heavy-bottomed frying pan until it sizzles if splashed with drops of water. Drop in the bruised cardamom, reduce the heat to low and slip the pastry circles into the *ghee* a few at a time. The *ghee* should simmer around them. Let them fry for about 6 minutes then turn them over. They should swell and be light golden in colour.

Remove with a slotted spoon onto absorbent paper and repeat until all the dough circles are cooked. Allow to cool.

3 tbsp blanched almonds
3 tbsp blanched pistachios

Crush the almonds and pistachios to a crumbly texture, mix together and sprinkle half onto a flat surface. Reserve the remainder.

Now, while the *balushahis* are cooling, prepare the syrup.

For the syrup:

8 tbsp sugar
1 1/2 tbsp water
2 tsp lime or lemon juice

Simmer the sugar and water together in a heavy-bottomed saucepan over a low heat until the mixture becomes a thick, heavy syrup which will stick to the *balushahis*. Then stir in the lime or lemon juice.

Coat the fried circles with syrup by dropping them into the hot syrup a few at a time. Remove with tongs onto the bed of crumbly nut mixture and sprinkle the tops with the other half of the nut mixture. Allow to cool.

Gajar Halwa

❧

Sweet Carrot Dessert

In India specialist cooks called *halwais* prepare many varieties of *halwas*, which seem to take forever to cook, for the commercial market.

I used to love watching the *halwais* stirring grated carrot or pumpkin or semolina and milk in enormous *karachis* (wok-like utensils). Seemingly endless quantities of sugar were poured in and the cooking and stirring went on and on until the moisture was absorbed. Large quantities of *ghee* were stirred in and a wonderful buttery aroma filled the air. The thick mixture was poured into huge shallow trays and nuts were poured on top. As the *halwa* cooled and the texture became firm, silver leaf was brushed across and the *halwa* was cut into diamond shapes ready to be served.

500 g/1 lb carrots	Wash, peel and finely grate the carrot.
4¹/2 cups milk *1/2 tsp cardamom powder* *1/4 tsp saffron threads,* *steeped for 15 minutes in* *1 tbsp hot milk*	Put the grated carrots, milk, cardamom powder and steeped saffron threads into a wide, heavy-bottomed saucepan. Bring to the boil, reduce the heat, simmer and stir as often as possible during this time until all the liquid is absorbed. Depending on the width of the saucepan, this can take up to 1 hour.
4 tbsp ghee or softened *unsalted butter*	Add the *ghee* or butter and keep stirring until the carrot mixture loses its milky look and turns a golden colour; this will take about about 7 minutes.

6 tbsp caster sugar
2 tbsp seeded raisins
4 drops rose essence
2 tbsp blanched and slivered
almonds
	Add the sugar, raisins, rose essence and half the almonds. Keep stirring on a low heat until the mixture starts to thicken and pull away from the sides of the pan.
	    Turn the *halwa* out onto a greased dish or tray and smooth and flatten the surface with the back of a spoon. Sprinkle over the remaining almonds and press lightly with the back of a spoon to make them adhere to the *halwa*. Allow to cool before cutting. The texture will firm up as the mixture cools.
	    The *halwa* can be served warm with a curl of whipped cream and a sprinkling of flaked almonds.

Sheermal

SWEET MILKY PASTRIES

Sheermal or *shirmal* is said to have been invented in Lucknow in the middle of the eighteenth century by a cook named Mahumdu. He became the acclaimed expert, opened a shop and, according to one account, turned out thousands of *sheermals* at a time.

The influence from Persia is evident in these *sheermals*. *Sheer* is the Persian for milk. *Sheermals* are large sweet dough disks about 15 cm/6 inches in diameter, though I prefer to make them slightly smaller. Traditionally, they are cooked in an iron *tandoor*-like oven and then liberally sprinkled or brushed over with milk flavoured with saffron threads. In this recipe the *sheermals* are first par-baked in a pre-heated oven for 3 minutes, then brushed over with milk and saffron threads and returned to the oven for 5 minutes. They are delicious served with a purée of apricots and whipped cream.

Allow about 3½ hours for the resting of the dough. The quantities given here will make 8 *sheermals*.

Pre-heat the oven to 180°C/350°F/gas mark 4 for about 15 minutes.

2 cups sifted plain flour *½ tsp salt* *2 tsp sugar* *2 drops kewra (screwpine) essence* *½ -¾ cup milk at room temperature*	Mix the sifted flour, salt and sugar into a bowl. Make a well in the centre, add the *kewra* essence and gradually mix and knead in the milk to a dough consistency. Cover with a moist cloth and allow to rest for 15 minutes.
3 tbsp melted ghee	Knead the melted *ghee* into the rested dough and continue kneading on a work surface until you have a very smooth, soft, pliable dough. This could take 10-15 minutes. Return the dough to the bowl and cover with a moist cloth. Set aside to rest at room temperature for 2 hours. Knead again lightly, cover with a moist cloth and set aside for 1 hour. Knead lightly once more. Divide into 8 portions, roll into balls and cover with a moist cloth for 10 minutes.

Extra flour for dusting	Dust the working surface and rolling pin with flour. Roll the balled portions out to 0.75 cm/¼ inch thick circles.
½ tsp saffron threads, steeped for 15 minutes in 2 tbsp hot milk *2 tbsp melted ghee*	Grease a large baking tray with some of the melted *ghee*. Prick the surface of the *sheermals* with a fork. Bake in a pre-heated oven for 3 minutes. Take out of the oven and very quickly brush over with saffron-flavoured milk, allowing threads to cling to the *sheermals*. Return to the oven and bake for 5 minutes. Remove from the oven, brush with melted *ghee* and serve with puréed fruit.

Kulfi
ﮊ
FIRM-TEXTURED ICE-CREAM

Ice-cream made in the Moghul style is delicious, much firmer than Western ice-cream. Flavouring can come from fresh fruits or nuts, cardamom and rose or *kewra* essence. This version is flavoured with almonds and pistachios. A slow cooking of milk to a condensed consistency gives *kulfi* its characteristic flavour. The mixture is traditionally frozen in conical metal containers with screw-top lids (like cream-horn containers) which are rolled between the palms and fingers during the freezing process to break the ice crystals.

2½ tbsp cornflour *4 tbsp milk*	Make a thin, pouring-consistency paste with the cornflour and milk. Set aside.
8 cups milk	Bring the milk to a boil in a heavy-bottomed saucepan, stir and keep it on a rolling boil for 10 minutes. Remove from the heat, add the cornflour paste and stir to prevent lumps forming. Return to the heat and allow the milk to simmer rapidly, stirring frequently until it acquires a thick creamy consistency and reduces to about one-third of the original quantity.
6 tbsp caster sugar *1 tsp cardamom powder* *2 tbsp blanched and pulverised almonds*	Add the sugar, cardamom, almonds, condensed milk, cream, rose essence and saffron threads in milk. Keep stirring and simmer gently for 5 minutes to dissolve the sugar.

2 tbsp condensed milk
1/2 cup thick cream
4 drops rose essence
1/4 tsp saffron threads,
steeped for 15 minutes in
1 tbsp hot milk

1 tbsp pistachios, blanched
and coarsely crushed

Allow the mixture to cool, but stir it frequently and mix in any skin that forms. When cool, stir in the crushed pistachio nuts. Pour into ice cube trays with the divisions removed, cover with foil and put into the freezer for 20 minutes.

Remove after 20 minutes and mix well to break up the ice crystals. Repeat this three times over the next hour. You will notice the *kulfi* becoming firmer and more solid so that, eventually, it is almost impossible to mix.

Cover the tray with foil and return to the freezer. The mixture will take about 4 hours to freeze solid. Before it reaches the solid stage, take the tray out of the freezer and dip a sharp knife in hot water to cut into portions for serving.

Shahi Tukre

BREAD SLICES IN CREAMED SYRUP

Culinary experts in Lucknow claim that this dessert was originally made there, but Hyderabadi cooks became the acknowledged specialists in the preparation of this tasty bread pudding.

Slices of bread, preferably a couple of days old, are deep-fried to a golden brown colour in *ghee* and then steeped in a sugar and water syrup. The syrup undergoes a further transformation with the addition of milk, cream and flavours of cardamom, nutmeg, raisins and rose essence, simmered to a creamy thickness and spread over the syrupy bread slices and served chilled.

Use a shallow serving dish large enough to take half the bread pieces side by side and deep enough to take two layers.

6 thick slices day-old bread
6 tbsp melted ghee

Trim the crusts off the bread and cut each slice in half. In a wide heavy-bottomed frying pan heat the *ghee* until it sizzles if splashed with drops of water. Fry the bread a few pieces at a time, turning to get an even all-over golden brown. Depending on the thickness of the bread, you may need to add more *ghee* for frying. Remove and drain on absorbent paper. Set aside.

³/4 cup caster sugar
¹/2 cup water

Put the sugar and water into another heavy-bottomed saucepan and bring to the boil. Reduce the heat and simmer until the sugar is dissolved. Raise the heat and boil for 4-5 minutes or until the syrup begins to thicken slightly.

Remove the saucepan from the heat and drop the fried bread pieces a few at a time into the syrup. Remove each piece with a slotted spoon, squeezing gently against the side of the saucepan to allow excess syrup to drain back. Place half of the bread pieces onto a shallow serving dish and keep the remainder to one side.

¹/4 tsp cardamom powder
¹/4 tsp nutmeg powder
¹/4 tsp saffron threads,
steeped for 15 minutes in
1 tbsp hot milk
³/4 cup cream
4 tbsp milk
2 tbsp seedless raisins
3 drops rose essence

Return the syrup to a medium heat, add the cardamom and nutmeg powder, saffron threads, the milk and cream and stir gently while bringing to the boil. Reduce the heat and keep stirring, allowing the liquid to simmer until it thickens to a light creamy consistency. Add the raisins and rose essence and continue to simmer for 2 minutes. Now spread half the cream mixture over the first layer of bread pieces.

1 tbsp ghee
3 tbsp blanched and slivered
almonds

Heat the *ghee* in a small frying pan and fry the slivered almonds to a golden colour. Sprinkle half of the almonds on top of the layered cream mixture.

Make another layer with the remaining bread pieces, spread the remainder of the cream mixture on top and scatter with the remaining almonds. Serve chilled.

Chukandar Halwa

BEETROOT DESSERT

This colourful *halwa* is made from grated beetroot and flavoured with cardamom and raisins and a crunch of almonds. It is not an everyday dessert and, like most of the milk- and sugar-based desserts, requires lengthy cooking and constant stirring. The result will be well worth the effort.

500 g/1 lb beetroot	Wash and peel the beetroot, grate it coarsely and set aside.
2¹/2 cups milk *³/4 cup sugar*	Put the milk and sugar in a heavy-bottomed saucepan and bring to the boil. Reduce the heat, add the grated beetroot and stir while simmering until the liquid has evaporated. This can be a lengthy process and will depend upon the size, type and thickness of the saucepan used.
5 tbsp ghee *1 tbsp seedless raisins* *1 tbsp blanched and slivered almonds* *¹/2 tsp cardamom powder*	Gradually add the *ghee* while stirring, then add the raisins, slivered almonds and cardamom powder. Stir until the mixture is thickened and the *ghee* starts to separate out.
Whipped cream *1 tbsp slivered almonds*	Serve warm in individual glass bowls with a swirl of cream and a sprinkling of slivered almonds.

DRINKS AND SHARBATS

'Upon his auspicious arrival let him drink fine *sharbats* of lemon and rosewater cooled with snow.' So said Tahmasp the Shah of Persia on greeting the Moghul Emperor Humayun and his Persian wife Hamida when they sought refuge at his court in 1544. Sherbets or *sharbats, nimbu pani* (lime juice) and *lassi* (yoghurt diluted with water) are drinks with a beneficial cooling effect and are high on the list of drinks taken in India. Persian-style, syrup-based sherbets are a colourful sight at roadside stalls throughout the subcontinent. As summer approaches, syrups are made up and bottled. Guests are welcomed with a refreshing *sharbat*: a couple of tablespoons are poured into a tall glass, topped up with crushed ice and iced water and stirred vigorously. Finally, a spoonful of swollen *tookmuria* seeds is added. *Tookmuria* are small seeds from a plant of the basil family which, when added to liquid, swell and form a coating. They are added to *sharbats* to give texture and are said to have cooling properties. *Tookmuria* seeds are available from some, but not all, Indian food shops.

If you can't obtain *tookmuria* seeds, *sharbat* is still a very pleasant drink. Make up a few bottles of syrups and keep them in the refrigerator to use like cordial. When using acidic fruits like lime, lemon or sour cherries, use an enamelled pan. *Sharbats* are normally fruit-based, but there is one that is very obviously Persian in origin, the *badam sharbat* (p.226). *Badam* means almonds in Persian and today *badam sharbat*, made from almonds, sugar and rosewater, is served in both Iran and India. And so the Persian influence lingers on.

Narangi Sharbat

ORANGE CORDIAL

3 cups juice from freshly squeezed oranges
4½ cups sugar
1 cup water

Grate the rind from one of the oranges and set aside. Put the orange juice, sugar and water in an enamelled saucepan. Bring to the boil over a medium heat and stir to dissolve the sugar. Reduce the heat and simmer until the syrup begins to thicken. Add the grated orange rind and simmer gently for a further 5 minutes. Strain through a fine sieve, allow to cool and then bottle.

1 tsp tookmuria seeds soaked in 1 cup of water until swollen and sealed in a jelly-like substance

If used, add the swollen seeds when serving.

Serve like a cordial, topped with crushed ice and diluted with water. To decorate, slit a slice of orange to the centre and slip onto the rim of the glass.

Nimbu Sharbat

LIME OR LEMON CORDIAL

2 cups juice from freshly squeezed lemons or limes
8 cups sugar
4 cups water

Grate the rind from 2 of the lemons or limes. Put the lemon or lime juice, sugar and water into an enamelled saucepan. Bring to the boil over a medium heat and stir to dissolve the sugar. Reduce the heat and simmer until the syrup begins to thicken. Add the grated lemon or lime rind and simmer gently for a further 5 minutes. Strain through a fine sieve, allow to cool and then bottle.

1 tsp tookmuria seeds soaked in 1 cup of water until swollen and sealed in a jelly-like substance

If used, add the swollen seeds when serving.

Serve like a cordial, topped with crushed ice and diluted with water. To decorate, slit a slice of lemon to the centre and slip onto the rim of the glass.

Istabari Sharbat

STRAWBERRY CORDIAL

6 *cups sugar*
3 *cups water*
750 *g/1½ lb strawberries,
well ripened, hulled and
puréed*
6 *drops rose essence*
A *few drops red food
colouring (optional)*

Put the sugar and water in a saucepan and bring to the boil. Reduce the heat and simmer gently for about 20 minutes or until the syrup begins to thicken. Add the puréed strawberries, rose essence and food colouring. Continue to simmer gently until the syrup thickens. Strain through a sieve, cool and bottle.

1 *tsp tookmuria seeds
soaked in 1 of cup water
until swollen and sealed in a
jelly-like substance*

If used, add the swollen seeds when serving.
Serve like a cordial, topped with crushed ice and diluted with water. To decorate, float a couple of strawberry slices on the surface.

Ananas Sharbat

PINEAPPLE CORDIAL

1 *cup water*
3½ *cups pineapple juice
(available in tins or cartons,
or extracted from fresh
pineapple)*
4 *tbsp sugar, or more if
required*
5 *cm/2 inch cinnamon stick*
4 *cloves*
4 *small, light-coloured
cardamoms, bruised*
12 *mint leaves*

Put the water, pineapple juice, sugar, cinnamon stick, cloves, cardamom and mint leaves in a saucepan. Bring to the boil and simmer gently for 10 minutes, stirring occasionally. Strain through a sieve, discard the solids, cool and bottle.

1 tsp tookmuria seeds
soaked in 1 cup of water
until swollen and sealed in a
jelly-like substance

If used, add the swollen seeds when serving.

Serve like a cordial, topped with crushed ice and diluted with water. To decorate, place a sprig of mint in the centre.

Badam Sharbat
🫖
ALMOND DRINK

185 g/6 oz blanched
almonds
1 tsp cardamom seeds
4 tbsp water

Blend the almonds, cardamom seeds and water to a smooth paste in a food-processor and set aside.

1½ cups water
5 cups sugar

Dissolve the sugar in 1½ cups water in heavy-bottomed saucepan. Add the almond paste and simmer on a low heat. Stir until the mixture becomes thick and syrupy.

3 drops rose essence
4 drops almond essence

Stir in the rose and almond essence. Strain through a sieve, discard any solids, cool and bottle.

Serve like a cordial, topped with crushed ice and diluted with water.

Lassi Namkeen
🫖
SALT YOGHURT DRINK

Nutritious yoghurt-based drinks are enjoyed all over India. Yoghurt beaten smooth with iced water, *lassi* is served in two ways: sweet *lassi meethi* and salted *lassi namkeen*. This salted *lassi* is a welcome drink during the long, hot Indian summers and can be very cooling. Serve in tall glasses with ice cubes or crushed ice.

2 cups yoghurt
3 cups iced water
1/2 tsp salt
A pinch of ground black pepper
Cubed or crushed ice
1/2 tsp dry-roasted and ground cumin seeds

Put the yoghurt, iced water, salt and pepper in a bowl and whisk briskly until frothy. Serve in tall glasses with ice cubes or crushed ice. Sprinkle the dry-roasted ground cumin seeds on the top.

If not serving immediately, leave the *lassi* in the bowl or jug without the ice. Whisk the *lassi* before serving in tall glasses half-filled with crushed ice or ice cubes.

Decorate with a sprig of mint.

Lassi Meethi

SWEET YOGHURT DRINK

This rose-flavoured yoghurt drink is cooling, sweet and refreshing. *Lassi* is a popular welcoming drink and is also served with meals.

2 cups yoghurt
3 cups iced water
3 tbsp sugar dissolved in a little hot water
5 drops rose essence
Ice cubes or crushed ice

Put the yoghurt, iced water, dissolved sugar and rose essence into a bowl and whisk briskly until frothy. Fill tall glasses with ice and pour over.

Kanji

VEGETABLE JUICE

This unusual concoction of carrot and beetroot with mustard seeds and a dash of chilli powder is almost a pickled juice. Traditionally, a type of red carrot is used which imparts a particular flavour. I have substituted the orange carrot familiar in the West. The beetroot adds to the colour and enhances the flavour.

You will need a wide-mouthed screw-top jar to take about 6 cups of juice.

250 g/8 oz small carrots, washed and cut into julienne strips
1 small beetroot, peeled and sliced
1/2 tbsp crushed black mustard seeds
1/2 tsp chilli powder
2 tsp salt
1 tsp ajowan seeds
5 cups water

Pack into the jar alternating layers of the julienne carrots and sliced beetroot. Sprinkle in the crushed mustard seeds, chilli powder, salt and ajowan seeds. Cover with water, secure the top and allow to steep at room temperature for 8-10 days. Then strain through a fine sieve, pushing against the sieve to extract all the juice. Discard the seeds, chill and bottle. Serve over ice cubes or crushed ice.

Kesari Badam Doodh

ALMOND-FLAVOURED MILK

This delicately flavoured, aromatic milk drink may be served hot or cold.

3 tbsp hot milk
1 1/2 tbsp blanched almonds

Blend the hot milk and almonds to a smooth paste in a food-processor.

4 1/2 cups milk
1/4 tsp crushed cardamom seeds
1 tbsp sugar, or to taste
1/4 tsp saffron threads
3 drops rose essence
1/4 tsp grated nutmeg

Put the blended almond paste, milk, cardamom seeds, sugar and saffron threads in a heavy-bottomed saucepan. Bring to the boil, reduce the heat and stir and simmer for 10 minutes. Add the rose essence. Serve in heat-proof glasses (if serving as a warm drink) with a pinch of grated nutmeg on the top. If serving cold, whisk to a froth and then pour over the ice cubes.

Thandai

﹖◈

SPICED ALMOND DRINK

The ladies at the courts of Oudh put great faith in this almond milk drink. 'Good for the skin, good for the heart, good for the body… you must take it every day in the summer,' was the advice given to me by an elderly lady whose forebears had held high positions at court at the decline of the Moghul empire.

3 tbsp blanched almonds *1 tbsp sunflower seeds* *2 cups hot water*	Blend the almonds, sunflower seeds and hot water to a smooth paste in a food-processor. Leave in the bowl and set aside.
3 tsp fennel seeds *1/2 tsp cardamom seeds* *3 cloves* *6 peppercorns*	Grind the fennel and cardamom seeds, cloves and peppercorns to a fine powder in a spice-mill or coffee-grinder.
2 tbsp sugar *1 1/2 cups boiling water*	Add the ground spices, the sugar and boiling water to the paste in the blender and blend to dissolve the sugar. Put muslin or cheesecloth over a bowl and drain the blended mixture. Squeeze to extract any remaining liquid. Discard the solids. Cool and chill.
2 cups chilled milk *6 drops rose essence*	When cool, add the almond liquid to the chilled milk and stir in the rose essence.
1 tbsp flaked almonds	Add crushed ice just before serving and sprinkle a few flaked almonds on the crushed ice.

Kashmiri Kawa

SPICED GREEN TEA

Kashmiri green tea is available in most Indian food shops. Kashmiris normally prepare this sweet, aromatic tea in a samovar, but this recipe uses a saucepan and jug.

4 cups water
1 tsp Kashmiri green tea

Put the water and tea leaves into a small saucepan.

1/2 tsp cardamom seeds
2.5 cm/1 inch cinnamon stick

Grind the cardamom and cinnamon to a powder in a spice-mill or coffee-grinder. Add the ground spices to the saucepan and bring to the boil.

1/4 tsp crushed saffron threads
4-6 tsp sugar
20 almond flakes

Add the saffron threads and the sugar and boil for 1 minute. Transfer to a warmed jug and allow to steep for a couple of minutes. Put the almond flakes into Chinese tea bowls or small coffee cups and pour over the kawa.

BIBLIOGRAPHY

Achaya, K.T., *Indian Food, A Historical Companion*, Delhi 1994.

Ali, Meer Hassan, *Observations on the Mussulmanns of India* (2 vols), London 1973.

Babur, *Baburnama* (2 vols), trans. Annette Beveridge, London 1921.

Bernier, François, *The Empire of the Great Mogol*, trans. John Cooke, London 1671.

Brand, Michael and Lowry, Glen D., *Akbar's India*, London 1986.

Caunter, Robert, Elphinstone, Monstuart and Lane-Poole, Stanley, *Nur Jahan and Jahangir*, Calcutta 1950.

Chakravarty, I., *The Saga of Indian Food: A Historical and Cultural Survey*, New Delhi 1972.

Chopra, P. N., *Social Life During the Mughal Age*, Agra 1963.

Edwards, Michael, *Niccolao Manucci; Memoirs of the Mogul Covert*, London n.d.

Fazl, Abul, *Ain-i-Akbari* (3 vols), trans. H. Beveridge, Calcutta 1907.

Fazl, Abul, *Akbar-Nama* (3 vols), trans. H. Beveridge, Calcutta 1907.

Gascoigne, Bamber, *The Great Moghuls*, London 1971.

Godden, Rumer, *Gulbadan: Portrait of a Rose Princess at the Mughal Court*, London 1980.

Gulbadan, Begum, *Humayunnama*, trans. Annette Beveridge, London 1902.

Hamblyn, Gavin, *Cities of Mughal India*, New Delhi 1977.

Ikram, S.M., *Muslim Civilization in India*, ed. A.T. Embree, New York 1964.

Isacco, Enrico and Dallapiccola, Anna L., (eds), *Krishna, The Divine Lover*, London and Boston 1982.

Jaffrey, Madhur, *A Taste of India*, London 1985.

Jahangir, *Memoirs of Jahangueir*, trans. Major David Price, Lahore n.d.

Kalra J. Inder Singh and Das Gupta, Pradeep, *Prashad, Cooking with Indian Masters*, New Delhi 1986.

Lamb, Harold, *Babur the Tiger: First of the Great Moghuls*, London 1961.

Lane-Poole, Stanley, *Aurangzib*, Oxford 1893.

Lynton, Harriet Ronken and Rajan, Mohini, *The Days of the Beloved*, Los Angeles 1974.

Majumdar, R. C., Raychaudhuri, H. C. and Datta, Kalikinkar, *An Advanced History of India*, Delhi 1974.

Manucci, Niccolas., trans., Irvine, William, *Storia Do Mogor, Or Mogul India 1653-1708* (4 vols), New Delhi 1981.

Mazumdar, K.C., *Imperial Agra of the Moghuls*, Agra 1946.

McNeill, William H. and Sedlar, Jean W., eds, *Classical India*, New York 1969.

Moreland, W. H., *India at the Death of Akbar*, New Delhi 1983.

Norman, Jill, *The Complete Book of Spices*, London 1990.

Patnaik, Naveen, *A Second Paradise, Indian Courtly Life 1590-1947*, New York 1985.

Prawdin, Michael, *The Builders of the Moghul Empire*, London 1963.

Pruthi, J. S., *Spices and Condiments*, New Delhi 1979.

Rao, Shivaji and Holkar, Shalini Devi, *Cooking of the Maharajas: The Royal Recipes of India*, New York 1975.

Rau, Santha Rama, *The Cooking of India*, New York 1972.

Sahni, Julie, *Classic Indian Cooking*, New York 1980.

Sharar, Abdul Halim, *Lucknow: The Last Phase of an Oriental Culture*, trans. and ed. E.S. Harcourt and Fakhir Hussain, London 1975.

Sharma, P. V., *Fruits and Vegetables in Ancient India*, Delhi 1979.

Siddiqui, Iqtidar Husain, *Mughal Relations with the Indian Ruling Elite*, New Delhi 1983.

Solomon, Charmaine, *The Complete Asian Cookbook*, Sydney 1976.

Stobart, Tom, *The Cooks Encyclopedia*, London 1982.

INDEX

An independent publishing house, Serif publishes a wide range of international fiction and non-fiction.

If you would like to receive a copy of our current catalogue, please write to:

Serif
47 Strahan Road
London E3 5DA

or

1489 Lincoln Avenue
St Paul
MN 55105

BENGALI COOKING: SEASONS AND FESTIVALS

Chitrita Banerji

Foreword by Deborah Madison

We are just beginning to appreciate the culinary diversity of the Indian subcontinent's numerous regions. Bengal is home to both Hindus and Muslims and her people farm the fertile Ganges delta for rice and vegetables and fish the region's myriad rivers. As recipes for fish in yoghurt sauce, chicken with poppy seeds, aubergine with tamarind, duck with coconut milk and other delights in *Bengali Cooking: Seasons and Festivals* testify, Bengal has one of Asia's most delicious and distinctive cuisines.

This highly original book takes the reader into kitchens in both Bangladesh and the Indian state of West Bengal by way of the seasons and religious and other festivals which have shaped the region's cooking. Chitrita Banerji offers her readers the wonderful recipes of Bengali home-cooking – dals, fish, vegetables and kedgerees – rather than the standard fare of Indian restaurants. Hers is much more than a cookbook: it is also a vivid and deeply-felt introduction to the life, landscape and culture of the Bengali people.

'Delightful ... written with a rare grace and zest'
Matthew Fort, *The Guardian*

'Chitrita Banerji gives her reades a keen appetite for the subtle flavours of India's most interesting region'
Paul Levy

paperback

also published by Serif

TRADITIONAL MOROCCAN COOKING: RECIPES FROM FEZ

Madame Guinaudeau

Foreword by Claudia Roden

Moroccan cuisine is famous for its subtle blending of spices, herbs and honey with meat and vegetables. In Fez, the country's culinary centre, the cooking has numerous influences – Arab and Berber, with hints of Jewish, African and French. The country's classic dishes are the famous *couscous, tagines* or stews, and *bistilla,* an exquisite pie made with a flaky pastry.

Capturing the atmosphere of Fez, cultural capital of the medieval Moorish world, Madame Guinaudeau takes us behind closed doors into the kitchens and dining rooms of the old city. She invites us to a banquet in a wealthy home, shopping in the spice market and to the potter's workshop; shares with us the secrets of preserving lemons for a *tagine*; shows us how to make Moroccan bread.

Traditional Moroccan Cooking is the perfect introduction to a splendid culinary heritage and a vivid description of an ancient and beautiful city. It offers a taste of the delights to be found in one of the world's great gastronomic centres.

'Successfully evokes the magic flavours of Fez'
Nigel Slater, *The Observer*

'Wonderful descriptions of the food and how to cook it'
Thane Prince, *Daily Telegraph*

paperback

also published by Serif

CLASSIC JAMAICAN COOKING: TRADITIONAL RECIPES AND HERBAL REMEDIES

Caroline Sullivan

Foreword by Cristine MacKie

Okra, plantains, sweet potatoes and mangoes: these and the other essential ingredients of Jamaican cooking are now widely available in Britain and North America, bringing the island's delicious cooking within anyone's reach.

Covering all aspects of Jamaican cuisine from soups to preserves, fish to ices, *Classic Jamaican Cooking* also presents a range of traditional herbal remedies and drinks. With recipes as varied as plantain tart and okra soup, salt fish patties and coconut ice-cream, this book dispels forever the myth that Jamaican cookery begins with curried goat and ends with rice and peas.

Needing only occasional modification for the modern reader ('Take seven gallons of rum, three gallons of seville orange-juice ...'), Caroline Sullivan brings alive the wealth and variety of the island's food. With its blending of African and European influences, Jamaican cooking rests on a foundation of tropical fruits and vegetables, and the author draws out the full range of their flavours in one of the New World's tastiest cuisines.

'A wealth of very good recipes' Frances Bissell, *The Times*

'Wonderful ideas that will appeal to adventurous cooks'
Lindsey Bareham

'A useful addition to your kitchen library' *The Voice*

paperback

also published by Serif

HOME BAKED:
A LITTLE BOOK OF BREAD RECIPES

George and Cecilia Scurfield

Foreword by Paul Bailey

Home baking has once again become one of the most popular forms of cookery, and this highly praised book is the perfect introduction to the subject for anyone who has wanted to make their own bread but feared that baking is too complicated or time-consuming. *Home Baked* starts with a clear summary of how to go about quickly acquiring the skills of kneading, rising, proving and baking itself. As in all forms of cookery, a bread's appearance is almost as important as its flavour, and the Scurfields describe how to transform a tasty but ordinary-looking bread into something supremely attractive and appetising.

Home Baked is essential kitchen equipment for those who suspect that bread-making can be more rewarding than warming up a deep-frozen 'French stick' from a super-market but fear that they could never get the dough to rise.

'That lovable little volume on yeast cookery'
Elizabeth David

'An inspiring, comprehensive and apparently fool-proof little book'
Times Literary Supplement

paperback

HOME-MADE CAKES AND BISCUITS

George and Cecilia Scurfield

Foreword by Geraldene Holt

What could be more useful than a short, unpretentious introduction to the art of cake-making? Starting with simple recipes, the reader is gradually introduced to a full range of cakes including those made with nuts, chocolate and fruit both fresh and dried. Unlike over-sweet cakes bought from shops, those made at home can be completely free of additives and colouring – and twice as tasty.

Home-Made Cakes and Biscuits contains recipes for cakes that will appeal to children as well as adults, cakes for special occasions and for every day. There are also clear, concise and practical recipes for pastries, biscuits, icing and fillings. The recipes come from England, America, France and Austria. With easy-to-follow recipes for such delights as Rich Chocolate Cake, Viennese Orange Cake, Nusstorte, Hazel Nut Macaroons and French Plum Cake, tea-time need never again be reduced to a packet of biscuits fast approaching its sell-by date.

'Delightful' *A La Carte*

'As welcome as the return of the swallows'
Elisabeth Luard, *The Scotsman*

paperback

COOKING IN TEN MINUTES

Edouard de Pomiane

Foreword by Raymond Blanc

300 uncomplicated *and* delicious recipes by France's most creative cookery writer, the witty, irreverent and super-efficient Edouard de Pomiane. Whizzing from stove to table, and still keeping everything under control, he delights us with his joy in cooking and with his belief that good food need not be the sole preserve of people with vast amounts of time and money to spend. This book is a must for anyone who leads a busy life but is determined to create the space in which to eat well.

'The very best kind of cookery writing'
Elizabeth David

'An utter delight'
Philippa Davenport, *Financial Times*

'Both timeless and timely, Pomiane's stylish good sense never dates'
Geraldene Holt

'An inspirational energy and joy in cooking'
The Guardian

paperback

COOKING WITH POMIANE

Edouard de Pomiane

Foreword by Elizabeth David

Dashing, mocking, conspiratorial, *Cooking With Pomiane* gives the best advice you could ever hope for on the making of meals both simple and spectacular. Writing in clear, logical language, Pomiane describes how to prepare each recipe with wit, ease and fluency. Like a good friend, he understands the difficulties of real cooking and shopping; he sympathises, makes a joke of our blunders, brushes them aside and breezes on. Throughout, he refuses to show off with his specialist's expertise and explains things with great common sense in a most engaging way, infecting us with his sheer love of food and zest for good cooking.

'Both serious and funny, never pompous, and agreeably anti-slimming'
Michèle Roberts, *Sunday Times*

'Besides being practical – de Pomiane really makes you understand what goes on when you boil, fry, roast, grill and braise – these books are enormous fun to read'
Paul Levy, *Daily Mail*

'You will love him and his writing'
Spectator

paperback

also published by Serif

THE ALICE B. TOKLAS COOKBOOK

Foreword by Maureen Duffy

The Alice B. Toklas Cookbook is one of the few books which genuinely deserve the label 'legendary'. Toklas lived with Gertrude Stein, the American writer and art collector, in Paris and the Bugey, a rural area in south-eastern France famous for its cooking and as the home of Brillat Savarin. For more than 25 years she collected and adapted recipes with which she entertained Picasso, Matisse and others. The fruit of hundreds of hours in the kitchen, market-place and vegetable-garden, this entertaining culinary companion ranges from inventive responses to wartime austerity to full-blown French bourgeois cooking at its richest and best. Always delicious, the recipes here vary from simple snacks – mushroom sandwiches and tricolour omelette made with spinach and tomato – to more complex dishes like *suprême of pike à la Dijonaise* and pheasant with cottage cheese.

The Alice B. Toklas Cookbook has long enjoyed a reputation as one of the most original cookbooks of the twentieth century. Available once again, it is certain to delight a new generation of readers as well as find its way back onto shelves from which it has mysteriously disappeared.

'A delightful concoction of reminiscences and recipes'
Time Out

paperback